VRIJE UNIVERSITEIT

Honour Killings, Moral Panic and
the Emergence of an Organizational Field

A Case Study of the Processes, Actors and Actions Involved
in the Emergence of an Issue-based Organizational Field

ACADEMISCH PROEFSCHRIFT
ter verkrijging van de graad Doctor aan
de Vrije Universiteit Amsterdam,
op gezag van de rector magnificus
prof.dr. V. Subramaniam,
in het openbaar te verdedigen
ten overstaan van de promotiecommissie
van de Faculteit der Sociale Wetenschappen
op maandag 29 januari 2018 om 9.45 uur
in de aula van de universiteit,
De Boelelaan 1105

door
Nicole Veronika Brenninkmeijer
geboren te Wimbledon, Verenigd Koninkrijk

promotoren: prof.dr. H. Ghorashi
prof.dr. M.B. Veenswijk
copromotor: dr. C.M. Roggeband

Honour Killings, Moral Panic and the Emergence of an Organizational Field

A Case Study of the Processes, Actors and Actions
Involved in the Emergence of an
Issue-based Organizational Field

Nicole Brenninkmeijer

VU University Press, Amsterdam

VU University Press
De Boelelaan 1105
1081 HV Amsterdam
The Netherlands

www.vuuniversitypress.com
info@vuuitgeverij.nl

© 2018 Nicole Brenninkmeijer

Design jacket: Haags Blauw, Den Haag (Bianca Wesseling)
Type setting interior: Jaap Prummel, Amsterdam (Japes)

ISBN 978 90 8659 772 7
NUR 761

All rights reserved. No part of this book may be reproduced, stored in a retrieval system, or transmitted, in any form or by any means, electronic, mechanical, photocopying, recording, or otherwise, without the prior written consent of the publisher.

This book is dedicated to all victims of violence
and to the professionals who help them.

Contents

Prologue	13
Introduction	17
How to make sense of these activities	18
Institutional theory and organizational fields	19
Reintroducing Bourdieu into institutional theory	22
Central research questions	23
Outline	24

Part I   Studying an organizational field

1. **Institutional theory's pendulum swings** — 28
   - 1.1   In search of a balanced theory of action — 29
   - 1.2   Swinging back and forth — 33

2. **Bringing Bourdieu back into institutional theory** — 36
   - 2.1   Applying Bourdieu in a piecemeal fashion: a critique — 36
   - 2.2   A theory of practice — 39
   - Concluding remarks — 50

3. **Methodological contemplations** — 52
   - 3.1   Bourdieu and the interpretive perspective — 52
   - 3.2   Reconstructing the issue's emergence — 55
   - 3.3   An organizational field ethnography — 58
   - 3.4   Reflection — 62

Part II   How honour-related violence became an issue within the Dutch public discourse

Introduction	66
Part II: theoretical underpinnings	67
Part II: outline	69

4. **Defining honour-related violence** — 71
   - 4.1   The emergence of a contested label — 71
   - 4.2   Developing a new label: honour-related violence — 77
   - 4.3   How these labels contributed to the emergence of a Dutch HRV field — 82

5. **Honour killings as field-configuring events** — 85
   - 5.1   Analysing field-configuring events — 85

	5.2	How honour killings become critical events	87
	5.3	Discussion about the attribution of the "honour killing" label	95
	5.4	Disputes about the cultural background to honour killings	104
	5.5	How these events contributed to the emergence of a Dutch HRV field	109

6. **Changing macro-cultural discourses** — 111
   - 6.1 Multiculturalism and gender-inequality — 113
   - 6.2 Social cohesion, national imaginaries and the creation of the other — 118
   - 6.3 How the changes in macro-cultural discourses contributed to the emergence of a Dutch HRV field — 121

7. **The moral panic driving the attention for honour killings** — 123
   - 7.1 Amplifying issue attention: the moral panic concept — 124
   - 7.2 Honour killings, moral panic and the emergence of an issue-based field — 127
   - 7.3 How the moral panic about honour killings contributed to the emergence of a Dutch HRV field — 131

Part III State practices and emerging field configurations

Introduction — 134
- Bourdieu on state power — 136
- Part III: outline — 138

8. **The political field as a field of struggle** — 140
   - 8.1 Field-configuring events within the political field — 141
   - 8.2 Accelerating the honour-related violence debate: Gül's murder — 146
   - 8.3 Developing a better understanding of the problem: two studies and a pilot — 149
   - 8.4 Assigning honour-related violence "priority project status" — 152
   - 8.5 Questioning the priority project's adequacy — 155
   - 8.6 Presenting the interministerial programme — 157
   - 8.7 How these state practices contributed to the emergence of a Dutch HRV field — 160

9. **Key actors and their capital** — 166
   - 9.1 Key actors and their roles within the emerging HRV field — 167
   - 9.2 The agenda setters — 169
   - 9.3 The experts — 171
   - 9.4 The bridge builders — 173
   - 9.5 The financiers — 175
   - 9.6 The regular function — 176
   - 9.7 Concluding remarks — 178

10. **Discussions about the label of honour-related violence** — 181
    - 10.1 The Working Definition versus the Definition-in-use — 183

10.2	Moving beyond the definition	191
10.3	Concluding remarks	194

11. Collaborative practices within the HRV field — 197
    11.1 Emerging field configurations: a schematic representation — 198
    11.2 Collaborative practices between the state and umbrella organizations — 201
    11.3 Collaborative practices between the state and local network partners — 206
    11.4 Network collaboration within the HRV field — 210
    11.5 Network partners and migrant organizations: lack of trust — 214
    11.6 Concluding remarks — 218

Conclusion and discussion — 222
    The emergence of the Dutch honour-related violence field — 223
    Field emergence: a multi-layered process — 224
        The three phases of issue-based field emergence — 238
        Critical preconditions for field emergence — 257
    Bringing Bourdieu back into institutional theory: an update — 235
        Bourdieu and the structure-agency dilemma — 256
        The added value of Bourdieu's theory in practice — 257
        Updating Bourdieu's framework with the addition of
        institutional concepts — 258
    Future research — 238
    Lessons for the public domain — 239

Epilogue: Newsletter of the Platform for Honour and Freedom — 240

References — 242

Appendixes

Appendix 1: Occurrences of the "honour killing" and "honour-related violence" labels in the media and in politics — 254

Appendix 2: Example from the matrix on Gül's murder — 256

Appendix 3: Observations — 257

Appendix 4: Information on the respondents and their backgrounds — 258

Appendix 5: Interview schedule — 263

Summary — 267

Acknowledgments — 280

List of Abbreviations and Acronyms

CDA	'Christian Democratic Appeal', Dutch Christian-Democratic Party	*Christen Democratisch Appèl*
CU	Dutch Christian Party	*Christen Unie*
D66	Dutch Progressive Liberal Party	*Politieke Partij Democraten*
FO	Umbrella for women's shelter organizations	*Federatie Opvang*
GL	'GreenLeft', Dutch political party, greens	*Groen Links*
HTIP	Leftish Turkish migrant workers' society	
HRV field	Honour-Related Violence field	
IOT	Umbrella Organization for Turks in the Netherlands	*Inspraak Orgaan Turken in Nederland*
LEC	National Expertise Centre on honour-related violence	*Landelijk Expertise Centrum eergerelateerd geweld*
LPF	'List Pim Fortuyn', Dutch political party founded by Pim Fortuyn	*Lijst Pim Fortuyn*
LOM	National minorities consultation platform	*Landelijk Overleg Minderheden*
MEP	Unit for Multi-Ethnic Policing	*Multi-Etnisch Politiewerk*
MP	Member of Parliament	
NCB	Dutch Centre for Foreigners	*Nederlands Centrum Buitenlanders*
NGO	Non-Governmental Organization	
PvdA	'Labour Party', Dutch Social-Democratic Party	*Partij van de Arbeid*
PVV	'Party for Freedom', Dutch Anti-Immigrant Party	*Partij voor de Vrijheid*
ROC	Regional Training Centres	*Regionaal Opleidings Centrum*
SGP	Dutch Conservative Christian Party	*Staatkundig Gereformeerde Partij*
SMN	Cooperative Association for Dutch people of Moroccan ethnicity	*Samenwerkingsverband Marokkaanse Nederlanders*
SP	Dutch Socialist Party	*Socialitische Partij*
STO	Cooperating Turkish Organizations	*Samenwerkende Turkse Organisaties*
VON	Refugees Organizations in the Netherlands	*Vluchtelingen-Organisaties Nederland*
VVD	'People's Party for Freedom and Democracy', Dutch Conservative-Liberal Party	*Volkspartij voor Vrijheid en Democratie*

List of Tables

Table 1. Key instigators and their roles

Table 2. Actors and their claims about the attribution of the "honour killing" label

Table 3. Letters and parliamentary debates on honour-related violence, 2004-2006

Table 4. Key actors and their roles

Table 5. Distribution of capital over the key actors within the emerging HRV field

Table 6. Critical preconditions for the emergence of the Dutch HRV field

List of Figures

Figure 1. The interrelationship between habitus, field and capital

Figure 2. Occurrences of the label of *eerwraak* in Dutch newspapers, 1990-2010

Figure 3. Occurrences of the label of *eerwraak* in Dutch parliament, 1996-2010

Figure 4. Occurrences of the label of *eerwraak* in Dutch newspapers and parliament, 1996-2010

Figure 5. Occurrences of the labels of *eergerelateerd geweld* and *eerwraak* in Dutch parliament, 1996-2010

Figure 6. Occurrences of the *eergerelateerd geweld* and *eerwraak* labels in Dutch newspapers, 1996-2010

Figure 7. Collaborative practices within the Dutch HRV field

Figure 8. Key events in the emergence of the Dutch HRV field

Prologue

Black pearls
Have you ever seen them?
I saw you lie there
An outspoken woman turned illiterate
Unrecognized, unheard
Each attempt to express yourself ending in a cry
Alienated from your own sentences
Caught in tears
Blonde on the outside, black inside
Back and forth between night and day

All hands were knocked together: 'why not?', you thought
On the day you said yes to him
The stars glistened intensely
A promise of hope and expectation
But the great Light shrivelled to a tiny light
You wanted your light to shine
You didn't want to be a drop in the ocean
Hope fighting against injustice

Your direction is no longer the faculty of law
Your steps no longer on their way to the future
Your willpower never left you
But the shots forced you to go
It was too late...

Which revengefulness
Which ancient tradition robbed you of your willpower, your sparkling eyes
and your soft smile?
There is no key that fits the door of my questions
Each drop of rain will now be a sign of your pain and suffering
Your dreams live on in everyone's soul
There was no full moon on June the 25th
Your love for life is like dandelion fuzz
Carried away on the wings of the wind
Your struggle for self-determination will rise again next spring
Unlimited
And unforgotten

(*Black Pearls* by Yeter Akin (2008))[1]

---

1. Translated by Saskia Stehouwer (2016).

It is a sunny day in June and I am holding a white rose as I walk through the streets of Alkmaar. I am not the only person holding a rose: about a hundred others walk beside me. Alkmaar is an old city, founded more than 750 years ago. It is a favourite among tourists, famous for its beautiful canals, its enclosed gardens and its traditional cheese market. However, we are not here to visit these attractions. We are on our way to Alkmaar's train station, where Zeynep Boral was shot dead by her ex-husband Serdar almost a year ago. When we reach our destination, Zeynep's mother is the first to tie her rose to the big tree standing outside the front of the station. As I walk up to the tree to add my rose to the circle of the red and white blooms now surrounding it, my eye is caught by a poem between the roses, called *Black Pearls* (11 June, 2008)[2].

Remembering Zeynep: Rafide's story

Just a few days before Zeynep's memorial walk, Zeynep's mother Rafide had narrated the story of her daughter's "honour killing" in a television interview that was broadcasted by current affairs programme NOVA (7 June 2008). She explained her contribution in the following words:

> The most important thing for me is that the police admit that they did nothing with the reports, that they didn't take us seriously, that's why I want to talk to you today. (...) If they'd done things differently from the start, then, maybe, he [Serdar] wouldn't have been free to act as he wanted. (...) I hope that the police in Alkmaar, as well as other police stations that work in a manner similar to the Alkmaar police, that in future they'll take cases more seriously. To prevent the same thing from happening to other Zeyneps. It's too late now for my Zeynep...[3]

In this excerpt, Zeynep's mother Rafide plainly points toward an accountable party in the event formed by her daughter's murder: the Alkmaar police. Earlier in the interview she had already explained, "If a member of an ethnic group walks into your office, you should take this seriously, since she wouldn't be there without reason. (...) [Since] in our culture we aren't used to airing our dirty laundry." Obviously, in Rafide's eyes, the police did not take them seriously and underestimated the danger to Zeynep.

According to Rafide the events leading up to Zeynep's death started in 2003. In that year Zeynep, only twenty at the time, married her cousin Serdar: the son of her father's brother, who lived in the city of Batman in Turkey and was four years older than Zeynep. When asked if this was a forced marriage, Rafide responds with,

---

2. This narration is based on my own observations during the commemoration that was organized one year after Zeynep's death.
3. The quotes have been translated from Dutch and are as close to verbatim as possible.

> Absolutely not! Initially she didn't want to marry, as she was too busy with her studies, she had no time for anything else. However, at a certain point she said, "Yes, I want to marry him".
>
> The offer came from the other side [of the family], they'd wanted this for a while, but Zeynep said, "No, I don't want to get married." Not because it was Serdar, she just didn't want to marry anyone at that point. However, during our holiday, after a night out with her cousins, she suddenly told us that she'd said "yes" to the proposal.

The interviewer then asks, "How do you explain that Zeynep, an independent woman, suddenly decided to marry her cousin?" Rafide replies,

> The uncle really wanted this; he wanted Zeynep to marry his son. (…) Besides, by coincidence my parents were also on holiday, they were in Batman at the same time. Moreover, they too had told Zeynep that they'd be very happy if Zeynep said yes to this marriage. So maybe that also played a part, that her grandfather, her grandmother and an uncle all told her to do this.

However, the marriage was not a happy one. It took less than a month after the wedding for Serdar to start abusing Zeynep. Rafide recalls,

> It quickly became clear that they weren't a good match. He wasn't the person he appeared to be. (…) Twice she reported him to the police. However, the first time she withdrew her report, the second time she didn't. This was nine months before she, before she … died. Nevertheless, in between we had contact with our local police officer. I don't know if this can also be interpreted as bringing charges, but in the meantime, we regularly contacted him.

As she did not want the outside world to see her bruises, Zeynep, a law student at the VU University Amsterdam, started to miss classes due to the abuse. Her mother recalls,

> Zeynep didn't dare to do anything anymore, she didn't go to school, didn't go outside. She didn't go to school for two months. I said to her, "Surely this isn't right?"

The interviewer asks, "Did you not tell her to leave that man?" Rafide immediately replies,

> I did, I did. After the first time, I told her, "He needs to go back." Because, I said, "someone who does something like this will never change, he'll always keep on doing this. I'm scared for you. I'm scared that I'll find you dead in your home when I come to visit you." (…)
>
> What I wanted, what I wanted from the police, and I literally said this, "I want you to arrest him and tell him that he can't do this." So as to scare him a little. To tell him that he can't hit a woman just like that. He [the police officer] told me, "We can't do that." So I said, "What good are you then? I've come to file a complaint. Don't you see what she looks like? This isn't normal, this can't be happening.'

Finally, at the end of 2005, and much to Rafide's relief, Zeynep left her husband and moved back into her parent's home. However, Serdar continued to intimidate them:

> At that point, my anxiety lessened, as she was close to me. Nevertheless, I told the police that Serdar was still threatening us. Told them that he'd said, "If Zeynep doesn't come back to me, if we don't stay together, then I'll kill her and myself as well. There's no other way…"

On the morning of 25 June 2007, a few weeks after they were officially divorced, Serdar turned this threat into reality and killed Zeynep on the stairs of Alkmaar's train station. He then shot himself in his head and died soon after in the hospital. According to Rafide, their upcoming holiday had triggered Serdar's actions:

> Two weeks later, on 7/7/2007, we intended to go on a holiday. Zeynep was supposed to join us. In their eyes, though, this was a problem: "How could Zeynep come back [to Batman] with her parents, while she was married to Serdar?" This way everybody would know that they'd had a divorce. He said, "I'm a nobody if Zeynep doesn't return to me. Within the family I won't mean anything to anyone anymore."

However, this threat did not cause Zeynep to change her plans and Rafide remembers that final morning vividly:

> It was strange, that morning she missed her bus. (…) I asked, "Shall I take you to the train station?" Zeynep answered, "There's no need. I can still catch the train if I take the second bus." She wanted to go by herself. When she got off the bus, he approached her. At first he tried to convince her. However, according to what witnesses have told me, she didn't want to talk to him. They did speak a little, but then she wanted to leave. She went up the stairs to the platform and then he –

At this point Rafide falls silent, looks at her hands and bites her lip, unable to continue.

Introduction

In 2007, honour-related violence was at the very forefront of public, political and scientific attention in the Netherlands. A trip to a bookshop would turn up books with titles such as *A veil of silence, On the run from an honour killing* (Djura 2005) and *Violated, I survived an attack on my life* (Soaud 2004). These books told the life stories of women like Hanife, Souad, Djura, Safiya, Aysel, Karima and Ayşe, all of whom were confronted with honour-related violence and lived to tell their tales (Gashi 2006, Soaud 2004, Djura 2005, Hoesseini & Masto 2004, Çalişkan 2006, Reysoo & Ouchan 1999, Ayşe 2005).

National newspapers ran articles about the murder of Zeynep Boral at Alkmaar train station and deliberations on whether her murder was an honour killing or a crime of passion. At the same time, an article appeared about a new project called "*Honour-related violence at and around schools*" at two ROCs[4]. The purpose of this project was to develop a manual that would instruct teachers and social workers on how to recognize signals of honour-related violence before it was too late.

At theatres, visitors could watch a play called *Is.man* by Adelheid Roosen. This play portrayed the story of the death of "green eyes", viewed from the perspective of three generations of migrant men: a grandfather who feels that his granddaughter has shamed his family's honour and therefore wanted her killed; a desperate father who killed his daughter to cleanse his family's honour and now feels an agonizing guilt; and a son who tries to understand why his beautiful sister had to die. This play also ran at local community centres, where it was used to trigger discussions between people from communities in which honour-related violence occurs.

People with a more scientific interest could have attended a dissertation defence at a university and listened to a presentation on how the Dutch criminal justice system deals with "cultural offences" such as honour-related violence and female circumcision (Ten Voorde 2007), or listened to an analysis of the offline and online debates on immigration in the Netherlands and on honour killings as a sign of the failures in migrant integration (Witschge 2007).

Anyone choosing to visit a get-together organized by a local migrant organization could have watched the documentary *Differences of Opinion are a Blessing*.

---

4. ROCs are Regional Training Centres, where students and adults can follow vocational training classes.

Contemporary Interpretations in Islam (Fatusch Productions 2007). In this documentary, a number of prominent and internationally respected Islamic thinkers elaborate on the Quran's position with respect to honour-related violence. The visitor could have joined the discussion afterwards, where the participants expressed their views on honour, shame and violence.

Lastly, visitors to the Dutch parliament building could have followed a debate in which members of parliament discussed the availability of shelters for men threatened by honour-related violence (Dutch House of Representatives 2007-2008, 30 388, no. 27). Visitors would have learned that the Dutch government had launched a large-scale interministerial programme against honour-related violence in 2006. This programme brought together civil servants, the State Secretaries and the Ministers from the Ministry of Justice, the Ministry of Health, Welfare and Sport and the Ministry of Housing, Spatial Planning and the Environment, and the Minister of Housing, Communities and Integration (Ministry of Justice 2010: website).

These examples serve to illustrate the widespread public, political and scientific attention that honour-related violence and honour killings were given in the Netherlands in 2007. A diverse group of actors (e.g. media, politicians, non-governmental organizations and academics) can be identified in the production processes of these activities, each working in their own distinct settings and sometimes from opposing perspectives. However, honour-related violence seemed to unite these actors and create a field centred around this particular issue: the honour-related violence field (HRV field).

How to make sense of these activities

Academic study can help to make sense of the described activities. This can be done from a number of different angles. For instance, the researcher could focus on the judicial aspects of honour-related violence cases (Ter Voorde 2007). Alternatively, he or she might focus on the framing of the issue within the media (Kortweg & Yurdakul 2009), or else study how migrants themselves define and perceive honour-related violence (Brenninkmeijer et al. 2009). Yet the diversity of actors and activities described above also evokes other questions: how, for instance, did the issue of honour-related violence become such a prominent issue within public discourse in the Netherlands in the first decade of the twentieth century? Why did the issue trigger the attention of some actors, while other actors did not take any interest in the issue whatsoever? And how did the relevant actors come to a shared understanding of the problem and its solution?

In my effort to find answers to these and other, related questions I considered various theoretical schools. For instance, to answer the question on where actors stand in relation to each other, I could have turned to *network analysis*. Alternatively, to study how the government has sought to handle the problem of honour-related violence I could have used *governance studies*. To determine how honour-related violence became such a prominent issue within Dutch public discourse I might subsequently have applied *framing analysis, critical discourse analysis* or *social movement theory*.

Nevertheless, using any one of these schools of thought would have meant limiting myself to the study of a particular actor or studying only specific aspects of the dynamics that I witnessed within the field of research. I therefore went in search of an alternative framework that would encompass all the different aspects that puzzled me. I found such a framework by combining Bourdieu's *theory of practice* with *institutional theory of organizational analysis*.

Institutional theory and organizational fields

The first step in finding this theoretical approach came during a research project that I conducted in 2007 and 2008. My research led me to conclude that the way in which honour-related violence was being tackled in the Netherlands was best described as a joint effort of organizations working together within a field centred around this particular issue (Brenninkmeijer et al. 2009). My present thesis builds on that initial research and studies the issue of honour-related violence from an organizational field perspective. The notion of a "field" is derived from Bourdieu (1977) and in the present study refers to a field comprised of a diverse group of actors, all of whom are concerned with the same societal problem and whose positions and powers within the field are defined by both their capital and their habitus.[5]

Besides Bourdieu's efforts, the concept of "field" has mainly been given shape within *institutional theory in organizational analysis*[6]. Inspired by Bourdieu's work, DiMaggio and Powell (1983) were the first to launch this concept within the domain of institutionalism. They used the concept of an organizational field to better locate where institutional processes take place (Scott 2008b:16). Others quickly picked up on this concept and it became a central construct within institutional theory (Wooten & Hoffman 2008:130). Yet Bourdieu's initial contribution to the concept of "field" was rapidly forgotten and his two additional concepts of "capital" and "habitus" have scarcely been considered by institutionalists (Emirbayer & Johnson 2008).

---

5. See Chapter 2 for an elaboration on the concepts of capital and habitus.
6. According to some, it is easier to define what institutional theory *is not* than to define what it actually *is* (DiMaggio & Powell 1991:1) Scott (2008b: 1-18), for example, distinguishes between institutional theory in economics, political science and sociology. Still, the present thesis primarily builds on literature developed from an organizational perspective on institutions, sometimes referred to as *institutional theory in organizational analysis* (Christensen et al. 1997).

The concept of an "organizational field" was initially introduced within institutional theory to explain stability, e.g. why organizations generally develop similar organizational structures and organizational behaviour patterns[7] within the delimited area of an organizational field (Scott 2008a:430). A familiar and often-cited definition of organizational fields is provided by DiMaggio and Powell (1983:148). Their work focuses on organizational fields centred around markets and technologies. They define organizational fields as fields formed by

> (…) those organizations that, in the aggregate, constitute a recognized area of institutional life: key suppliers, resource and product consumers, regulatory agencies, and other organizations that produce similar services or products. (DiMaggio and Powell 1983:148)

However, this perspective on organizational fields, which focuses on homogenizing pressures within fields, was criticized for its inability to explain the persisting diversity of practices within a single field. Moreover, institutionalists found themselves unable to explain processes of change within organizational fields (Scott 2008a:431, Wooten & Hoffman 2008:134).

These clearly felt limitations lead to, among other things, a reconceptualization of the idea of an organizational field. In contrast to previous definitions, which emphasized the stable and static character of organizational fields, these fields are now seen as dynamic and contested, "evolving both through the entry or exit of particular organizations or populations (…) and through an alteration of the interaction patterns and power balances among them" (Wooten & Hoffman 2008:135). Moreover, fields are no longer seen as separate and distinct from organizations, but as both the medium and the outcome of the reproduction practices of field members. As Wooten and Hoffman (2008:136) state by paraphrasing Scott, "the essence of the field perspective was its ability to analyse the ways in which organizations enact their environment and are simultaneously enacted upon by the same environment."[8]

Recently, a new step has been taken in the study of organizational fields: a focus on the processes involved in organizational field *emergence*. However, research into this topic is still rare (Wooten & Hoffman 2008: 139, Kluttz & Fligstein 2016:197) and generally focuses on the emergence of technological fields or specific industries (for examples, see Grodal 2007, Grodal & Granqvist 2014, Gustafsson 2010). Hoffman (1999), and in addition directs attention towards a different type of organizational field, the *issue-based organizational field*. From this perspective, organizational fields are not formed around shared products or markets, but around issues that materialize within societal discourses (Hoffman 1999:352).

---

7. This is generally referred to as *isomorphism*.
8. Chapter 1 presents a more detailed review of the developments in institutional theory in organizational analysis over the past thirty years.

Issue emergence on this level might lead to localized activity between actors whose interests and objectives are triggered by this issue, which in turn leads to the creation of links between organizations that previously did not exist and thus to field emergence (Hoffman 1999:352, Lawrence & Phillips 2004:690).

Honour-related violence appears to be a case in point. Various scholars have connected the increased attention for honour-related violence to changes within macro-cultural discourses on multiculturalism, integration and nationalism. Pratt Ewing (2008), for example, presumes that honour killings generate such extensive attention because they are perceived as emblematic of migrants' failure to assimilate to their host country's culture (see also Hellgren & Hobson 2008; Meetoo & Mirza 2007; Dustin 2006). Other scholars link the increased focus on honour-related violence to disenchantment with the ideals of multiculturalism. According to these scholars, multiculturalism is blamed for the failure of migrants' economic and social integration. Moreover, following the terrorist attacks of 2001 (Twin Towers, USA), 2004 (Theo van Gogh, Netherlands) and 2005 (London), multiculturalism is seen as an impediment to the political integration of Muslim migrants in particular (Vertovec & Wessendorf 2010, Phillips & Saharso 2008:291-292).

As illustrated by the examples at the start of this chapter, the issue of honour-related violence has indeed triggered the interest and objectives of a wide variety of actors, including a theatre maker, migrant organizations and politicians. Moreover, these observations fit Hoffman's (1999:352) understanding of the emergence of an issue-based field. According to Hoffman, the presence of such a field can be observed through 1) increased interaction between particular actors, 2) an increase in the shared information load and 3) the development of a mutual awareness between actors that they are involved in a common debate. He therefore describes fields as "relational spaces that provided organizations with the opportunity to involve itself with other actors" (Wooten & Hoffman 2008:138).

The fact that the emergence of an issue-based organizational field is strongly connected to the emergence of an issue, moreover, means that these types of organizational fields have specific characteristics. For instance, these types of organizational fields might not always be in use. As Downs (1972:38) noted regarding the concept of the *issue-attention cycle,* the attention that an issue receives is not permanent. Instead, issues become important rather suddenly, remain important for a short while and then gradually fade away. In a similar vein Hoffman explains, "Field membership may also be for a finite time period, coinciding with an issue's emergence, growth, and decline" (1999:352). In his more recent work he therefore urges researchers to turn their attention towards the moment that "fields come alive" in order to answer questions on the processes involved in the emergence of an issue-based organizational field (Wooten & Hoffman 2008:139).

The Dutch HRV field case appears to offer a great opportunity to do just that, as the initial research period (2007-2008) coincided with the field's emergence and the issue's emergence is still traceable through document analysis and media analysis. In this thesis, I therefore take up Wooten and Hoffman's invitation and study *the processes involved in the emergence of the Dutch HRV field*. Studying the processes that contribute to the emergence of a new issue-based field calls for exactly the type of questions described previously. When and why do actors take an interest in a certain issue, for example? How do actors come to develop a shared understanding of the problem? Who has the ability to decide how the problem is tackled? In other words, this perspective enables me to make sense of the observed field dynamics and to study the emerging field configurations.

Reintroducing Bourdieu into institutional theory

As hinted above, Bourdieu's contribution to the concept of organizational field was soon forgotten within institutional theory. Nevertheless, this thesis argues that his *theory of practice* offers the theoretical framework needed to make sense of the emerging field configurations. For instance, by describing fields as *fields of power* and *fields of struggle* Bourdieu (Bourdieu & Wacquant 1992:98-99, 101) offers a way to understand the power dynamics within the emerging HRV field. His concept of *capital* additionally helps to explain why some actors are better equipped than others to steer the emerging field in a particular direction. Lastly, his concept of *habitus* might shed some light on why different actors define the problem of honour-related violence in slightly different ways[9].

This thesis argues that institutional theory would benefit greatly from a reintroduction of Bourdieu's theoretical framework into institutional theory. I start my argument by demonstrating how some of the main drawbacks of institutional theory have remained unresolved despite institutionalists' best efforts to resolve them (Chapter 1). In short, institutional theory seemingly remains unable to develop a *theory of action* that adequately incorporates processes of power (Clegg 2010, Suddaby 2010, Munir 2014, Hirsch & Lounsbury 2014, Willmott 2015).

I then go on to argue that piecemeal application has prevented Bourdieu's work from reaching its full potential within organizational analysis, and more specifically within new institutional theory in organizational analysis (Emirbayer and Johnson 2008; Golsorkhi et al. 2009). I conclude this line of reasoning by showing that reintroducing Bourdieu into institutional theory is exactly what institutional theory needs: a balanced theory of action. However, this holds true only insofar as his complete *theory of practice* and thus his theoretical triad of field, capital and habitus are applied.

---

9. The examples above only hint at the applicability of his framework to the present case study. Further elaborations of his key concepts can be found in Part I. Parts II and III go on to present an analysis of this case study from a Bourdieu-inspired perspective.

Still, new institutional theory is not without its own merits and Bourdieu developed his theory of practice many years ago (1977). Thus, while taking Bourdieu's work as my starting point, where necessary I "update" it by introducing some concepts and ideas from institutional theory, for example the concept of issue-based fields, its focus on field emergence and the idea that critical events can hold field-configuring powers.

A final and perhaps more trivial reason why Bourdieu's theoretical framework appears particularly suitable for this study lies in the origin of his theory of practice. He developed this theory based on his study in Kabylia, Algeria (Bourdieu 1977). Honour is a key concept within Kabyle society. In their everyday lives, the Kabyle use the concept of honour as a measure to determine adequate forms of behaviour. In his book *Outline of a Theory of Practice*, Bourdieu (1977) consequently uses numerous examples in which the Kabyle and their honour-related practices appear. It seems particularly fitting that a theory that was developed within a strict honour-based society should now be applied to a new and emerging field in which honour again plays a crucial role.

Research goal and relevance

The goal of this research is twofold. On the one hand, I want to *make sense of the empirical reality* with which I was confronted when I started the initial research in 2007. To use a different phrasing, I want to make sense of all those things within the research field that puzzled me: I want to disentangle the field dynamics that I witnessed between and within the actors involved in the issue of honour-related violence and make sense of the emerging field configurations. Moreover, I want to understand how the issue of honour-related violence emerged in the first place.

I therefore conducted a case study of firstly the emergence of the issue and secondly the emergence of the honour-related violence field. This case study encompasses three components: 1.) a media analysis of Dutch national newspapers between 1990 and 2010, 2.) an analysis of the parliamentary debates on honour-related violence between 1990 and 2010 and 3.) an ethnographic field study that took place in 2007-2008.

With this thesis I also hope to make a *theoretical contribution*. I do this firstly by investigating the processes involved in the emergence of an issue-based field. Secondly, I investigate the potential of reintroducing Bourdieu's work into new institutional theory in organizational analysis. I will explore this potential by applying Bourdieu's theoretical triad of field, capital and habitus to a case study of an emerging issue-based field. Lastly, I wish to help bring Bourdieu's work into the twenty-first century by updating it with some of institutional theory's strong concepts and ideas.

By combining an empirical goal with a theoretical one, I adhere to *an interpretive research tradition* (Schwartz-Shea & Yanow 2012). During my research I constantly moved back and forth between studying empirical material and exploring theoretical considerations. This *iterative process* made it possible to study the issue of honour-related violence and the subsequent field emergence from a variety of angles, enabling me to develop a full understanding of both the issue's and the field's emergence.

Several years have passed since the initial research that inspired this case study. Part of the reason for this delay lies in the aforedescribed iterative working method: theoretical and empirical findings regularly inspired me to include additional research and explore additional theoretical schools of thought. Personal circumstances also occasionally forced me to take a step back from the research and writing process. While these breaks drew out the research, they also gave me the opportunity to view the data from a fresh perspective, which helped crystalize the overall patterns. The key questions that this case study addresses also remain as relevant as ever. Despite the intervening years studies into the processes involved in organizational field emergence are still rare, as are studies that apply Bourdieu's theoretical triad of habitus, capital and field.

Central research questions

The topics outlined above come together to form the following main research questions:

What actors and processes contributed to the emergence of the issue-based organizational field on honour-related violence in the Netherlands?

How does Bourdieu's theory of practice contribute to an understanding of the processes involved in organizational field emergence?

Outline

In a way, this thesis is presented in reverse. As explained in this introduction it were the results of a study conducted in 2007 and 2008 that led me to investigate the work of the new institutionalists and Bourdieu on organizational fields and field emergence. The results of this investigation are presented in *Part I*. *Chapter 1* describes institutional theory's pendulum swings between a focus on structure and a focus on agency. I then describe Bourdieu's theory of practice in *Chapter 2*. *Chapter 3* then addresses the methodological groundwork of this case study.

The results of my theoretical investigations in turn motivated me to reconstruct how the issue of honour-related violence first materialized in the Dutch public discourse. This reconstruction is presented in *Part II*. I start by explaining how the labels of honour killing and honour-related violence first emerged within Dutch media and parliament. The emergence of these labels is subsequently represented in a series of charts to illustrate how the issue of honour-related violence reached a sequence of peaks in issue attention in 1999, 2003 and 2004 (*Chapter 4*). I go on to describe the four events that triggered these attention peaks: the actual and attempted honour killings of Kezban (1999), Hassan (1999), Zarife (2003) and Gül (2004). By describing the media's representation of these murders, I hope to illustrate some of the micro dynamics that contributed to the issue's emergence (*Chapter 5*). *Chapter 6* then describes the macro-cultural discourses that other scholars have linked to the emergence of the issue of honour-related violence. Next, *Chapter 7* argues that both the developments at the macro level and the activities at the micro level of relevant actors helped create a sense of *moral panic* about honour killings, which in turn facilitated the development of a Dutch HRV field.

In *Chapter 8*, I describe the political debates that followed Gül's murder. In 2006 these debates eventually led to the announcement of a large-scale interministerial programme against honour-related violence. The subsequent chapters of *Part III* present the data that led me to believe that it is indeed possible to speak of the emergence of a HRV field. These chapters provide answers to a series of empirical questions: What actors play key roles in the field of honour-related violence, and what is the basis from which they derive their positions (*Chapter 9*)? What do the actors involved understand the term "honour-related violence" to mean (*Chapter 10*)? Lastly, the ways in which the various actors organize themselves in relation to this problem is analysed in *Chapter 11*.

The thesis ends with a discussion and conclusion, in which I phrase an answer to the central research questions. I also reflect on the theoretical and practical implications of this case study.

Part I
Studying an organizational field

1. Institutional theory's pendulum swings

How and why do organizations behave the way they do, and what are the consequences of their behaviour? These are key questions within organizational theory (Greenwood et al. 2008:1). They are also key questions in this study. Why did the topic of honour-related violence trigger the attention of such a diverse group of organizations? How did these organizations subsequently position themselves within the emerging field? And how did taking those positions contribute to the emerging configurations of this issue-based field?

Until the late 1970s these types of questions were answered predominantly from a *functionalist perspective* on organizations and organizational practices. The general line of reasoning within this perspective was that a particular subsystem – for example a certain form of organizational behaviour – emerges, functions and flourishes as a result of its functioning within a broader system: a sector or market, for instance (Lammers et al. 2000:80). This view of organizations was challenged by the introduction by Berger and Luckmann (1967) of *social constructionism* within organizational theory (Scott 1987; Phillips & Malhotra 2008:703), which specifically highlights the importance of meaning making in the production and reproduction of organizational practices.

Berger and Luckmann's line of inquiry was introduced within institutional theory in organizational analysis by a series of papers (Meyer & Rowan 1977; Zucker 1977; DiMaggio & Powell 1983; Tolbert and Zucker 1983) that are now regarded as the initiators of what has been termed *new institutional theory*[10] (DiMaggio & Powell 1991). Within this research tradition, *institutions* are generally defined as cognitive frameworks which, through processes of meaning making, guide actors' behaviour[11] (Scott 2008b:49, Fligstein 2001:108). By accentuating how institutions shape the actors' interpretations of social life, new institutionalism has shifted the emphasis to the structural dimension of institutions. As a consequence the source of action is perceived to exist primarily exogenous to the actor. As Wooten and Hoffman (2008:130) phrase it, "Action is not a choice among unlimited possibilities but rather among narrowly defined set of legitimate options". Institutions are thus perceived as structures acting as social facts that actors subsequently take into consideration when determining appropriate forms of action. As social facts

---

10. New institutional theory is sometimes referred to as "neo" institutional theory (see for example Christensen et al. 1997). DiMaggio and Powel (1991) contrast it with *old institutionalism*, which departs from a functionalist perspective on actors and their actions.
11. Within this thesis the concept of *actor* can denote an organization or an individual.

are transmitted from one actor to another, they take on a rule-like and taken-for-granted status and become *institutionalized* (Wooten & Hoffman 2008:131).

Contributions within new institutionalism initially focused principally on how institutional pressures support and/or constrain organizational processes, thereby seeking to explain the convergence and stability of organizational practices within an organizational field (Battilana, 2006a:654; Garud et al. 2007:957; Boxenbaum & Jonsson 2008:78). From its inception new institutional theory's focus on the structural dimension of institutions has been criticized, however, for lacking an adequate *theory of action* (Christensen et al. 1997:392; Westenholz et al. 2006). This shortcoming was summarized neatly by Fligstein:

> Institutional theory in organizational analyses had a limited theory of action because it generally focuses on how meanings become taken for granted in organizational arenas. To the degree that institutional theory in organizational analysis has a theory of action, it treats shared meanings as constrains on action that limit and determine what is meaningful behaviour. (Fligstein 1997:397)

Nevertheless, this very limited conceptualization of action – action as being constrained by shared meaning systems – cannot explain processes such as institutional change or the emergence of a new organizational field. Institutionalists have therefore looked for ways to develop what Hirsch and Lounsbury (1997) term a "more balanced approach to the action - structure duality" (1997:406) (see also Scott 2008a:428).

The following section first describes the quest in new institutional theory for an adequate theory of action. It then discusses the pendulum swings that can be deduced from this review. Chapter 2 then addresses some of the more recent criticisms of institutional theory by reintroducing Bourdieu's work, and more specifically his *theory of practice*, into institutional theory.

1.1 In search of a balanced theory of action

How is it possible that a theory that started out from Berger and Luckmann's social constructionism, which postulates that "[s]ocial order exists *only* as a product of human activity" (Berger & Luckmann in Scott 1987: 495, italics in the original), lost sight of its focus on actors and their activities? Although the founding publications of new institutional theory did indeed focus on the micro processes involved in the processes of institutionalization (see also Scott 1987), researchers building on these seminal works, and specifically on that of DiMaggio and Powell (1983), "somewhat blindly" pursued the more structural implications of their work by focusing on the concepts of isomorphism and decoupling (Suddaby 2010:16).

Moreover, according to Suddaby, institutional theory might have stretched beyond its core purpose, viz. to understand how organizational practices acquire meaning, by focusing on the study of macro-organizational phenomena (Suddaby 2010:14). Yet he also notes that attempts by new institutionalists to remedy this deficiency go back as far as 1988, when a paper by DiMaggio urged institutional scholars to "attend to the agentic and often creative ways in which organizations inculcate and reflect their institutional environments" (Suddaby 2010:15), a process that DiMaggio labelled *institutional entrepreneurship*. Moreover, in 1991 DiMaggio and Powell (1991:16) again called for a more thorough investigation of the micro foundations underpinning the macro structures that had become the focal point of new institutionalism. In other words, they sought to bring these two levels of analysis together.

These early calls for a reintroduction of micro-level analysis, interest and agency did not go unnoticed within the domain of new institutional theory. Between 1997 and 2007 four special issues appeared that respectively concentrated on *Actors and Institutions* (1997), *Institutional Theory and Institutional Change* (2002), *Institutions in the Making: Identity, Power, and the Emergence of New Organizational Forms* (2006) and *Institutional Entrepreneurship as Embedded Agency* (2007). Each of these special issues highlighted the importance of actors and action in the production and reproduction of institutions. At the same time they recognized that institutional theory still lacked an adequate theory of action.

The editors of the first issue, for instance, stress that while institutionalists study the rise and diffusion of new practices, they do so at a macro level, therefore losing sight of the role of actors and action in the process of institutionalization (Christensen et al. 1997:393). In the subsequent issue Dacin et al. (2002:47) advocate a return of agency, interest and power to institutional theory. The importance of agency and power is also stressed in the next special issue, which focuses on how institutions emerge within and between organizations (Westenholz et al. 2006:890). These editors follow Christensen et al. (1997:393) in emphasizing the importance of the micro level of analysis, stating that "[p]aying attention to the local and global simultaneously is key to understanding the construction of new institutions" (Westenholz et al. 2006:894). Lastly, the fourth special issue (Garud et al. 2007) introduces the *paradox of embedded agency* as a solution to institutional theory's quest for a more "balanced approach to the action-structure duality" (Hirsch & Lounsbury 1997:406). This paradox relates to the following question:

> (…) if actors are embedded in an institutional field and subjective to regulative, normative and cognitive processes that structure their cognitions, define their interests and produce their identities (Friedland and Alford, 1991; Clemens and Cook, 1999), how are they able to envision new practices and subsequently get others to adopt them? (Garud et al. 2007:961)

In other words: how can actors who are institutionally embedded distance themselves from institutional pressures and innovate their beliefs and actions? Scholars adhering to new institutionalism developed the following answer to this question: while organizations are indeed shaped by their context, that context is first and foremost the product of human action (Battilana 2006a:654; see also Garud et al. 2007:961).

For instance, organizational fields do not simply emerge out of nowhere: it takes local activity, individual or organized, to bring a field into existence (Lawrence & Phillips 2004). It is in the ambiguity of the structures that actors themselves have created in the first place that they find a platform for agency. This solution to the puzzle of embedded agency corresponds to the more general explanation of the structure-agency relationship as developed in Giddens's structuration theory. His theory conceptualizes structures as processes, existing only through their continual production and reproduction by the actions of knowledgeable agents (Scott 2008a:438).[12]

Following its initial introduction by DiMaggio, the concept of *institutional entrepreneurship* was further developed by others as a means to solve the paradox of an embedded agency. According to Garud et al. (2007:598) the juxtaposition of two concepts that respectively focused on continuity and conformity – the institutional side – and on action, interest and power – the entrepreneurial side – "generates a promising tension" that "opens up avenues for inquiry into how processes associated with continuity and change unfold, and, how such unfolding processes can be influenced strategically".

A variety of studies have sought to understand, for instance, what institutional entrepreneurs do to propagate new organizational forms (Perkmann & Spicer 2007, Child et al. 2007) and under what conditions institutional entrepreneurship is possible (Laurence & Philips 2004, Garud et al. 2007, Maguire et al. 2004) and to capture the qualities necessary to become an institutional entrepreneur (Battilana 2006a, 2006b; Garud et al, 2007; Levy & Scully 2007, Mutch 2007).

However, while some emphasize the benefits of this new line of inquiry, others are more critical. In 2010 the Journal of Management Inquiry published an essay with the provocative title *The State, Power and Agency: Missing in Action in Institutional Theory?*, in which the author takes issue with the concept of the institutional entrepreneur. According to Clegg (2010:5), the concept of an institutional entrepreneur is nothing but a theory-saving devise in the form of a type of "hypermuscular agency". Instead he advises institutionalists to take the role of the state in the production of institutions more seriously. He also criticizes institutionalists' tendency to downplay the role of struggle and conflict, and thus of power, by focusing on how most actors take their institutional environments for granted and so do not question their domination by this environment (Clegg

---

12. See Chapter 2 for Bourdieu's answer to this conundrum.

2010:6). Clegg in contrast accentuates the role of power: "The concept of power is absolutely central to any understanding of society" (Clegg 2010:11).

Sharing the views put forward by Clegg (2010), Suddaby (2010:15) concludes that the stream of literature that developed to bring the actor and agency back into new institutional theory "overshot the mark". He goes on to state,

> Instead of passive cultural dopes, institutional theory now presents organizations as hypermuscular supermen, single handed in their efforts to resists institutional pressure, transform organizational fields and alter institutional logics. Any change, however slight, is now "institutional" and any change agent is an "institutional entrepreneur". (Suddaby 2010:15)

Suddaby subsequently identifies a number of challenges for new institutional theory. Just as the editors of the various special issues had previously, Suddaby (2010:16) suggests that institutionalists need to shift their gaze from macro studies on institutionalization to case studies and interpretive methods "that pay serious attention to the subjective ways in which actors experience institutions". In doing so, Suddaby (2010:18) also suggests a shift from studies that focus on the outcome of institutions to studies that focus on the processes of institutionalization.

Four years later, Kamal Munir repeated Clegg's appeal to better incorporate the concept of power within institutional theory. In 2014 the Journal of Management Inquiry published an essay with the title *A Loss of Power in Institutional Theory*, in which Munir criticized the lack of engagement on the part of new institutionalists with more critical theories that had developed a better understanding of the concept of power. According to Munir (2014:1-2) institutionalists present an overly "sanitary view of the world" by "accepting organizational hierarchies and their inherent power differentials as given."

In their rejoinders to Munir's essay both Willmott (2015) and Hirsch and Lounsbury (2014) subscribe to Munir's criticism. For instance, the latter write,

> We agree with Munir that institutional theory's allergy to power, conflict, and morality has held back organizational studies. In fact, this indictment should not be limited to institutional theory, but is a problem with the field of organization studies more generally. Not only do we risk losing significance but also by avoiding controversial issues and seeing everything as too legitimate, the pages of our journals have become increasingly boring. (…) A more critical institutional perspective will not only focalize attention on issues of power, domination, and inequality, but can also uncover alternative possibilities for change and reformation. (Hirsch and Lounsbury 2014:1)

Willmott (2015:109) subsequently argues that new institutional theory comes from a *conservative tradition* in which "institutions and institutionalization are analysed as if they were a *given* object of scientific investigation, rather than an object embedded in, and reproductive of, relations of domination and oppression" (italics in the original).

Thus, while in 2008 Scott put forward that institutional theory was "approaching adulthood", the above review suggests otherwise. Although institutionalists acknowledged early on that new institutional theory needed to focus on both the macro and the micro processes involved in the production and reproduction of institutions, they still seem to struggle to develop a theory of action that is capable of providing an even-handed approach to the action-structure duality that, moreover, adequately incorporates processes of power and domination.

1.2 Swinging back and forth

While seeking to develop an adequate theory of action, over the past forty years institutionalists seem to have switched from overemphasizing the institutional forces to which actors are subject to overemphasizing the power of the actors to develop and/or change institutions (Clegg 2010, Suddaby 2010). Moreover, while shortcomings were identified as early as in 1988 (DiMaggio) to date scholars still urge new institutionalists to turn their attention to these same deficiencies (Clegg 2010; Suddaby 2010; Munir 2014, Hirsch & Lounsbury 2014, Willmott 2015).

As argued before, this is caused by the inability of new institutionalists to develop an adequate theory of action, one that is capable of incorporating both structural and agent-based forces and so surmounting the macro-micro divide plaguing institutional theory. Developing such a theory is admittedly a daunting prospect, and many have tried to do so and failed. Moreover, balancing structure and agency is not only a challenge that has troubled new institutionalism, it is one that is faced by all scholars working in the social sciences, and organizational analysis in particular. Essentially the challenge is that theories that prefer structure over agency lead to deterministic models, in which humans can act only according to the structures by which they are governed, while preferring agency over structure conversely leads to heroic models of actors, in which contextual and historical influences are not taken into consideration (Garud et al. 2007:961).

As alluded to above, scholars working within the domain of institutional theory appear to have alternated from a functionalist heroic model (old institutionalism) to a deterministic model (new institutionalism) and back again to a heroic model of agency (which could be described as "new" new institutionalism). These developments have been described by Cooper et al. (2008:675) as "flip-flopping" between

> (…) (functional) structuralist and action-theorist accounts of action. The dynamic of the flip-flop depends upon each pole being simultaneously recognized and denied as one or the other side of the dualisms [is] privileged, and subsequently found to be unbalanced by advocates of the alternative pole. (Cooper et al. 2008:676)

In a similar vein, Hirsch and Lounsbury (1997:409) described the development from old to new institutional theory as a pendulum swing towards structuralism.

Yet Clegg (2010) and Suddaby (2010) pointedly describe how the pendulum now seems to have returned to the agency side of the swing.

Although Hirsch and Lounsbury (1997:415) predicted such a swing, it is not what they advocated. On the contrary: they specifically warned institutionalists against these types of swings, stating that "it is important to develop a theory that incorporates both rather than risk alternating excommunications each time the intellectual pendulum shifts."

Three schools of thought have emerged within institutionalism for resolving the most recent criticisms of the institutional entrepreneur. A first development was the advancement of a concept that allows the pendulum to swing back towards a more nuanced form of agency, i.e. *institutional work*. Lawrence et al. (2011) put forward this view in an attempt to bring back the individual into institutional theory. Moreover, they sought to draw attention to

> the myriad, day-to-day equivocal instances of agency that, although aimed at affecting the institutional order, represent a complex mélange of forms of agency – successful and not, simultaneously radical and conservative, strategic and emotional, full of compromises, and rife with unintended consequences (…). (Lawrence et al. 2011:52-53)

The authors go on to define institutional work as the practices of both individuals and collectives that create, maintain or disrupt institutions. However, these actions are always embedded in the institutional structures that they simultaneously produce, reproduce and transform. As such, institutional work represents a new answer to the paradox of the embedded agency.

In their 2011 paper Fligstein and McAdam introduced the concept of *strategic action fields* as another solution to the most recent criticisms of new institutional theory. Their theoretical frameworks bring together elements from various theories, including social movement theory, institutional theory in organizational analysis and the works of Bourdieu and Giddens. Their goal was to develop a "general theory of social change and stability rooted in a view of social life as dominated by a complex web of strategic action fields" (Fligstein and McAdam 2011:2). *Strategic action fields* are subsequently defined as the "fundamental units of collective action in society" (Fligstein & McAdam 2011:3). They represent a meso-level social order in which actors, both individual and collective, "interact with knowledge of one another under a set of common understandings about the purpose of the field, the relationships in the field (including who has power and why), and the field's rules" (Fligstein & McAdam 2011:3).

Fligstein and McAdam's concept of a strategic action field represents an attempt to develop something new, something that rises above the structure-agency dialectic. However, as the authors themselves admit, they borrow heavily from other theories and specifically from Bourdieu's conceptual framework. This raises the question whether it is truly necessary to develop a completely new theory, since Bourdieu's work on the study of organizations has not yet reached its full potential (Emirbayer & Johnson 2008; Golsorkhi et al. 2009).

A final development was the advancement of *the institutional logics perspective* (Thornton et al. 2012). According to Hirsch and Lounsbury (2014) this perspective is well positioned to engage more fully with critical theories and thus the concept of power. The institutional logics perspective, according to Thorneton et al. (2012:5), is a "metatheoretical perspective for studying how individual and organizational actors are influenced by and create and modify elements of institutional logics – which conceivably changes values". Hirsch and Lounsbury (2014:2) subsequently define institutional logics as "configurations of symbolic and material elements (e.g. beliefs and practices) whose effects can be understood via mechanisms that operate in both bottom-up and top-down ways".

Nonetheless, both the institutional work and institutional logic perspectives still depart from an institutional theory framework, and according to Willmott (2015), referring to institutionalists' lack of sensitivity to processes of power, that framework is "fundamentally conservative". Willmott therefore doubts that a solution to institutional theory's lack of power conceptualization can be found within this theory, and he provocatively poses the following question: "If you are actually concerned about domination, oppression, and resistance including its (re)production through "institutional work", why begin with, or stick with a theory in which power lacks a "fundamental role?" (Willmott 2015:110). He consequently wonders if it would not be better to start from a critical form of analysis that has a well-developed understanding of the concept of power, and subsequently add elements of institutional theory that could enrich this analysis.

Following Willmott's suggestion, I do indeed depart from a theory that incorporates an explicit power conceptualization, viz. Bourdieu's theory of practice. Moreover, Bourdieu's theory represents an active attempt to bridge both the structure-agency duality and the macro-micro divide. Nonetheless, new institutional theory is not without its own merits. While taking Bourdieu's work as starting point, where necessary I "update" it by introducing some concepts and ideas from institutional theory.

2. Bringing Bourdieu back into institutional theory

Over the past forty years organizational scholars have increasingly shown an interest in the work of Pierre Bourdieu, facilitated in part by the translation of Bourdieu's work into English (Emirbayer & Johnson 2008:2; Golsorkhi et al 2009:780). This has also been the case within new institutional theory. In their introduction to the edited volume *The New Institutionalism in Organizational Analysis* DiMaggio and Powel (1991) for instance already refer to his work as a means for tackling institutional theory's quest for a theory of action. They particular highlight the potential offered by the concept of habitus, as it explains why strategically oriented actors repeatedly reproduce structures that are not in their best interests. As such, according to DiMaggio and Powell (1991:26), Bourdieu's framework "offers a particular balanced and multifaceted approach to action."

Hirsch and Lounsbury (1997:413) similarly refer back to Bourdieu's work in their critique of DiMaggio and Powel's demarcation between old and new institutionalism. They qualify the dichotomy between "old" and "new" institutionalism as "false" and "misleading". They subsequently advocate returning Bourdieu to institutional theory as a way to end this "family quarrel"; they feel that Bourdieu's grand theory encompasses elements that appeal to both old and new institutionalists.

Despite these appeals only a small number of empirical studies have indeed sought to incorporate Bourdieu's work into an institutional framework (for instance, see Oakes et al. (1998) and Kurunmäki (1999)). Even then, these examples can be criticized for the piecemeal fashion in which they apply Bourdieu's framework.

2.1 Applying Bourdieu in a piecemeal fashion: a critique

While the concepts of field and capital are widely used in organizational literature, the same cannot be said of the concept of habitus. In their review entitled *Bourdieu and organizational analysis*, Emirbayer and Johnson (2008) therefore conclude that

> (...) the specific ways in which these terms are being used provide ample evidence that the full significance of his relational mode of thought has yet to be apprehended. Moreover, the almost inattention to habitus, the third of Bourdieu's major concepts, without which the concepts of field and capital (at least as he deployed them) make no sense, further attest to the misappropriation of his ideas and to the lack of appreciation of their potential usefulness. (Emirbayer and Johnson 2008:2)

Emirbayer and Johnson go on to conclude that "Bourdieu has had virtually no impact on organizational analysis" (2008:2). They argue that the added value of Bourdieu's theoretical framework lies in the combined use of his main concepts: field, capital and habitus. Phrased differently, the whole of his theory is greater than the sum of its parts (Dobbin 2008:53). Nonetheless, in the past these concepts have mainly been applied in a piecemeal fashion (Emirbayer & Johnson 2008:1-2; Swartz 2008:45; Golsorkhi et al. 2009:780). For instance, while the concept of field has been embraced within institutional theory, it is seldom used in combination with the two other concepts.

In their introduction to a special issue on Bourdieu's relevance to organizational analysis Golsorkhi et al. (2009:780) subscribe to the foregoing conclusion. They additionally emphasize the significance of Bourdieu's work in making sense of processes of domination and power. The issue of domination, they argue, and more specifically the conscious and unconscious ways in which domination and systems of domination are produced and reproduced within and between organizations, is an understudied issue within organizational theory. They go on to state that by engaging more fully with Bourdieu's writing organizational theorists could "become more critical in an unstigmatized way" (Golsorkhi et al. 2009:781).

Where these scholars are quite harsh in their criticism of organizational theorists' engagement with Bourdieu, Dobbin (2008) is more apologetic. In his rejoinder to Emirbayer and Johnson's paper, Dobbin (2008:54) argues that applying Bourdieu's theory in a holistic manner is a challenge. He also remarks that American organizational theorists, in particular, work according to quite different epistemological and evidentiary standards, using regression coefficients rather than ethnographies. Where Bourdieu uses broad strokes to paint the whole picture, American sociologists have worked in a more compartmentalized manner, "flashing out different parts of a bigger story" (Dobbin 2008:55): while Bourdieu tried to paint the whole of the elephant, scholars such as institutionalists have meticulously worked on painting its legs, an ear or its tail (Dobbin 2008:55).

Even so, studies by Vaughan (2008) and Wright (2009) illustrate how rewarding it can be to indeed make an effort to apply all Bourdieu's concepts in an integrated manner. In her 2008 paper, Vaughan describes the National Aeronautics and Space Administration (NASA) as an organizational field in its own right. Within the confines of that field, she studied the 1986 space shuttle *Challenger* accident by focusing on NASA's decision to launch despite the engineers' objections. Vaughan found that NASA personnel had developed a disposition (habitus) that a certain amount of deviance in research results was an "acceptable risk". Where it intersected with the power configuration within the field – the manager was positioned above other decision-makers such as engineers – and the structure of the field, which hindered communication between the separate engineering departments, this disposition was what led to the fatal decision launch in the face of the objections.

Wright (2009) also applied Bourdieu's theoretical triad of habitus, field and capital in her study focusing on the development of institutions within the field formed by England's first-class county cricket. Using a historical narrative method, Wright examined the changing positions of professionals and amateurs in English cricket. Within this field the "professional" label was used to denote sportsmen who were paid to play cricket, while the "amateur" tag referred to the gentlemen players, i.e. the English elite who financed the sport. Initially, in the mid-19th century, cricket as a field was dominated by the latter group. Based on their economic and social capital, which was generated by their "shared habitus of cricket as moral character arising from socialization in elite schools, universities, church and service of Empire" (Wright 2009: 866), the amateurs were in a position to establish the rules of the game within this field. However, England's development from an agricultural society of privileged birthright into an industrial society permitting social mobility led professional cricketers to question this status quo. These structural changes opened up the opportunity for professionals to acquire economic capital and thus the power to challenge the status quo, which in the end led to a breakdown of the amateur-professional classification (Wright 2009:865).

These analyses of both Vaughan (2008) and Wright (2009) convincingly illustrate how a Bourdieusian framework helps in the study of the micro dynamics of position-taking, conflict and domination, while at the same time placing these dynamics in their historical context and so relating these micro processes to macro-level developments. These inspiring examples, in combination with the convincing appeal by Emirbayer and Johnson (2008) and Golsorkhi et al. (2009:780) to more fully exploit the potential of Bourdieu's theory of practice, encouraged me to apply Bourdieu's framework to study the emergence of an issue-based field. In doing so, I hope to contribute to institutional theory's quest for an adequate theory of action.

Still, as Swartz (2008:51) critically points out, the proof of the pudding is in the eating. While Emirbayer and Johnson (2008:2) give us a generative reading of Bourdieu's work by translating it to organizational analysis, "the strength of any conceptual framework in the social sciences lies in its ability to generate new empirical investigations with fresh theoretical insights" (Swartz 2008:51). In the final chapter of Part I, I therefore explain how I conducted the research that will provide the "pudding" for my proposition that Bourdieu's original framework could offer institutional theory an adequate theory of action. The two following parts of the present thesis then display the empirical data that is analysed using a Bourdieusian framework. In the final chapter of my thesis I return to this proposition and critically examine how a reintroduction of Bourdieu's work does indeed solve a number of institutional theory's more persistent challenges, for example the macro-micro divide, the structure-agency duality and the inclusion of processes of power.

2.2 A theory of practice

Institutional theory's quest for a theory of action has never been a unique one. Various other areas of research have experienced similar challenges, for instance social movement theory and organizational culture studies. More generally, it can be concluded that it is a quest that has troubled, and still troubles, the social sciences overall. In his oeuvre Bourdieu explicitly sets out to fulfil this quest by developing a *theory of practice*. That theory is intended to transcend ancient dichotomies such as the macro-micro divide and the structure-agency dialectic. In order to transcend these dichotomies Bourdieu starts from an epistemological dichotomy, namely the *subjectivist-objectivist dichotomy* (Thompson 1991:11, Wacquant 1992:3).

Bourdieu (1977:1-5) finds that *subjectivism* falls short of delivering scientific knowledge by settling for a representation of reality that is based on the meaning attributed to that reality by the research population. This, he postulates, is merely a layman's representation of reality, and science should strive to deliver more than this practical knowledge alone. In contrast, *objectivism* seeks to represent reality in terms of objectified structures, and so breaks with immediate (i.e. lay) experience as the basis for knowledge. However, by completely ignoring this lay experience, objectivism neglects the temporal dimension of any sequence of actions, and consequently only grasps half the truth of any series of actions.

For example, when studied from a subjectivist perspective the exchange of gifts may be perceived as token of appreciation. However, this ignores the unconscious principle of the reciprocity of gifts. In contrast, when studied from an objectivist perspective the exchange of gifts is considered in a mechanical manner, i.e. viewed as a cycle of reciprocity, in which the obligation to give is followed by the obligation to give in return. Nonetheless, this model-like mechanical approach does not take into consideration that the meaning attributed to the gift exchange depends on the response that it triggers. Moreover, actors can play on time, meaning that the time that elapses between gift and counter-gift may vary, which has consequences for the meaning attributed to the gifts. For instance, if the gift immediately has the response of a counter-gift that is identical to the primary gift, this is perceived as a refusal to accept the gift in the first place (Bourdieu 1977:4-5). Bourdieu therefore concludes that it is the combination of these two perspectives that "defines the full truth of the gift" (Bourdieu 1977:5)[13].

The present thesis follows Bourdieu's ambition to move beyond the subjectivist-objectivist dichotomy and aspires to combine both subjectivist and objecti-

---

13. Bourdieu (1977:4) here puts forward not only a theory of action; in the same instance he also puts forward a theory of scientific practice. The next chapter elaborates further on the position that Bourdieu takes with regard to scientific knowledge, where I present the methodological contemplations included in this research process.

vist types of knowledge by incorporating both the reality representations given by the research population and an analysis of the patterns that can be deduced from these representations. The epistemological and ontological grounding of this research is explained at greater length in Chapter 3.

Habitus

Bourdieu's theory of practice is intended as a theory that surmounts the dichotomy of objectivism-subjectivism described above. In this theory the concept of *habitus* takes centre stage. In a typical Bourdieusian manner, he defines habitus as

> systems of durable, transposable *dispositions,* structured structures predisposed to function as structuring structures, that is, as principles of the generation and structuring of practices and representations which can be objectively "regulated" and "regular" without in any way being the product of obedience to rules, objectively adapted to their goals without presupposing a conscious aiming at end or an express mastery of the operations necessary to attain them and, being all this, collectively orchestrated without being the product of the orchestrating of action or conduct. (Bourdieu 1977:72, italics in the original)

With this definition Bourdieu seeks to detach the habitus concept from the more mechanical (objectivist) explanations of action, which emphasize the model-like or rule-like manner in which action B follows action A. At the same time, Bourdieu distances himself from the idea that any action is the result of conscious deliberations and thus the result of free will (Bourdieu 1977:73). In other words, this concept attempts to balance the internalized structural forces that drive actions and the agnatic forces that determine actions (Bourdieu 1977:82).

The general idea behind the habitus concept is that it incorporates past experiences through the formation of dispositions that in the present guide an actor's interpretation of reality, which subsequently informs all his future actions. In guiding an actor's interpretation of reality the concept of habitus directs attention towards the layman's interpretation of reality (subjectivism), while at the same time directing attention towards how this interpretation of reality is structured by past experiences (objectivism).

Moreover, the habitus concept helps Bourdieu (1977:72-94) to integrate a historical component into his theory of practice. Besides the individual's own past experiences the habitus is also informed by processes of socialization within a particular group: the past experiences of the social group or class within which the individual is socialized are integrated in the individual's own dispositions. A habitus, consequently, is not individually owned.

Bourdieu's work (1977:80-87) stresses the shared nature of the habitus. He describes this as *class habitus,* by which he refers to a social group that shares a similar history and thus similar dispositions. An actor's habitus subsequently is

> never anything other than a certain specification of the collective history of his group or class, *each individual system of dispositions* may be seen as a *structural variant* of all the other group or class habitus, expressing the difference between trajectories and positions insides or outside the class. (Bourdieu 1977:86, italics in the original)

Moreover, social classes are not alone in developing common dispositions. The same form of development may be presumed to occur within occupational classes. It could subsequently be presupposed that differences in occupational habitus might lead to the variances in issue interpretation. This proposition is investigated further in the course of the present research.

The habitus, however, does not work in a conscious manner: actors do not consciously invoke their past experiences, or their socialization, when determining their future actions. Rather, the habitus functions in a somewhat unconscious manner, invoking tacit knowledge. Actors unconsciously invoke past experiences to calculate the possible outcomes of future actions. This calculation of possibilities then leads them to take certain actions (Bourdieu 1977:76-78).

For instance, in her study of the *Challenger* launch, Vaughan (2008) concluded that NASA personnel had developed a disposition to the effect that a certain degree of deviance in the research results was acceptable. Consequently, when they identified a minor deviance in the Challenger's research results, this did not automatically lead to the conclusion that the launch needed to be aborted.

Bourdieu summarizes this unconscious integration of history within the habitus as follows:

> The "unconscious" is never anything other than the forgetting of history which history itself produces by incorporating the objective structures it produces in the second natures of habitus (...) It is because subjects do not, strictly speaking, know what they are doing that what they are doing has more meaning than they know. The habitus is the universalizing mediation which causes an individual agent's practices, without either explicit reason or significant intent, to be none the less "sensible" and "reasonable". That part of practices which remains obscure in the eyes of their own producers is the aspect by which they are objectively adjusted to other practices and to the structures of which the principle of their production is itself the product. (Bourdieu 1977:79)

This excerpt further clarifies Bourdieu's perception of the workings of the habitus. In a somewhat intricate manner, the quote alludes to the actors' lack of awareness of how their calculations of possibilities are mediated through their habitus. What actors perceive as feasible action options varies depending on their past experiences and processes of socialization. As a consequence, actors are inclined to reproduce and thus affirm the historical structures that are engraved on their habitus.

These elaborations on the concept of habitus offer some lines of enquiry for studying an emerging issue-based field such as the influence of an actor's occupational habitus on his or her perception of the issue of honour-related violence.

The more general question that can be inferred from this presupposition is how variances in the habitus of field members contribute and/or influence the processes of field formation.

Processes of power: the symbolic violence concept

Bourdieu (1977:196-197) connects the processes described above to the concept of *symbolic violence*, by which he means the way both dominating and dominated actors unknowingly contribute to the persistence of unequal power relationships. Based on their habitus, dominant actors will assess certain actions as feasible, while the dominated in contrast will not even contemplate such actions or will assess them as impossible. Both types of actors therefore display / reproduce the types of actions that correspond to their respective positions and / or classes in society. Moreover, habitus causes both the dominant and the dominated actors to perceive this unequal relationship as legitimate.

However, this gentle and invisible form of violence, "which is never recognized as such, and is not so much undergone as chosen" (Bourdieu 1977:192), is preceded by a more visible form of violence. Bourdieu (1977:184) distinguishes two modes of domination: first, a *direct form of domination*, which is acted out between agents, and second, the *subtle mode of domination* that is described above. The latter form of domination, according to Bourdieu (1977:184), is only possible if and when the structures that support a certain distribution of power are in place. The more a recognized area of life is institutionalized, the fewer overt struggles for power will occur and thus the less the actor's cost will be to retain his or her dominant position. In such instances, "the dominant class have only to *let the system they dominate take its own course* in order to exercise their domination" (Bourdieu 1977:190, italics in the original).

In contrast, new and emerging fields require agents to invest in the development of such configurations. Consequently, the struggles for power become more open and above all more costly. These overt power conflicts require agents to invest time and effort to bring into place the structures that support their dominant positions. Bourdieu summarizes these types of processes as follows:

> (...) until such a system exists, they have to work directly, daily, personally, to produce and reproduce conditions of domination which are even then never entirely trustworthy. Because they cannot be satisfied with appropriating the profits of a social machine which has not yet developed the power of self-perpetuation they are obliged to resort to *the elementary forms of domination,* the direct domination of one person by another (...). (Bourdieu 1977:190, italics in the original)

This elaboration on processes of power triggers some questions. Firstly, on what basis are particular actors able to exert power over other actors? In other words, what defines who is in a position to dominate another actor? Secondly, how do some actors come to develop a habitus that supports their dominant position within society, while others develop a habitus that leads them to assume and reproduce a dominated position? These questions on domination call for the introduction of two of Bourdieu's other concepts: *capital* and *field*.

Capital and field

According to Bourdieu (Bourdieu & Wacquant 1992) it is the amount and type of capital that actors possess which determines whether they are in a position to dominate others. However, the relative worth of the types of capital depends on the field in which they are deployed (Bourdieu & Wacquant 1992:101).

Bourdieu distinguishes three "fundamental species" of capital: economic, cultural and social capital (Bourdieu & Wacquant 1992:119). *Economic capital* denotes an actor's material welfare, the possession of money and property, for example buildings and raw materials. *Cultural capital*, or informational capital as it is also known, denotes an actor's cultural goods. Bourdieu breaks cultural capital down into three separate forms. The first is the *embodied* form, which through processes of socialization is engraved on an actor's habitus: verbal facility, ecstatic preferences and knowledge of educational systems, for example. The next is an *objectified* form, meaning books and instruments that require particular cultural abilities to utilize. The last is an *institutionalized* form, by which Bourdieu refers to educational credentials – titles – that have become crucial to determining an actor's status and his ability to gain access to particular jobs (see also Swartz 1997:75-77). Bourdieu's third type of capital, *social capital*, denotes an actor's "durable network of more or less institutionalized relationships of mutual acquaintance and recognition" (Bourdieu & Wacquant 1992:119)[14].

Bourdieu additionally distinguishes a fourth type of capital: *symbolic capital*. Any of the above forms of capital can become symbolic capital and thus the most valued type of capital within a given field (Bourdieu & Wacquant 1992:119, Bourdieu 1989:17). In the same way as symbolic violence, symbolic capital represents the type of capital that is intrinsically connected to a field. Consequently, even though it is the dominant force of structuration within the field, its workings go largely unrecognized (Bourdieu 1977:171-183).

While the value attributed to any type of capital depends on the field in which it is put to use, at the same time the distribution of capital over a field determines the potential positions of actors within a field and thus the structure of the field. The following quote further exemplifies the close relationship between field and capital:

---

14. Bourdieu's work connects these types of capital, and their interconnectedness to habitus, to the reproduction of social classes. He particular highlights the role of educational systems in reifying the cultural differences between social classes.

(...) a field may be defined as a network, or a configuration, of objective relations between positions. These positions are objectively defined, in their existence and in the determinations they impose upon their occupants, agents or institutions, by their present and potential situation (*situs*) in the structure of the distribution of species of power (or capital) whose possession commands access to the specific profits that are at stake in the field, as well as by their objective relation to other positions (domination, subordination, homology, etc.). (Bourdieu & Wacquant 1992:97)

The concept of field, just as the concept of habitus, thus refers to an *objectified structure*: a concept developed by Bourdieu to interpret an empirical reality in which he observed that particular groups of actors operate under one and the same logic – a logic, moreover, that is distinct from the logic that governs other groups of actors. In sum, fields are "relatively autonomous social microcosms, i. e., spaces of objective relations that are the site of a logic and a necessity that are *specific and irreducible* to those that regulate other fields" (Bourdieu & Wacquant 1992:97, italics in the original).

Consequently, a field is *not* formed by a group of actors[15], but rather by the relationship between the positions that compose the field. Those positions in turn are defined by the type and amount of capital available to the actor occupying this position (Bourdieu & Wacquant 1992:107). A study of a field may subsequently lead to a study of how actors are distributed within that field across two dimensions: firstly according to the overall capital they possess, and secondly according to the structure of their capital, i.e. "the relative weight of their different species of capital, economic and cultural, in the total volume of their assets" (Bourdieu 1989:17).

For example, within the field of England's first class county cricket, amateurs and professionals were historically positioned as follows. In the first dimension, professional players were positioned according to their access to cultural capital, specifically the objectified and the institutionalized form; they knew how to use the bat and held the title of professional. Amateur players, in contrast, were positioned according to their access to cultural capital, specifically embodied capital; they shared a "habitus of cricket as moral character" (Wright 2009:866). Moreover, as the sport's financers they also had access to economic capital. Lastly, they had broad networks of relationships, developed during their "socialization in elite schools, universities, church and service of Empire" (Wright 2009:866) and thus had access to social capital.

It is not only the greater variety of capital that initially placed amateur players in a dominant position. In the mid-19th century relatively little weight was attributed to the cultural capital of the professional players while economic and social

---

15. This position is what sets Bourdieu's framework apart from institutionalists, who equate a field with its field members (see DiMaggio & Powell 1983).

capital carried a great deal of weight within the field of cricket. Amateur players were placed in a dominant position on account of both the first and second dimensions (see Wright 2009).

This example also illustrates how the value of a certain type of capital within the delimited space of a field is influenced by broader societal developments and thus the broader field in which the sub-field is *nested*. Emirbayer and Johnson (2008:22-32) refer to this idea by the concept of nested fields: the organizations that make up the *organizational field* can in turn be studied as fields on their own account. They describe this phenomenon using the phrase *organization-as-field*. Within an organization-as-field the same processes can be observed as in an organizational field: for example, individual actors within the organization-as-field are able to hold particular positions within this field according to their capital and the dispositions inscribed on their habitus.

The authors describe the relationship between separate organizational fields and an organization-as-field as a vertical relationship of "self-similarity across levels" (White 1992 in Emirbayer & Johnson 2008:22). They illustrate that the same processes that can be observed at the organizational field level can also be seen at the organization-as-field level. However, while the same concepts may be used to analyse processes within an organization-as-field (the micro level) and the organizational level (the meso level), the material reality to which they allude might differ. The concept of an actor at the organizational field level, for example, most commonly refers to an organization, not to an individual. In contrast, actors within an organization-as-field are often individuals, or representatives of smaller sub-populations within an organization.

This offers further lines of inquiry for studying organizational field emergence. Empirically the following questions come to mind: 1.) How are actors positioned within the emerging HRV field on account of both how much capital they possess and the value attributed to the relevant type (or types) of capital? 2.) Can we thus identify the capital deemed most important and/or worthwhile pursuing within the emerging field?

The game metaphor

Bourdieu often compares the workings of fields with playing a game[16]. In this game the separate players hold a variety of cards, representing the various types of capital. The purpose of the game is to retrieve the card (i.e. capital) that represents the trump card in that specific game. A field can therefore also be described as a *field of struggles*. However, besides functioning as the stake in this struggle,

---

16. At the same time, Bourdieu cautions that unlike a game a field "is not the product of a deliberate act of creation, and it follows rules or better, regularities, that are not explicit and codified" (Bourdieu & Wacquant 1992:98).

these cards also function as "weapons". The total number of cards, in combination with their composition, determines a player's power and influence. Fields are therefore described as *fields of power* at the same time. The cards determine a player's relative strength in the game – his or her *position* – and the player's strategic orientation toward the game – his or her *position-taking*. For instance, players can choose to increase the number of cards or hold on to their cards, or alternatively they can try to change the stakes of the game and thus the card denoted as the trump card (Bourdieu & Wacquant 1992:98-99, 101).

This game metaphor offers further insight into how Bourdieu perceives field dynamics. For the field under investigation, this metaphor gives rise to questions such as what forms of struggle can be witnessed within the emerging HRV field, and how actors deploy the capital to which they have access in order to move the emerging field in a particular direction.

The logic of a field: illusio and doxa

A field's configuration depends not only on the distribution of positions across it. A field's configuration also depends on the field members' *illusio* and the field's *doxa*. The concept of illusio denotes a specific type of interest[17], described by Bourdieu as being "invested, taken in and by the game. To be interested is to accord a given social game that what happens in it matters, that its stakes are important (...) and worth pursuing" (Bourdieu & Wacquant 1992:116). Each field subsequently calls for a specific type of illusio. Moreover, each actor within the field holds his or her own illusio, depending on field position (Bourdieu & Wacquant 1992:117). Consequently, players who do not believe in the "game" and its stakes cannot partake in the game. Even actors who oppose the game need to invest in the game in order to change it.

It is therefore safe to presuppose that the actors who actively participate in the Dutch HRV field at a minimum agree on the fact that honour-related violence is indeed a social problem. Moreover, it may be presupposed that in order for a field to emerge enough actors need to develop an illusio of the game played within that particular field – in this case, to combat honour-related violence.

The concept of *doxa* forms the second element of a field's logic. It adds a further layer to Bourdieu's concept field. Besides containing a field of struggle and a field of power, a field also contains a doxa. The concept of doxa refers to the political order, the classifications in use, within a given field (Bourdieu 1977: 165-169). For instance, within the HRV field the emerging doxa includes a definition of the issue of honour-related violence. By unconsciously integrating a field's

---

17. Bourdieu contrasts his conceptualization of illusio with a state of indifference, which he describes as being "unmoved" by the game.

doxa into their habitus over time, actors contribute to the creation of a "quasi-perfect fit" between the objective order, the field and the subjective principles of organization, their habitus (Bourdieu 1977:164). This reproduction of a doxa within the habitus subsequently helps actors to make sense of the world around them and to act according to the rules of the "game".

These types of synchronous situations are, nevertheless, more likely to occur in fields that are mature and therefore have developed more stable taxonomies. Under such circumstances,

> the established cosmological and political order is perceived not as arbitrary, i.a. as one possible order among others, but as a self-evident and natural order which goes without saying and therefore goes unquestioned, the agents' aspirations have the same limits as the objective conditions of which they are the product. (Bourdieu 1977:166)

The order represented by the doxa thus represents the order that is perceived as the legitimate, taken-for-granted order within a field. As such it is often supported by some or all of the field's dominant actors: it is through this *doxic order* that they exert symbolic violence. Only in times of crisis is this order questioned, since such times potentially disrupt the intimate fit between the subjective structures (habitus) and the objective structures (field) and thus create space for a critique of the existing order (Bourdieu 1977:169).

In an emerging field, the doxa may be presupposed to still be under construction. Moreover, actors will most probably seek to actively influence the developing doxa to fit their specific interests, their illusio. In studying the emergence of a Dutch HRV field, it is therefore interesting to consider the debates on the issue's definition and how actors attempt to manipulate that definition. Moreover, field members might also deem other definitions to be important, for instance how domestic violence is defined. However, what other definitions are under negotiation within the emerging HRV field is a matter of empirical observation.

Development of the field over time

Lastly, Bourdieu directs attention to the aspect of time in the workings of fields,

> (...) the strategies of a "player" and everything that defines his "game" are the function not only of the volume and structure of his capital *at the moment under consideration* and the game chance (...) they guarantee him, but also of the *evolution over time* of the volume and structure of this capital, that is, of his social trajectory and of the dispositions (habitus) constituted in the prolonged relation to a definite distribution of objective chances. (Bourdieu & Wacquant 1992:99, italics in the original)

According to Bourdieu the structure of a field is fluid: "*At each moment*, it is the state of the relations of force between players that defines the structure of the field" (Bourdieu & Wacquant 1992:99, italics by NVB). Therefore, a field is constantly in a state of flux, particularly if it is a new field in which actors still "have to work directly, daily, personally, to produce and reproduce conditions of domination" (Bourdieu 1977:190), e.g. the field's doxa and symbolic capital.

Time not only influences the structure of a field at a particular moment in time, the development of a "game" *over time* also has consequences. As the quote indicates, an actor's accumulation of capital and thus his or her position in the field may change over time, which in turn might lead to changes in the actor's habitus. Moreover, as time passes actors can incorporate a field's doxa, which in turn might lead to changes in their perception of reality. Bourdieu sums up this type of process neatly with his phrase, "the field structures the habitus". However, the relationship between field and habitus works both ways. An actor's habitus in turn "contributes to constituting the field as a meaningful world (...)" (Bourdieu & Wacquant 1992:127).

In considering the element of time with regard to this study of field emergence, various questions spring to mind. For instance, it is possible to distinguish separate stages in field emergence? And if issue emergence and field emergence refer to different stages, how do those stages then relate to one another? Lastly, within the processes of its emergence a field is supposedly in a constant state of flux; it is therefore crucial to constantly bear in mind the situationality of any empirical observations.

[(Habitus) (Capital)] + Field = Practice

By integrating the concepts of field and capital into his theory of practice Bourdieu adds further layers to the workings of the concept of habitus. As explained above, actors unconsciously invoke past experiences to calculate the possible outcomes of future actions. Yet as has also been shown above, this calculation of possibilities always takes place within a certain context. Any calculation will therefore also take into account the individual's current position and thus his or her power within a given field. Consequently, the actions taken by the actor are the result of the actor's habitus, in combination with his or her capital, whose value is determined by the field's logic. Figure 1. offers a schematic representation of Bourdieu's *theory of practice*.

The following example also illustrates the workings of Bourdieu's theory of practice. As described previously, Vaughan (2008) showed in her study of the *Challenger* launch how NASA personnel had developed a disposition in which a certain amount of deviance in the research results was acceptable. However, the decision to launch was inspired not only by the jointly developed disposition. The action taken was the result of the intersection of the developed disposition *and* the configuration of the NASA field, which was defined by the value attributed to the various forms of capital. Within the NASA field, the engineers' cultural capital, their knowledge of the *Challenger*'s machinery, was outclassed by the manager's capital. His social capital, in the form of his position within the organization, was perceived as the legitimate source of power in the decision-making process. Consequently, the NASA engineers did not oppose the manager's decision to launch (see Vaughan 2008).

Figure 1. The interrelationship between habitus, field and capital

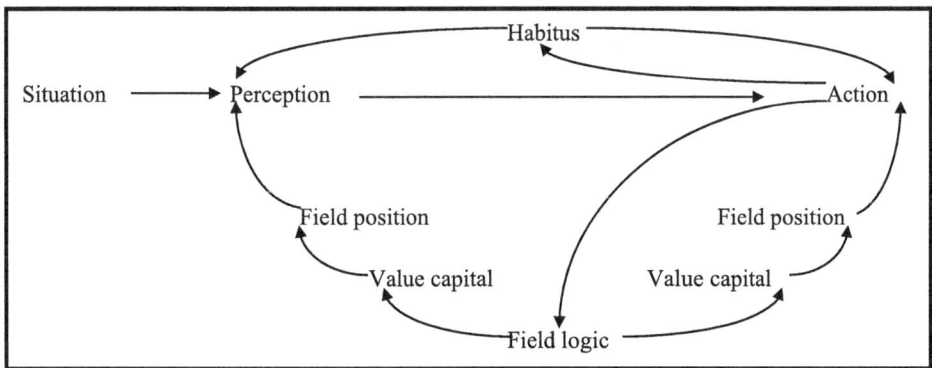

Figure 1 further illustrates that the actions taken as the result of a calculation of possibilities – based on the actor's habitus *and* his or her field position – lead to a feedback loop into a field logic. It is in this manner that actors determine and/or change the field's configurations, e.g. its doxa and illusio.

Moreover, the actions taken as a result of the calculation of possibilities also lead to a feedback loop into the actor's dispositions. Over time, the actor's position within the field will be integrated into his habitus (field structures habitus). Bourdieu labels this process *the logic of adjustment of dispositions to position* (Bourdieu & Wacquant 1992:81, 127). Consequently, actors whose capital places them in a dominant position within a certain field may display practices that reaffirm this position of dominance in other fields. It is through the logic of adjustment of dispositions to position that Bourdieu explains how some actors come to develop a habitus that supports their dominant position within society, while others develop a habitus that leads them to assume and reproduce a dominated position.

Bourdieu connects this line of reasoning to the concept of *homology*, which he defines as "resemblance within a difference" (Bourdieu & Wacquant 1992:106). Bourdieu uses this concept in various ways. For instance, he shows that fields, while functioning according to differing sets of logic, accommodate the same types of struggle – struggles over a trump card. In a similar vein, homology also refers to the idea that actors hold the same types of position within different fields. Based on their past experiences, which were accumulated from either a dominant or a dominated field position, actors will have developed dispositions which reflect this position. While the logic of a field might be different, the actor's habitus remains the same when entering a new field and consequently his or her actions are likely to be the same.

Concluding remarks

I have argued that Bourdieu's theoretical framework might offer a solution to institutional theory's quest for an adequate theory of action. Moreover, similar to Emirbayer and Johnson (2008) I have argued that a reintroduction of Bourdieu to institutional theory is only useful insofar as his framework is employed in a relational manner, i.e. incorporating not only the concept of field, but also the concepts of capital and habitus.

This presentation of Bourdieu's *theory of practice* illustrates that the whole of his theory is indeed greater than the sum of its parts (Dobbin 2008:53). Moreover, it is in their combined use that the concepts of habitus, field and capital offer solutions to the various problems facing institutional theorists. For instance, Bourdieu's framework presents a way to combine micro and macro levels of analysis. The concept of habitus offers a way of focusing on the micro, while at the same time offering insight into the macro context in which it was formed. The concept of field presents the next level of analysis, while the idea of nested fields offers a means of studying multiple research levels at once.

The discussion of Bourdieu's framework also illustrates its potential for studying processes of change and struggle, and thus for viewing fields as dynamic spaces. By presenting fields as fields of struggles Bourdieu accounts for changes within fields. Moreover, this concept offers a first way to incorporate processes of power into the study of fields. His work on symbolic violence, fields of power and capital offers further avenues for studying these types of power processes.

Finally, similar to institutionalists, Bourdieu sets out to develop a balanced approach to action. While some have argued that Bourdieu, and notably his concept of habitus, ultimately favours structuralism over agency, he himself maintains that

> Habitus is not the fate that some people read into it. Being the product of history, it is an *open system of dispositions* that is constantly subjected to experiences, and therefore constantly affected by them in a way that either reinforces or modifies its structures. It is durable but not eternal! (Bourdieu & Wacquant 1992:133)

Moreover, as the diagram shown above illustrates, an actor's actions are the result of the combined effort of habitus, field and capital. Figure 1 also shows that the actions taken by an actor lead to a feedback loop into the field's logic. Therefore, the structures in which a habitus develops are also subject to change.

In this thesis I use Bourdieu's framework as a lens to study action, and specifically organizational action. Consequently, I view an actor's action as the result of a combination of factors: the situation confronting him, his historically developed dispositions (i.e. habitus), his position within a certain field (i.e. his capital) and the field's logic. By keeping these various factors in mind, it becomes possible to understand the actors, actions and processes that contributed to the emergence of the Dutch HRV field.

3. Methodological contemplations

> (...) the enduring significance of Bourdieu's enterprise does not reside in the individual concepts, substantive theories, methodological prescriptions, or empirical observations he offers so much as in the manner in which he produces, uses, and relates them. To borrow an opposition dear to him, it is the *modus operandi* of Bourdieu's sociology, not its *opus operatum*, that most fully defines its originality. (Wacquant in Bourdieu and Wacquant 1992:ix, italics in the original)

In his work Bourdieu not only presents a theory of practice, he also develops a theory of scientific practice, a *methodology*[18]. Moreover, by presenting empirical observations, methodological contemplations and theoretical thoughts alongside each other he offers us an insight into his *modus operandi*. Similarly, the aim of Part I is to present the modus operandi in the present research. Nevertheless, while building on both his theoretical and his methodological contributions, I present them separately, following the more conventional way of presenting research results.

This separate presentation of theory and methodology was motivated in part by the theoretical point I wish to make. In the previous chapters I argued that institutional theory would benefit from a reinvestigation of Bourdieu's theoretical work. In the present chapter the argument is less provocative. I first argue that Bourdieu's methodological thoughts can be related to a particular school of methodological thought that is gaining ground within the social sciences: interpretive methodology (Schwartz-Shea & Yanow 2012). I then turn to the three studies that were conducted as part of the present case study: a media analysis, an analysis of parliamentary debates and an organizational field ethnography. I end the chapter with a critical reflection on my own position as a researcher.

3.1 Bourdieu and the interpretive perspective

Scholars working from an interpretive perspective seek to bridge the dichotomy between qualitative and quantitative research by way of the concept of abduction. *Abduction* offers a third logic of inquiry, besides deduction in quantitative research and induction in qualitative research. *Deduction* generally refers to re-

---

18. I follow Haverland and Yanow (2012:401) in using the label of *methodology* to denote "the applied philosophical positions that underpin and inform" the methods that are used in the research. *Methods* then refer to the "tools and techniques that are used to carry out the research: surveys, questionnaires, interviews, observations, participation, and the like".

search that is theory-driven; hypotheses are deduced from theory and subsequently tested against research results. The starting points for *inductionists*, in contrast, are empirical observations which may lead to the development of general laws (Schwartz-Shea & Yanow 2012:26-27).

The distinction between deduction and induction can be related to the dichotomy that Bourdieu seeks to bridge in his work, i.e. between objectivism and subjectivism. While Bourdieu criticizes both the idea that science should strive to present the objectified structures behind the empirical reality and the idea that science should present a lay representation of reality (Thompson 1991:11, Wacquant in Bourdieu & Wacquant 1992:3), interpretativists object to the idea that science should start from either theory or empirical reality. Like Bourdieu, scholars working from an interpretative perspective argue that both ways of knowing should be combined. Schwartz-Shea and Yanow (2012) describe this third way of knowing as follows:

> (...) abductive reasoning begins with a puzzle, a surprise, or a tension, and then seeks to explicate it by identifying the conditions that would make the puzzle less perplexing and more of a "normal" or "natural" event. (...) In this puzzling-out process, the researcher tacks continually, constantly, back and forth in an iterative-recursive fashion between what is puzzling and possible explanations for it, whether in other field situations (e.g., other observations, other documents or visual representations, other participations, other interviews) or research-relevant literature. The back and forth takes place less as a series of discrete steps than it does in the same moment: in some sense the researcher is simultaneously puzzling over empirical materials and theoretical literature. (Schwartz-Shea and & Yanow 2012:27)

Scholars working from an interpretative perspective thus combine knowledge derived from empirical observations with knowledge derived from theory. In other words, they are interested in both the lay representation of reality (subjectivist knowledge) and the objectified structures that help to explain this reality (objectivist knowledge). Bourdieu (1977:4) labels this combination of types of knowledge the third-order knowledge.

The description of abductive reasoning that is put forward by Schwartz-Shea and Yanow (2012:27) very adequately describes how the present research was conducted. It all started with a puzzle. In 2007 and 2008 I was part of a research team that conducted a large-scale study into honour-related violence. The aim of that study was twofold. On the one hand, we wished to explore the perceptions of three different migrant communities on honour, violence and their interconnectedness[19]. On the other, we wanted to map out how honour-related violence was combatted in the Netherlands. What actors played key roles in this process? What

---

19. We particularly studied the perception of honour among the Turkish, Moroccan and Hindu communities in the Netherlands. See Brenninkmeijer et al. (2009) for further details of that earlier study.

were their perceptions of honour-related violence? How did those actors believe that the problem should be handled? The findings from that second part of the research in particular left me with a number of queries.

Firstly, I was amazed by the great variety of actors that had some form of involvement in the issue of honour-related violence. Moreover, I was intrigued by why this issue should surface at that particular moment in time. To understand this puzzle I first explored various theories that could help me understand the empirical reality confronting me. The results of that theoretical exploration are presented in the preceding chapters. While these theories offered some answers, they also triggered new empirical questions. For instance, how was the field's emergence connected to the issue's emergence? This question convinced me to conduct an additional study of the issue's emergence. The results of this second study are presented in Part II. In Part III I present the results of the study conducted in 2007-2008. However, those empirical results have now been complemented by Bourdieu's theoretical work and concepts from institutional theory in organizational analysis.

This iterative process, moving back and forth between theory and empirical study, also matches Bourdieu's description of scientific development. Moreover, not only does he explicitly reject the distinction between methodology and theory, he also opposes a rigid separation between separate types of data collection (Bourdieu & Wacquant 1992:224-227). Elsewhere he eloquently summarized his position as follows:

> (...) how artificial the ordinary opposition between theory and research, between quantitative and qualitative methods, between statistical recording and ethnographic observation, between the grasping of structures and the construction of individuals can be. These alternatives have no function other than to provide a justification for the vacuous and resounding abstractions of theoreticism and for the falsely rigorous observations of positivism, or, as the division between economists, anthropologists, historians and sociologists, to legitimize the limits of *competency*: this is to say that they function in a manner of *social censorship*, liable to forbid us to grasp a truth which resides precisely in the *relations* between realms of practice thus arbitrarily separated. (Bourdieu and De Saint Martin 1978:7 in Bourdieu & Wacquant 1992:28, italics in the original)

Clearly, Bourdieu's work debunks methodological *rigidity*, i.e. the idea that various methods should not be combined within a single research project. According to Bourdieu, a researcher should always strive to use whatever methods provide the best answer to the research question: "We must try, in every case, to mobilize all the techniques that are relevant and practically usable, given the definition of the object and the practical conditions of data collection" (Bourdieu & Wacquant 1992:227). However, Bourdieu is quick to add that the "extreme liberty" that he advocates "has its counterpart in the extreme vigilance that we must apply to the conditions of use of analytical techniques and to ensuring that they fit the question at hand" (Bourdieu & Wacquant 1992:227).

The present case study adopts Bourdieu's position on data collection and combines various types of data collection. Each type of data provides answers to different but related questions. Both the media analysis and the analysis of the parliamentary debates provide answers about the processes involved in the emergence of the issue of honour-related violence in Dutch public discourse. Moreover, the present thesis argues that the manner in which the issue emerged within both fields influenced the emerging field configurations of the Dutch HRV field. The organizational field ethnography then provides information on the emerging HRV field. Below I elaborate further on these methods as a way to illustrate the *scientific rigor* of this study.

3.2 Reconstructing the issue's emergence

In order to reconstruct the emergence of the issue of honour-related violence I focus on its emergence within two specific fields: the media field and the political field. The media and political fields both play a crucial role in transforming a private issue into a social problem. Bourdieu et al. (1994:2), for instance, explicitly draw attention to the state's role in the "production" of social problems. Moreover, Bourdieu explicitly urges scholars to critically analyse the emergence of social problems, as they might otherwise unknowingly and/or unwillingly contribute to the construction of an issue as a social problem;

> To avoid becoming the object of the problems that you take as your object, you must retrace the history of the emergence of these problems, of their progressive constitution, i.e., of the collective work, oftentimes accomplished though competition and struggle, that proved necessary to make such and such issue to be known and recognized (…) as legitimate problems, problems that are avowable, publishable, public, official. (…) Here one would need to analyse the particular role of the political field (Bourdieu 1981a) and especially of the bureaucratic filed. (…) the bureaucratic field contributes decisively to the constitution, and the consecration, of "universal" social problems. (Bourdieu & Wacquant 1992:238-239)

Consequently, retracing the emergence of the issue of honour-related violence serves multiple purposes. Firstly, it enables me to understand why the issue of honour-related violence became a social problem at that particular moment in time. Moreover, it enables me to explore the role of the state in the issue's emergence. In addition, it enables me to explore whether the manner in which the issue emerged affects the emerging configurations of the issue-based field. Lastly, by retracing the emergence of the issue I can take a step back and critically explore my own role in the construction of the problem of honour-related violence (this last point is addressed in further detail in the final section of this chapter).

Scholars working within the domain of the social construction of social problems[20] also draw attention to the role of the media in the construction of social problems. Among the first scholars to draw attention to the media's crucial role were Fritz and Altheide (1987). They explicitly urged other scholars to acknowledge the role of the media in transforming personal tragedies into major social problems. Moreover, while the media indeed function as a podium for actors to put forward claims about particular issues, they also function as a filter. According to Fritz and Altheide (1987:475) scholars should therefore not overlook the fact that it is the media that determine what actors are given a voice within the media field.

My study covers the media and parliament as fields in their own right. In the words of Emirbayer and Johnson (2008) I studied each as an *organization-as-field*. By focusing on the interactions between actors within both fields, I was able to capture some of the micro dynamics that contributed to the emergence of the issue of honour-related violence. I started this part of the case study by systematically retracing how and when the labels of honour killing (*eerwraak* in Dutch) and honour-related violence emerged within both fields. In this manner, the emergence of the labels formed the practical operationalization of the issue's emergence within societal discourse.

Conducting a media analysis

For the media analysis, I used the search engine *LexisNexis* to retrieve information on the emergence of labels of honour killings and honour-related violence in all national and local newspapers in the Netherlands. For each year in which either of these labels was mentioned, I counted the total number of publications that used the labels (see Appendix 1 for the number of publications per year). From these numbers I inferred that some type of critical event must have taken place in 1999, 2003 and 2004, being the years in which the occurrences of the label of honour killing rose explosively (see Chapters 4 and 5).

Further analysis of the news coverage during those years brought to the fore that it particularly concerned a number of actual and attempted honour killings. I

---

20. The works of Spector and Kitsuse (1977), and specifically their book *Constructing Social Problems*, have been pinpointed as a turning point in the sociological study of social problems (Schneider 1985:209; Hilgartner and Bosk 1988:53; Best 1993:132, 2002:700). Spector and Kitsuse (1973) urge researchers to take a social constructionist perspective on social problems by studying their natural history: how ordinary members of society transform private problems into social issues / social problems. It is through their claim-making activities that problems come into existence. However, actors may have different degrees of the power to mobilize support for a particular claim and / or problem definition (ibid:149) or have different motives for making such claims (Hilgartner & Bosk 1988:57). While Bourdieu's work might seem related to this approach, it differs substantially, "in that it grounds social work of symbolic and organizational construction in the objective structure of the social spaces within which" problems are socially constructed (Bourdieu & Wacquant 1992:239).

therefore conducted a second search in *LexisNexis* to specifically focus on those murders or attempts.[21] My analysis of the related articles focused on identifying what actors were given a voice by the media and what claims those actors made. Those claims include both the claims made during formal interviews with journalists and claims made by actors in other settings, for instance in court and in parliament, which were subsequently described by journalists.

For each murder or attempted murder, I subsequently developed a matrix in which I entered both the actor and his or her claims and how those claims developed over time (see Appendix 2 for an example of such a matrix). Next, I compared the four matrixes at various levels and asked questions such as the following:
- Who were the first actors to claim attention for these honour killings or attempts?
- How did these actors define the problem of honour-related violence?
- What solutions to the problem did these actors put forward?
- Can a change of tone be detected in the media coverage of the honour killings and attempts over time?

By conducting this qualitative content analysis of all articles related to the four actual and attempted honour killings, I was able to retrace some of the micro dynamics involved in the social construction of honour-related violence as a social problem. The results of my analysis are presented in Chapter 5, where I argue that the actual and attempted honour killings functioned as *unplanned field-configuring events* for the Dutch honour-related violence field.

The results of the media analysis are subsequently supplemented by the results of a literature review of papers discussing the emergence of the issue of honour-related violence in relation to changing macro-cultural discourses on multiculturalism, gender, social cohesion and nationalism. This literature review is presented in Chapter 6. Chapter 7 then presents the concept of *moral panic* as an objectified structure that further explains the emergence of the issue of honour-related violence.

---

21. This search generated the following numbers of hits: Kezban Vural n=147, Veghel + eerwraak n=272, Zarife + eerwraak n=291, Gül B. + eerwraak n=146. Nevertheless, these numbers must be qualified: for example they only include the articles in which the victim's name is mentioned, while some articles – in particular those published immediately after the murders occurred – only mention the act and not the victim's name. Moreover, in Gül's case various media used different ways of spelling her name, including Gul, Guel, Gül B., etcetera. Lastly, the names of the persons involved in the Veghel case were rarely mentioned; instead actors referred to this case by mentioning Veghel in relation to the *eerwraak* label. This means that the numbers presented above only function as indicators of the total amount of media coverage. Moreover, my analysis used several other search combinations in addition to the ones listed above.

Studying a political field

The emergence of the labels of honour killing and honour-related violence in parliament was retraced through a search using the search engine *Overheid.nl*. This search engine makes it possible to trace all official governmental publications, including transcripts of parliamentary debates. For each year in which the labels "honour killing" and/or "honour-related violence" were mentioned I counted the total number of publications in which these labels were used (see Appendix 1). This analysis revealed that the attention for the issue of honour-related violence in parliament grew significantly in the years 2004-2006 (see Chapters 4 and 8). I therefore subsequently conducted a qualitative content analysis of the parliamentary debates and letters sent to parliament about the issue of honour-related violence during these years.

This analysis included ten parliamentary debates and eleven letters sent to parliament on behalf of Members of Cabinet (see Table 3 in Chapter 8). When coding and analysing these debates and letters I particularly focused on the following elements:

- How was the issue of honour-related violence defined by the Members of Cabinet and by MPs?
- What solutions to the problem of honour-related violence did the Members of Cabinet and/or MPs put forward?
- What actors were mentioned by Members of Cabinet and/or MPs as key actors in the fight against honour-related violence?
- How did the MPs and Members of Cabinet interact – for instance, what instruments were used by MPs to push the Cabinet in a particular direction (e.g. petitions)?
- Demarcation processes: how was honour-related violence distinguished from other problems, such as domestic violence?

The results of this analysis are presented in Chapter 8, where I describe the micro dynamics within the political field.

3.3 An organizational field ethnography

Bourdieu regularly used ethnography as his research method, for instance in his classic study of the Kabyle, which forms the basis for his theory of practice (Bourdieu 1977). However, he did propagate a specific type of ethnography: one that combines insider knowledge with knowledge about the objective structures at work (e.g. third-order knowledge). Bourdieu termed this method *participant objectivation*. The following quote explains this principle:

> One does not have to choose between participant observation, a necessarily fictitious immersion in a foreign milieu, and the objectivism of the 'gaze from afar' of an observer who remains as remote from himself as from his object. Participant objectivation

undertakes to explore not the 'lived experiences' of the knowing subject but the social conditions of possibility – and therefore the effects and limits – of that experience and, more precisely, of the act of objectivation itself. It aims at objectivizing the subjective relation to the object which, far from leading to a relativistic and more or less anti-scientific subjectivism, is one of the conditions of genuine scientific objectivity. (Bourdieu in Wacquant 2004:398)

The quote not only alludes to how ethnographic research should be executed according to Bourdieu, it also illustrates how Bourdieu's thoughts on methodology, methods and theory are interrelated as it also illustrates his answer to the *puzzle of embedded agency*. The research objects (e.g. "knowing subject") display certain behaviours and interpretations of reality (e.g. "lived experience"), yet both the behaviours and the interpretations are limited by the "social conditions of possibility" (e.g. the subject's habitus, access to capital and position within the field). Consequently, within field ethnographies the researcher should combine insider knowledge about the "lived experience" (gathered through participant observation) with objectified knowledge (theoretical knowledge) about the "social conditions of possibilities".

Moreover, according to Bourdieu, researchers should combine this third-order knowledge with a thorough analysis of their own positions within the field, i.e. the researcher's own "social conditions of possibility". Bourdieu calls this process *epistemic reflexivity* (Bourdieu & Wacquant 1992). I explain my own position within the research field in the following section. I first elaborate on the methods that I used within the ethnographic field study.

Going into the field

In 2007 the Dutch Ministry of Justice, and more specifically the coordinator of the interministerial programme against honour-related violence, commissioned a study into honour-related violence in the Netherlands. That study was conducted by a research group within the Department of Culture, Organization and Management of the VU University in Amsterdam[22]. This project made us participants in the emerging HRV field, as we became part of the interministerial programme. At the same time, we remained *strangers*[23] in the field, as none of us had previously worked on the issue of honour-related violence.

From this insider-outsider position we were able to attend many relevant meetings and gatherings (see Appendix 3), gained access to relevant documents and

---

22. The research group was formed by two professors, two senior researchers, two junior researchers and a Ph.D. student.
23. The label "stranger" is borrowed from Schwartz-Shea and Yanow (2012:29) who define *strangerness* as "Being a stranger to one's physical setting (…) and trying to hold on to that quality for as long as one can – is desirable in order to see as explicitly as possible what for situated knowers is taken-for-granted, common sense, and tacitly known".

were able to interview many representatives of the organizations that were part of the emerging field (see Appendix 4). The aim of that earlier study was to understand how actors within the emerging HRV field defined the issue of honour-related violence and how they organized themselves around this particular issue. It invoked questions such as who the key actors within the emerging field were, and on what grounds they gained their positions; how the actors defined the issue of honour-related violence; and how did they work together?

To answer these and related questions, we combined three qualitative research methods. Firstly, we analysed relevant governmental and organizational policy documents, plus information on the relevant websites. Secondly, we conducted seventy-six open-end interviews with representatives of organizations involved in combatting honour-related violence (see Appendix 5 for the interview schedule). Lastly, we observed a number of relevant meetings and gatherings. These methods are described in greater detail below.

This combination of methods made it possible for us to learn about the field's members, their interrelations and their definitions of the problem. However, given the size of the field and its wide variety of members, it was clearly impossible to gain a proper understanding of the micro dynamics within each of the different actors – an occurrence that characterizes classic organizational ethnographies (Ybema et al. 2009; for recent examples see Smits 2013, Berendse 2013, Van der Raad 2015). Nonetheless, given the focus of this case study, namely the processes involved in the emergence of an issue-based organizational field, the level of analysis was not the individual organizations but rather the organizational field. Moreover, the present case study combines various different levels of analysis: micro (in both the media and parliamentary analysis), meso (in the ethnographic field study) and macro (in the literature review of macro-cultural discourses).

Document analysis

One purpose of the document analysis was to obtain an initial impression of the research field. The website analysis was used to identify what actors were actively working on the problem of honour-related violence. For example, by examining whether the website of *Federatie Opvang* (FO, the umbrella organization for women's shelters), municipal websites, police websites, etcetera, including any references to the issue of honour-related violence, it became possible to make a first assessments of the field's members.

The document analysis also included an analysis of documents produced and/or used by the field's actors. Examples of these documents include a risk assessment instrument developed for women's shelters, documents developed by the municipal partners in Rotterdam and Amsterdam, a PowerPoint presentation by the project leader of the honour-project for schools, papers published by the Multi-Ethnic Policing Unit (Unit-MEP) and protocols developed by migrant organizations. The purpose of this analysis was to establish the organization's formal definition of honour-related violence, the proposed solution and which partners they perceive as relevant in combatting honour-related violence.

Interviews

The research population for the interviews consisted of individuals working for organizations concerned with preventing, or implementing policy measures against, honour-related violence, or with protecting victims and/or dealing with offenders under criminal law. It therefore includes individuals working for organizations such as the police, women's shelters, municipal authorities, local and regional advice and support centres for domestic violence, youth care agency *Bureau Jeugdzorg*, the central government, educational institutions, migrant organizations, umbrella organizations for migrant organizations, citizens' initiatives, the media and experts in the field of honour-related violence.

The interviews were conducted according to an interview schedule (see Appendix 4). Most of the interviews were conducted by two researchers: one of the researchers would take the lead in the interview while the other took on the role of observer. Two Master students who conducted two case studies as part of their Master's degree programme "Culture, Organization and Management" also conducted some of the interviews.

The majority of the interviews were held at the respondent's offices. This had the added benefit of combining interview data with observational data on the respondent's working environment. Respondents without their own workplace – some experts and members of migrant organizations, for example – were interviewed in cafes or in their homes. On average, the interviews lasted ninety minutes, and all were recorded using a voice recorder for subsequent transcription.

Observations

A total of fourteen meetings, conferences and other gatherings were attended in the framework of this ethnographic field study. We visited those gatherings to establish how the relevant actors spoke about honour-related violence within the different settings. For example, what was the focus of the discussions at the national conference for the police force's points of contact for honour-related violence? And what thoughts were put forward by representatives of the country's four largest municipalities (G4) about combatting honour-related violence during their meetings?

Another objective was to establish what actors were present at the various gatherings, to map out the networks between organizations. For example, we studied who were present at the conference about honour-related violence organized by *Federatie Opvang* and what actors were represented at the presentation of Rob Ermers's book *Eer en Eerwraak* ("Honour and Honour Killings") (2007).

We gained admission to these gatherings through the contacts that we had built up during the course of our research. Some of the people we interviewed added us to their networks and notified us of relevant gatherings. Most of the observations were made by one or more members of our research team, some were made by the Master students involved. Observation reports were drawn up of all these gatherings, which served as input for the subsequent analysis.

Data analysis

The analysis involved an examination of the documents, observation reports and transcripts, which were coded using a series of topics. I specifically focused on the presented problem definition: what characteristics did the respondents ascribe to honour-related violence? For instance, what groups were involved in this type of violence? And what forms of violence did the respondents and the documents link to honour-related violence? I also studied how people viewed their own roles in the efforts to combat honour-related violence, and what responsibilities they assigned to others in the field of honour-related violence. Lastly, I considered which actors worked together and how their partnerships were given shape and/or experienced. The results of this first analysis were published in a report that was presented to the Ministry of Justice in 2009 (see Brenninkmeijer et al. 2009).

This first stage of data analysis clearly followed the line of analysis put forward by *grounded theorists*. Scholars adhering to *grounded theory* framework depart form an inductionist position (Glaser & Strauss 1967). I subsequently complemented these empirical findings with theoretical elaborations provided by institutional theory and Bourdieu. These theoretical findings subsequently stimulated me to conduct additional empirical studies, which in turn stimulated further theoretical explorations. This iterative process, going back and forth between theory and empirical reality, is also apparent in the way this thesis is structured. Both Part II and Part III start with some further theoretical elaborations, which are of particular relevance for the empirical findings that are presented in the subsequent section.

3.4 Reflection

(…) to make you see how difficult, indeed well-nigh desperate, the predicament of the sociologists is, that the work of production of official problems, that is, those problems endowed with the sort of universality that is granted by the fact of being guaranteed by the state, almost always leaves room for what are today called *experts*. Among those so-called experts are sociologists who use the authority of science to endorse the universality, the objectivity, and the disinterestedness of the bureaucratic representation of problems. (Bourdieu & Wacquant 1992:240)

This quote *could* have been about me. As a researcher who was being paid by the government to study the rather new issue of honour-related violence, I ran the risk of unwittingly and uncritically reaffirming the government's position on this issue. However, I averted this danger by critically examining how the problem and the field were constructed. My goal was to help explain why the field's actors felt compelled to frame honour-related violence as a distinct social problem, in need of its own definition and problem solution. However, it took some time for me to come to this conclusion.

Throughout most of the ethnographic field study I wondered whether it was reasonable and/or logical to define honour-related violence as an issue separate and distinct from domestic violence. Was it truly different? For instance, both types include the full spectrum of violence, both mental and physical. Moreover, both can be related to gender-related power dynamics. I initially felt that I needed to answer this question. As time passed, however, I realized that this research was not about finding an answer to that particular "puzzle". Mine was a different puzzle. I wanted to answer the questions of why and how the issue of honour-related violence emerged at that particular moment in time, and how the issue's emergence subsequently led to the emergence of the connected issue-based field.

Still, the fact that I was being paid by the government's interministerial programme might have influenced how respondents behaved around me, or how they answered my questions during interviews. When reflecting on the research results, I believe that this may very well have happened. Some respondents, for instance, actively voiced their criticisms of the honour-related violence programme when talking with us. Others, in contrast, may have voiced their concerns more carefully, depending on their positions within the field. However, by combining various sources of information, I was able to develop a complete picture of the field and its actors. Moreover, the fact that the government had commissioned the study afforded us access to all types of meetings and gatherings, respondents and documents that would otherwise not have been open to us. In general, I therefore feel that the government's support for this study opened more doors than it closed[24].

A final reflection concerns my own "social conditions of possibility". According to Bourdieu, scientists themselves are positioned in a particular manner within the scientific community. This position will influence the types of observations that researchers make while participating in the field. Moreover, it will influence

---

24. See also Marrewijk et al. (2010) on the *ethnoventionist approach*. According to the authors, being part of an organizational research field and even actively contributing to organizational interventions within this field is possible as long as this is combined with a reflective attitude. They particular highlight the potential of this approach within participative action research and organizational ethnographies.

the types of questions they ask and how they read organizational documents[25]. He therefore challenges scientists to know themselves well, as this leads to better science:

> (...) one knows the world better and better as one knows oneself better, that scientific knowledge and knowledge of oneself and one's own social unconscious advance hand in hand, and that primary experience transformed in and through scientific practice transforms scientific practice and conversely. (Bourdieu in Wacquant 2004:398)

Being a trained organizational anthropologist and adhering to an interpretative research tradition, I do indeed focus on certain processes within the emerging field (see Chapters 1 and 2). Likewise, I use certain techniques to uncover these processes. In order to be transparent about the choices I made during this research, I have disclosed my methodological choices in the foregoing.

Besides being positioned within a specific scientific community, my "social conditions of possibility" were also influenced by the context in which I studied the issue of honour-related violence. When I started this research in 2007 the moral panic about honour killings was still raging: the issue was at the very forefront of public, political and scientific attention in the Netherlands. Being forced by personal circumstance to occasionally take a break from the research and writing process proved to be useful in this respect. Instead of taking for granted the issue's relevance, these "forced" reflection periods allowed me to take a step back and critically examine why the issue of honour-related violence generated such heated debates within the Netherlands at that particular moment in time.

Still, I am not only a scholar: I am a native Dutch woman who has never encountered any form of honour-related violence in person. Consequently, I also remained a stranger on a different level: not only was I a stranger to the research field, I was also not a victim or potential victim of honour-related violence. The closest that I came to experiencing what it means to be a victim of honour-related violence was when I attended the service commemorating Zeynep Boral. I was confronted with her family's pain and suffering; they had lost someone dear to them. I felt bad about being there, since my interest was purely scholarly in nature: I wanted to know which actors were present and to hear what they had to say. It felt terrible to write research notes while her family sat before me and cried. To remind myself, and others who read this thesis, of the very real pain and suffering of the victims of violence, this book opens with Zeynep's story.

---

25. Scholars working from an interpretive perspective similarly call on scientists to be reflective with regard to "the role of his or her prior knowledge and positionality in generating knowledge claims, as well as in constructing this world through the writing of (scientific) text" (Berendse 2013:66).

Part II
How honour-related violence became an issue within the Dutch public discourse

Introduction

I've always worked with migrant and refugee women. In any case, I've had regular dealings with them and given them much of my attention, and especially in connection with sexual and domestic violence. I've only come to work with the terms honour-related violence and honour-revenge since I started at (…), five years ago, and I received an invitation from Sweden to work on a European project. I used to work as a social worker at a women's shelter and looking back, at the time we already offered shelter to large numbers of migrant women, and some of them were in fact dealing with honour-related violence. We didn't call it that, but things like threats from family members, it became apparent to us that this involved other issues than in Dutch families, but we didn't call it that.

So how did you cope with it?

I vividly remember one situation twenty years ago. A young Turkish woman was married off, but she didn't want to marry him and he didn't want to marry her. She left her husband and hooked up with her boyfriend from when she was a teenager. Her husband was okay with that, but her family wasn't.

She came to the shelter when she was pregnant from her boyfriend and was being threatened by her family. Eventually she decided, "I want to mend the relationship with my family." So we supported her and said. "Well, if that's what you want." As she didn't want her family to know about the pregnancy, she had an abortion when she was five months pregnant. I accompanied her to the midwife, it was really awful!

Then her father even visited us in the shelter. I was on call that night and I sat in the next room to keep an eye on everything. She'd hoped that it would be a reconciliation; instead, it went completely wrong. So I jumped between them and told him, "I think it would be better if you left now." She quickly left the shelter while he said things like. "She's doomed to die" and "We know where to find her." Luckily I was able to transfer her somewhere else that same evening.
Eventually everything calmed down and she had other children with her boyfriend. Apparently, time had healed the wounds. (…) This was by far the most extreme case I ever experienced. Other than that, we didn't do anything different from how we treated abused women in Dutch culture.

So did you find that this was enough, or did you feel that the support was inadequate?

Yes, I think it was often inadequate, because we weren't able to put ourselves in a position to understand what was really happening. We didn't realize, we didn't have a clue, we had a sense of it, but we didn't have the tools to really support them. (Interview with a former social worker, October 2007)

The introductory excerpt illustrates that somehow, during the past twenty years, domestic violence against migrant women has become *reconceptualized* as violence in the name of honour. It also reveals that this type of violence is not new. However, it is only of late that it has been perceived as a *discrete social problem* with its own specific characteristics, in need of a separate approach and policy.

In analysing the emergence of the Dutch HRV field it is not enough to establish that, objectively speaking, honour-related violence is a serious problem and therefore in need of specific policy measures. As the above excerpt illustrates, honour-related violence was already an issue twenty years ago, and it is only lately that this type of violence has been given its own label. Moreover, the first reliable figures about occurrences of honour-related violence in the Netherlands were only presented in 2010 (Jansen & Sanberg 2010) while the interministerial programme to combat this type of violence had been initiated in 2006. Clearly, honour-related violence was perceived as a distinct social problem long before the nature and extent of the problem were clearly understood. Why did actors suddenly start to perceive honour-related violence as a distinct social problem? Who were the first to define honour-related violence as a social problem? In Part II, I consider these and other questions as I study the emergence of the issue of honour-related violence within the Dutch public discourse.

Part II: theoretical underpinnings

Although Hoffman (1999) states that issue-based fields emerge after a particular issue has surfaced within society's discourse, he remains vague on how the issue emerges in the first place. I therefore draw on the work of other institutionalists and Bourdieu to make sense of these first stages of field emergence.

While Bourdieu does not elaborate much on the processes involved in field emergence, he does offer ideas on the processes involved in the social construction of social problems. He particularly points out the role of states in their construction. Based on their *informational capital*, according to Bourdieu et al. (1994:7), states are able to concentrate and redistribute information as means to advance *theoretical unification* about a social problem within a field. Theoretical unification (i.e. convergence in the way something is perceived) is made possible in particular by the state's ability to develop classification systems that subsequently impose common principles of vision and division within their societies (Bourdieu et al. 1994:7)[26]. For purposes of the present case study, it is therefore interesting to investigate how the classification and demarcation between domestic violence and honour-related violence came into being.

---

26. See Part III for a more thorough discussion of Bourdieu's position on state power.

Stine Grodal (2007) also highlights the importance of classification systems and clear labels in field emergence. Her doctoral thesis convincingly illustrates that the emergence of the nanotechnology field was made possible only through the development of the label "nanotechnology". The adoption of this label outside the scientific community, particularly by governments, futurists and venture capitalists, made it possible for this new field to emerge. Moreover, the government's subsequent allocation of resources to this field proved to be pivotal to its emergence. In her concluding remarks Grodal summarizes the process of organizational field emergence as follows:

> Communities' adoptions of labels co-evolve with the construction of meaning and the availability of resources within an emerging organizational field. (...) As an increasing number of communities adopted the label, they infused it with meaning that reflected their interests, values, and goals. The monetary, social, and human resources that flowed to the field depended on the label's meaning at the time. (...) A necessary condition for a field to evolve is, thus, new communities' adoption of the label. It is, however, not possible for new communities to adopt a label without changing the meaning of the label. By definition, communities possess different webs of meaning and they use symbols in different ways. (Grodal 2007: 172-175)

While Grodal makes very limited use of Bourdieu's work, her own work "translates" easily to Bourdieu's framework, as labels and definitions are part of a field's classification system (i.e. a field's doxa). The foregoing quote additionally illustrates that, like Bourdieu, she focuses on the actor's actions. Moreover, while she does not use the concept of habitus, it is apparent from this excerpt that she works from similar presumptions: the meaning that an actor attributes to something is determined by his or her disposition (webs of meaning). Her writings on monetary, social and human resources that flow into the field also focus on various types of capital that are relevant to field emergence. Lastly, her work shows a clear interest in processes of power, as she also focuses on the actor's interest, values and goals.

Two institutionalists who also have written about field emergence are Lawrence and Phillips. According to Lawrence and Phillips (2004:690) changes in macro-cultural discourses provide the critical preconditions for organizational field emergence. For instance, their study of the commercial whale-watching industry in Victoria in Canada shows that this industry could develop due to changes in the conceptualization of whales, in particular killer whales (e.g. orcas). While killer whales were previously seen as "horrifying monsters", for example, in the book *Moby Dick*, the movie *Free Willy* featured a killer whale as "an endearing creature worthy of empathy, compassion and even admiration" (Lawrence & Phillips 2004:695). This reconceptualization of killer whales as "endearing creatures" made it possible for the commercial whale-watching field to emerge: people were now eager to "meet" killer whales in real life.

In a similar vein, it may be argued that the development a Dutch HRV field was made possible through the reconceptualization of *domestic violence* against migrant women as *violence in the name of honour*. Clearly, if this type of violence had not been reconceptualized as a specific type of violence, the new organizational field would not have emerged. In part, the reconceptualization of domestic violence against migrant women can be regarded as the result of changing macro-cultural discourses. Various scholars studying honour-related violence have already connected the emergence of this issue to changes in discourses on multiculturalism, gender and nationalism (Dustin 2006; Pratt Ewing 2008; Phillips & Saharso 2008).[27]

Nevertheless, Lawrence and Phillips also note that "discursive activity at a macro level can act to provide the building blocks for new institutional fields[28], but how these building blocks are used to construct a field depends upon local action and the strategies of local actors" (Lawrence and Phillips 2004:690). They therefore direct attention to the activities of actors on the micro level: activities that are embedded in broader discourses that both facilitate and constrain particular forms of behaviour (embedded agency). It is at the micro level that Bourdieu's work once more becomes relevant, as his theory of practices helps us to understand how these activities are guided by internalized dispositions (i.e. an actor's habitus) and an actor's position within the field.

Part II: outline

The focus in Part II is on the actors, actions and processes contributing to the emergence of the issue of honour-related violence within the Dutch public discourse. Based on the theoretical notions presented above, I focus on the following combination of processes: 1) the development of a common label, 2) the actor's actions on a micro level and 3) changes in macro-cultural discourses.

I start this exercise in Chapter 4 by introducing the two labels that have come to dominate the Dutch public discourse on honour-related violence: *eerwraak* (honour killing) and *eergerelateerd geweld* (honour-related violence). By describing their application over time in the media field and the political field, I can clarify *when* the issue of honour-related violence emerged within the Dutch public discourse.

Chapter 5 then describes the four actual and attempted honour killings that functioned as pivotal events for the Dutch honour-related violence field. Based

---

27. See Chapter 6 for a further discussion of these changing discourses.
28. Like Bourdieu, and scholars of organizational science who use Bourdieu's work (Emirbayer and Johnson 2008), I use the term *organizational field* rather than *institutional field* for discussing field emergence. However, both terms refer to the same concept: fields that are formed by organizations that constitute a recognized area of life (DiMaggio & Powell 1983:148).

on an in-depth analysis of the media reports on these murders, I illustrate how various actors successively joined the honour-related violence field. Moreover, their claims help explain their interpretation and use of the labels of *eerwraak* and *honour-related violence*. As such, this chapter also answers the question of *how* the issue emerged within the Dutch public discourse.

Inspired by other scholars' work on honour-related violence, in Chapter 6 I link the emergence of this issue to changes in macro-cultural discourses on multiculturalism, gender and nationalism. That chapter answers the question of *why* this issue emerged at that particular moment in time.

In Chapter 7, lastly, I argue that both the macro-level developments *and* the micro-level activities of the relevant actors contributed to the development of a *moral panic* about honour killings, which in turn facilitated the development of a Dutch honour-related violence field.

4. Defining honour-related violence

> Honour-related violence means any form of physical or mental violence perpetrated from within a collective mentality, in response to a breach of honour (or the threat of such a breach) concerning a man or woman and therefore his or her family, where the outside world is or might become aware of the breach. (Ferwerda & Van Leiden 2005:25)

This policy definition of honour-related violence was developed by a research-consulting group in 2005. It was adopted for the purpose of replacing the earlier label of *eerwraak*, which translates literally as "honour revenge".

Part II of this study begins by systematically retracing how and when these labels emerged within the media field and the political field. This is relevant for variety of reasons. Firstly, the emergence of these labels is indicative of the issue's emergence within the Dutch public discourse. Secondly, the works of both Grodal (2007) and Bourdieu et al. (1994) indicate that the construction of a label is a critical precondition for field emergence. The goal of this chapter therefore is to describe how the labels of *eerwraak* and honour-related violence developed over time, rather than presenting a clear-cut definition of this type of violence.

4.1 The emergence of a contested label

The label *eerwraak* was developed in 1978 by "Turkologist" (specialist in Turkish studies) Ane Nauta and refers to the killing of a person in order to cleanse one's honour[29]. On his consultancy website Nauta writes that he developed this term given the lack of words in Dutch to describe "this newly imported cultural phenomenon" (Nauta & Nauta 2011:website). By coining this phrase, Nauta explicitly framed these types of killings as an issue with a cultural grounding that had been newly introduced into the Netherlands.

This is interesting, as the connection between honour and violence is not new in the Netherlands. For instance, two rather recent doctorates describe how honour played a prominent role in the daily life of Dutch citizens in the eastern (Gietman 2010) and northern (Nijdam 2008) parts of the Netherlands in previous centuries. Nevertheless, from its inception the concept of *eerwraak* (honour killing) has explicitly been linked to migrants and described as being distinct from crimes of passion and domestic violence.

---

29. In English this type of murder is referred to by the label "honour killing".

The use and development of the label of *eerwraak* in the media field

Though it was introduced in the 1970s, the *eerwraak* label only came into common use in the early 1990s. Its first appearance in a Dutch newspaper was in a 1990 article entitled "Honour killings not to be tolerated in our society". This pivotal moment is discussed in some detail to identify how the label was first used by various actors.

The article in question discusses the legal proceedings connected to the murder of Nihat Karaman in 1988. The accused, a Dutchman of Turkish decent, admitted to killing Karaman because his family's honour had been shamed. He claimed that he had killed Karaman because Karaman had raped the accused's married sister. However, some members of the Dutch-Turkish community believed that Karaman's murder had been triggered by his political involvement. Karaman was a prominent member of his community: he was the initiator of both the leftish Turkish migrant workers society HTIP and *Inspraak Orgaan Turken in Nederland* (IOT), the umbrella organization for Turkish migrant organizations in the Netherlands (Vermeulen 1990:2). Yet this interpretation of the murder was not raised during the legal proceedings.

Various actors can be identified in the description of the proceedings. The first is the public prosecutor, from whose quote "such an enactment of honour killing is not to be tolerated in our society" (Vermeulen 1990:2) the article's title was taken. The prosecutor's claim that this was indeed an honour killing follows the line of reasoning put forward by Ane Nauta, the scholar who had developed the label *eerwraak* and who had been engaged as an expert witness. According to Nauta, "[t]he motive of *eerwraak* is the only apparent and clearly grounded motive" (Vermeulen 1990:2). The defence lawyer also used Nauta's analysis to underpin his argument that the suspect was suffering from force majeure, as

> the suspect's actions were motivated exclusively by the sense that it was his duty to cleanse the family honour, which according to the legal customs of the suspects environment and according to his own views could only be done by killing the guilty party. (Vermeulen 1990:2)

However, the article also provides a claim to the contrary that challenged Nauta's position. According to Secretary Ibrahim Ozdemir of HITB, the murderer was hiding behind Turkish traditions:

> The cultural differences are put forward only for the purpose of obtaining a reduced sentence. (…) The basis for a traditional Turk's honour is his horse, his weapon and his woman. If any of these objects is violated, there is only one punishment for the offender and that is death. For example, if a Turkish woman is raped, it is a traditional husband's duty to kill first his wife and then the rapist, then turn himself in to the police. This will save his honour. The brother plays no part in this whatsoever. (Vermeulen 1990:2)

This actor, who was socialized within the Turkish community and as such had developed certain dispositions for interpreting this murder[30], argues that the murder was not an honour killing. According to Ozdemir, the murder does not match with how the concept of honour traditionally functions within the Turkish community.

An alternative account can be found in the doctoral thesis of Van Eck (2001:57-59, 97-99), a pupil of Nauta and one of the scientific experts who later came to dominate the emerging Dutch HRV field. Her study of twenty ethnic Turkish honour killing cases in the Netherlands provides an analysis of this case. Her hypothesis, based on an in-depth analysis of the court records, is that the husband was involved in planning the honour killing and functioned as a "perpetrator in the background", while the brother deliberately took full responsibility. Moreover, she assumes that the rape story was nothing more than a way to conceal the fact that the wife and the victim had had an affair during their children's summer camp. Presenting this relationship as rape made Karaman the one to bear the blame for shaming the family honour and therefore the designated victim.

These quotes and the accompanying analysis highlight differences in how the label of *eerwraak* was initially used and interpreted by various actors. They also offer a first opportunity to illustrate how Bourdieu's concepts of habitus, capital and field can help make sense of the actors' diverging positions. While the public prosecutor used the label as a means to substantiate a severe sentence, the defence lawyer used the same label to demonstrate that a number of mitigating circumstances needed to be taken into account. This makes sense from the perspective of Bourdieu's ideas, as the actors occupy different field positions and their interpretations of a single label are informed by diverging positions and dispositions.

This first case also introduced two types of experts: the *academic expert* and the *expert with insider knowledge*. It is striking that, while Nauta's analysis is seen as credible, the analysis given by insider Ibrahim Ozdemir is dismissed by both the public prosecutor and the defence lawyer. This demarcation between different types of experts has come to dominate the emerging HRV field and is addressed at greater length in Part III. I suffice by saying here that the difference in appreciation of the experts' respective explanations offers an indication of the type of informational capital that is deemed relevant within the Dutch honour-related violence field.

Lastly, the article illustrates that from its inception the use of the label *eerwraak* has been subject to debate. Subsequent cases of honour killings show similar disputes on whether or not a murder should indeed be labelled an honour killing (see Chapter 5).

---

30. The Dutch term for a person possessing this type of knowledge is *ervaringsdeskundige*: an "expert through experience" (as opposed to formal training).

Since that initial article the *eerwraak* label has flourished both in the Dutch media and elsewhere. An analysis of national and regional newspapers in the Netherlands shows that the label was still used only infrequently between 1990 and 1999 (n=67). However, starting in 2000 the use of the label rose explosively, with an issue-attention peak in 2004 (n=1341). Figure 2 is a chart showing the occurrences of the label of *eerwraak* in Dutch newspapers over time (see also Appendix 1 for the precise numbers per year).

Figure 2. Occurrences of the label of eerwraak *in Dutch newspapers, 1990-2010*[31]

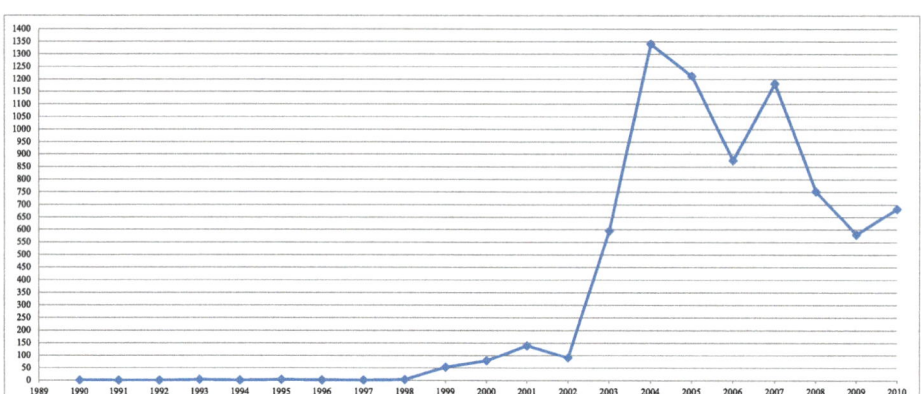

Obviously these numbers need to be qualified. First, not all articles that make use of the label actually refer to Dutch honour killings: some refer to books, movies or plays dealing with the subject, while others refer to honour killings in other countries. Second, in some instances one and the same article was published in multiple different regional newspapers and as such is counted more than once. Yet even given these limitations the numbers for the media field illustrate that the label of *eerwraak* had become a familiar one in the Netherlands by 2003/2004.

Use and development of the label of eerwraak in Dutch politics

A similar trend is revealed by an analysis of the occurrences of the *eerwraak* label in Dutch politics. The label was first used in parliament in two related research reports in 1996. One report described the nature, extent and severity of organized crime in the Netherlands (Fijnaut et al. 1996). The other described organized crime specifically in Amsterdam, Enschede, Nijmegen and Arnhem (Fijnaut & Bovenkerk 1996). Both research reports were written by prominent Dutch crim-

---

31. Numbers are based on an analysis of Dutch national and regional newspapers using the search engine LexisNexis, 24 March 2011.

inologists. The concept of *eerwraak* was therefore presented first of all as a criminological problem. However, as a more detailed analysis shows, both reports also explicitly represent *eerwraak* as an issue connected to Turkish culture.

In the first report, *eerwraak* is mentioned in a paragraph discussing the number of organized crime murders in the Netherlands. The authors found that various migrant communities were overrepresented in this segment: the numbers from non-native communities being three to four times higher than those among native Dutch people. With regard to the Turkish community they subsequently state,

> The Turkish heroin trade features the highest number of murders. Possible explanations are (a) political struggles that are exported, as evidenced by the involvement of the Grey Wolves and PKK, (b) the significant number of fire arms owned by Turkish and Kurdish men, both in Turkey and elsewhere, (c) a violent cultural tradition surrounding issues of honour killings (Yesilgöz, 1995). In this connection, however, another factor is (d) competition for market share. Following intervention from Turkey, a quarrel between an established crime family in Rotterdam and newcomers who challenged their power in 1992 resulted in no fewer than 11 deaths. The other ethnic crime groups display a much lower level of violence. (Fijnaut et al. 1996:68)

This excerpt again describes *eerwraak* as a "cultural tradition", one that is specifically linked to the Turkish community in the Netherlands.

The second report again mentions *eerwraak* in connection with members of the Turkish community in the Netherlands. The label is used in the description of the life of a first-generation Turkish migrant who was the head of a prominent narcotics organization in Amsterdam. Apparently this man, named A in the rapport, was wanted for murder in Turkey. In the following excerpt the authors contrast his murder, which they label as *bloedwraak*[32], with *eerwraak*:

> The head of the A family is a man of respect. In Turkey he is a *kabadayi*, a man of honour and experience whom people obey almost automatically. A true *baba*, the father of a crime family, will also show himself in public. Everyone knows what he does, as do the police and the judicial authorities, yet he displays his true greatness by being untouchable. The *babas* are happy to be depicted. Their exploits and opinions are shown to the people on television and on the front pages of the popular press. A could not do this: in Turkey he was wanted for a murder that he had committed in his youth as part of a blood vendetta [*bloedwraak*]. It is important to bear in mind that honour killings [*eerwraak*] are different, and in these cases the punishment for murder is less severe than in the Netherlands. However, the Turkish authorities comes down hard on blood feuds and punishments in those cases are much more severe than they are here. (Fijnaut & Bovenkerk 1996:75)

---

32. *Bloedwraak* refers to retaliation for the death of a family member through the murder of one of the killer's relatives (Van Eck 2001:14). In English these types of killings are labelled *blood feud* or *vendetta*.

This excerpt again links the concept of honour with Turkish culture, not to the criminal environment to which A clearly belonged.

Alternatively, the authors could have connected these types of honour-motivated murders to the conceptualization of honour within the criminal environment, rather than in terms of Turkish culture. For instance, in his book on organized crime killings Van de Port (2001:123-133) considers what role honour plays in criminal settings. He argues that honour plays a crucial role guiding criminal behaviour. While the motive for these killings is often described in economic terms, for instance the victim still owed the killer money, Van de Port (2001:94-100) believes there to be another dimension to organized crime killings: one that is more emotional and moral, a dimension in which honour, humiliation, shame and vengeance play a crucial role. Yet that dimension received no mention in these initial reports.

Following these initial reports, as document analysis shows, the label of *eerwraak* saw a moderate degree of use in parliament between 1996 and 2002 (n=19). In 2003, however, the use of the label started to rise dramatically, with an issue-attention peak in 2005 (n=99).

Figure 3. Occurrences of the label of eerwraak *in Dutch parliament, 1996-2010*[33]

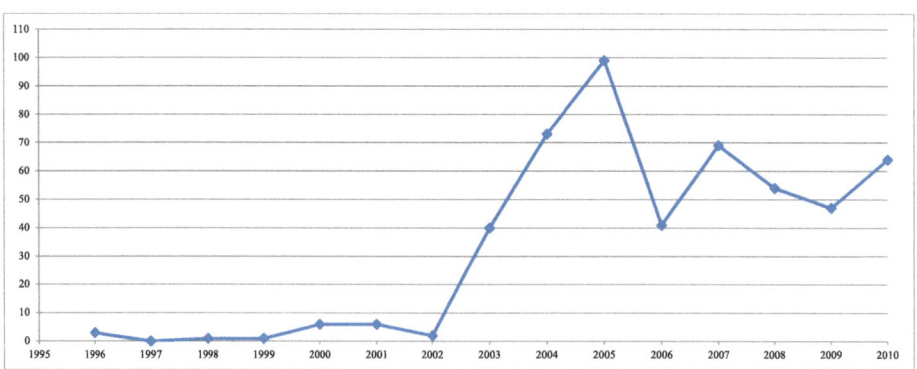

Figure 4 contrasts the occurrences of the *eerwraak* label in Dutch newspapers against the occurrences of the label in parliament. In both fields the numbers for the use of the label start to rise sharply in the same year, i.e. 2003. Moreover, both fields display the highest values in 2004 and 2005; after 2005 the numbers start to decline in both fields. Nonetheless, the occurrences remain at a higher level than before the sudden increase in 2003. Lastly, both fields show a revival of the label

---

33. Numbers are based on an analysis of "official announcements" by the Dutch national government using the search engine Overheid.nl, 30 March 2011.

in 2007. This might stem from a murder that drew the attention of many actors: the honour killing of Zeynep Boral (see the Prologue).

The striking concurrent decline in occurrences of the *eerwraak* label in both fields after 2005/2006 could be explained in part by the introduction of a new label in that same year. In 2005, the policy definition of *eergerelateerd geweld*, or "honour-related violence", came into being, following its use in a research rapport by Ferwerda and Van Leiden (2005).

Figure 4. Occurrences of the label of eerwraak *in Dutch newspapers and parliament, 1996-2010*[34]

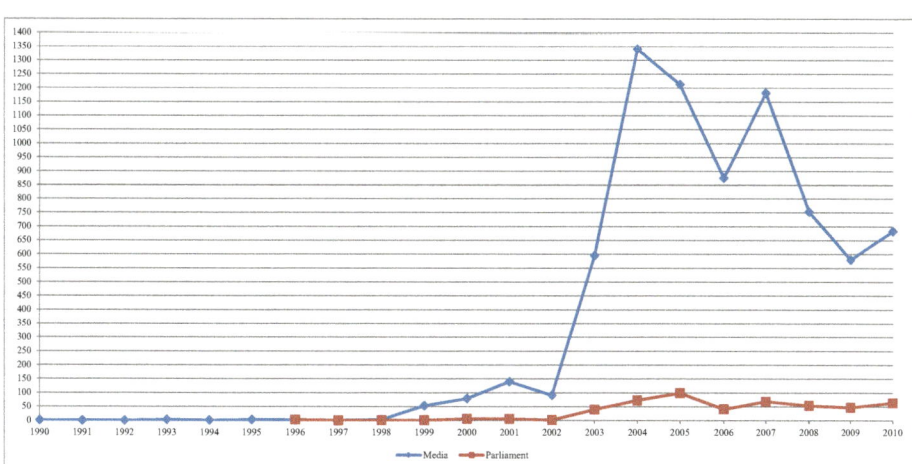

4.2 Developing a new label: *honour-related violence*

After a series of honour killings that generated a great deal of media attention (see Chapter 5), various members of parliament urged the Dutch government to develop specific measures to combat honour-related violence. In response, the government commissioned a series of studies that focused on a) mapping out the extent of the problem (Janssen 2006); b) developing a body of knowledge on honour-related violence (Van der Torre & Schaap 2005) and c) developing a clear definition of the problem[35] (House of Representatives 29 203, no. 15).

---

34. Numbers are based on an analysis of Dutch national and regional newspapers using the search engine LexisNexis, 24 March 2011, and on an analysis of "official announcements" by the Dutch national government using the search engine Overheid.nl, 30 March 2011. For the precise numbers, see Appendix 1, the table showing the occurrences of the *eergerelateerd geweld* and *eerwraak* labels in Dutch parliament and in the media, 2004-2011.

35. See Chapter 8 for an in-depth analysis of the political debates that followed these murders.

That final study was conducted by two members of an independent research firm, Ferwerda and Van Leiden. They found that the *eerwraak* label had several disadvantages and therefore proposed a new and broader definition for this type of violence:

> If the theory, practice and policy of 2005 are combined, it would seem advisable to abandon the phrase "honour revenge" [*eerwraak*], since that phrase is too limited in scope, referring to killing for the sake of the sexual honour (or a threat to that sexual honour) of – in most cases – a girl or woman. Even the most experienced Dutch experts on honour killings adopt the point of view that it is better to apply (as in various other countries) the term "honour-related violence" [*eergerelateerd geweld*]. Such a term (…) offers scope to cover both sexual honour and non-sexual honour, and as such the idea that both female and male honour might be at stake and both men and women could be the victims. Killing the person or persons causing dishonour is then the most extreme expression of honour-related violence. An honour killing is then the most extreme expression of honour-related violence where the sexual honour of the woman, and as such also the family honour, is at stake[36]. In the experts' view, the term honour-related violence also adds considerably to the possibilities for identification (risk assessment) and prevention. (Ferwerda & Van Leiden 2005:22)

In this quote, the authors go on to discuss a number of drawbacks to the *eerwraak* label. Ferwerda and Van Leiden (2005:17-23) for instance note that the label *eerwraak* (literally: "honour revenge") was not useful in an international context, where the label honour killing was much more widely accepted. It was in fact the international use of the label "honour-related violence" that inspired them to develop the Dutch label *eergerelateerd geweld*, a literal translation of the English (see for example Kvinnoforum 2003 and 2005). In addition, it was not entirely clear whether the *eerwraak* label referred exclusively to honour killings, or whether it had broader applicability and covered various forms of violence committed in the name of honour. Lastly, they conclude that *eerwraak* ("honour revenge") was in fact an inaccurate label. The second part of the term was perceived to be misleading, since the intention of an honour killing is not to achieve "revenge"; instead, the purpose of an honour killing is to cleanse the family's honour.

In order to develop a label and definition that could subsequently count on the support of a wide range of actors, Ferwerda and Van Leiden sought input from various experts. They first interviewed academic experts on this topic, including Nauta and Van Eck[37]. They also organized multiple group sessions and invited representatives from the police, women's shelter organizations, a Public Prosecution Service department and umbrella organizations for migrant organizations

---

36. However, the authors subsequently state explicitly that in future they will use the term "honour killing" for this, not "*eerwraak*".

37. In their report, Ferwerda and Van Leiden label these scholars *eerwraakdeskundigen*, meaning "honour-revenge experts" (2005:59).

(Ferwerda & Van Leiden 2005:10-13, 59). Based on their feedback they developed the following definition:

> Honour-related violence means any form of physical or mental violence perpetrated from within a collective mentality, in response to a breach of honour (or the threat of such a breach) concerning a man or woman and therefore his or her family, where the outside world is or might become aware of the breach. (Ferwerda & Van Leiden 2005:25)

In developing this broad definition, the authors sought to provide policymakers and practitioners with a definition that 1) offered information on the causes and expressions of this form of violence, 2) provided input for detecting, registering and assessing the risks of this type of violence and 3) enabled people to distinguish this type of violence from other types of violence such as domestic violence, crimes of passion and honour-related violence with a religious or nationalist basis (Ferwerda & Van Leiden 2005).

Key elements of the new definition

The new definition contains a number of key elements. The first of these is the definition's focus on *"any form of physical or mental violence"*, which therefore covers a broad spectrum of violence, including both punishable and non-punishable forms.

Next, the definition refers to the *collective mentality* that drives this type of violence. According to the authors this collective mentality is based on a "shared, persistent mentality that is a traditional element of a community or culture and that has remained as time has passed" (Ferwerda & Van Leiden 2005:26). Honour-related violence is therefore framed as a culture-based form of violence. Moreover, by using terms such as "persistent" the authors present this culture as static, unchangeable, like a package that is imported from the homeland and remains the same, despite contextual changes (Narayan 2000:1084). In their report Ferwerda and Van Leiden (2005: 15-16) also regularly utilize Turkish concepts such as *namus*[38] and *seref*[39] to explain the cultural component of specific honour killings. However, this focus on Turkish culture is absent from the definition; in fact, the definition does not make any reference to a specific community, and so is applicable to a broad range of communities and cultures.

---

38. According to Ferwerda and Van Leiden, *namus* refers to "a family's shared virtuous honour". The *namus* is communal property – belonging to both the female and the male members of the family – for which every member of the family must bear responsibility (Ferwerda & Van Leiden 2005:16).

39. According to Ferwerda and Van Leiden *seref* refers to "the man's reputation as a participant in a community. It concerns the man's ability to respond properly to insults or injuries to his possessions, i.e. all those matters that are collectively regarded as offences to his honour" (Ferwerda & Van Leiden 2005:15-16).

While Ferwerda and Van Leiden explicitly relate this type of violence to the cultural backgrounds of the offenders and their victims, elsewhere they explicitly deny any connection between this type of violence and Islam (Ferwerda & Van Leiden 2005:18). This denial contrasts markedly with the connection that is often made between honour-related violence and Islam in coverage that this issue receives in the media (Korteweg & Yurdakul (2009, 2010).

A third key element of this definition is its inclusion of both *male and female honour* and, by implication, the possibility of both female and male victims. According to the authors, the earlier label of *eerwraak* explicitly refers to murders committed to cleanse a family's shamed *sexual honour*, i.e. its female honour. However, they also refer to the *non-sexual elements* of honour, meaning predominantly male pride. They go on to introduce the label of *trotsmoord* ("pride murder") to refer to murders committed to cleanse the shamed male pride, as according to the authors the victims of these murders are generally male (Ferwerda & Van Leiden 2005:26)[40].

In the closing part of the definition the authors address the importance of knowledge by others of the shameful act or behaviour. According to Ferwerda and Van Leiden (2005) this is of "crucial importance" because

> [w]hen the environment suspects or is aware of a woman's or girl's premarital sexual relationship, for example, the pressure on the husband or the father increases. Very often, older relatives (a grandfather) play a very prominent role "seemingly in the background" in terms of the follow-up and as such also in terms of urging a response. (Ferwerda and Van Leiden 2005:28)

This point was apparently given particular emphasis by representatives of women's shelter organizations. To understand their preoccupation with this point, it is important to understand how *eerwraak* and subsequently honour-related violence became a key issue in the Dutch public debate and how women's shelter organizations became important actors in that debate. This is addressed at greater length in Chapter 5.

---

40. However, that label was never generally adopted in other fields. For example, within the media field only five articles ever employed it. Of those five articles, three only included the label because it was one of four hundred new words officially recognized in the *Van Dale* Dutch dictionary in 2005. Another article referred to the label in a quote from the report. In parliament, the label is mentioned in seven documents, including the report. Five of the remaining references appear in other scientific reports submitted to parliament, while the final reference concerns a letter introducing one of those reports. The label was never used by members of parliament, nor by the relevant ministers. (The numbers presented here are based on an analysis of Dutch national and regional newspapers using the search engine Lexis-Nexis, 24 March 2011, and on an analysis of "official announcements" by the Dutch central government using the search engine Overheid.nl, 30 March 2011.)

Use and development of the eergerelateerd geweld label

Parliament adopted the new policy definition relatively quickly. The label was introduced in 2004, even before the formal completion of Ferwerda and Van Leiden's report in 2005. Moreover, with 56 occurrences (versus 41 of *eerwraak*) in 2006 and 135 occurrences (versus 64 of *eerwraak*) in 2010, the label swiftly assumed the key position within this field. Nonetheless, as the chart below shows the *eerwraak* label was not replaced entirely by its new counterpart.

Figure 5. Occurrences of the labels of eergerelateerd geweld *and* eerwraak *in Dutch parliament, 1996-2010*[41]

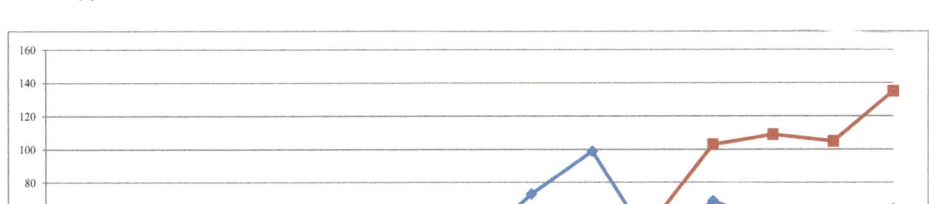

Within the media field, in contrast, the label of "honour-related violence" never met with much success. It was introduced in 2005 and with 70 occurrences (versus 1213 of *eerwraak*) in 2005 and 160 occurrences (versus 683 of *eerwraak*) in 2010 it never came close to matching the frequency of use of its competitor, *eerwraak*. See Figure 5 for a graph showing the occurrences of the *eergerelateerd geweld* label compared to the *eerwraak* label in the media.

While showing differences in development, both charts indicate that the label *eerwraak* remains particularly persistent. The final section of this chapter presents some possible explanations for the media's preference for the *eerwraak* label and the political field's preference for honour-related violence (*eergerelateerd geweld*).

---

41. Numbers are based on an analysis of "official announcements" by the Dutch national government using the search engine Overheid.nl, 30 March 2011.

Figure 6. Occurrences of the eergerelateerd geweld *and* eerwraak *labels in Dutch newspapers, 1996-2010*[42]

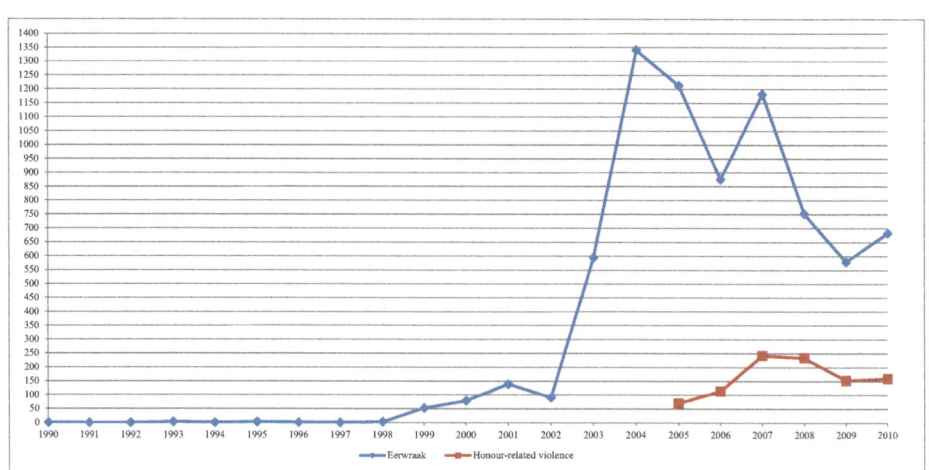

4.3 How these labels contributed to the emergence of a Dutch HRV field

This chapter describes how the labels of *eerwraak* (honour killing) and *eergerelateerd geweld* (honour-related violence) came into being and were adopted in the Netherlands. While the label of *eerwraak* had existed since the 1970s, it only came into popular use at the end of the 20th century. The label of *eergerelateerd geweld*, in contrast, was purposefully developed at the instructions of the Dutch government in 2005 and was used in parliament even before the report introducing the label had been officially presented.

The figures in this chapter additionally provide information about the years that are of particular interest in a study of *how* the issue of honour-related violence gained increasing prominence in the Netherlands. A first increase in the use of the *eerwraak* label is visible in 1999. The years 2003 and 2004 subsequently show a spectacular rise in the use of the label within the media field. This leads to the question of what triggered these developments.

A more in-depth analysis of the media reports during those years reveals that these were the years in which one or more murders or murder attempts took place that were labelled as honour killings: the murders of Kezban in 1999, of Zarife in 2003 and of Gül in 2004 and the attempted murder of Hassan in 1999.

---

42. Numbers are based on an analysis of Dutch national and regional newspapers using the search engine LexisNexis, 24 March 2011.

An analysis of media reports on these murders also provides further information about the micro dynamics that contributed to the issue emergence within the Dutch public discourse (see Chapter 5).

Grodal (2007) also highlights the importance of a shared label for field emergence. In this case study of the Dutch HRV field, not one but two labels contributed to the emergence of the field: *eerwraak* and *eergerelateerd geweld*. Together, these labels define an important part of the field's emerging *doxa*. In the following chapters, I therefore study how both these labels were used and disputed by various actors within the HRV field.

Nevertheless, the foregoing analysis already introduces some of the key actors within this emerging issue-based field: scholars, the media and the government. Moreover, the media's preference for the label of *eerwraak* and the government's active contribution to the development of an alternative label offers an insight into why they took an interest in this field and thus into their respective *illusios*.

The media's preference for the label of *eerwraak* is not surprising. Various scholars have pointed out that drama gives a social problem a strong competitive advantage over other problems (Downs 1972; Hilgartner & Bosk 1988, Loseke 1999). As Downs says, "A problem must be dramatic and exciting to maintain public interest because news is 'consumed' by much of the American public (and publics elsewhere) largely as a form of entertainment" (Downs 1972: 42). Moreover, according to Loseke (1999:181) people tend to unite at extremes, by which she means that extreme cases are the ones that lead to a shared sense of unjustness: "We tend to agree only at the extreme, at those places that are clearly and most certainly and without a doubt immoral".

Honour killings are clearly extreme cases of violence. Moreover, the public nature of some of these killings creates the drama needed to sell newspapers, while other types of honour-related violence are less dramatic in nature and therefore tend to generate less media attention. The subsequent media analysis of four honour killings and attempted killings shows that overall everyone agrees that killing a person for shaming the family's honour is not tolerated in Dutch society. This position was already expressed by the title of the very first news item that discussed this issue: *"Honour killings not to be tolerated in our society"*.

It is precisely this overall agreement that honour killings would not be tolerated in Dutch society that led politicians in unison to call on the government to take action against this type of violence. However, the government needed a clear definition that would help it to tackle the problem of honour-related violence. By giving instructions to develop a definition, the government helped to develop a clear classification of the problem – what Bourdieu et al. (1994) term "*theoretical unification*". Moreover, the government's swift adoption of the label of honour-related violence indicates the power of experts such as Ferwerda and Van Leiden in the construction of a field's classification system (i.e. the field's doxa).

By combining both labels in its emerging doxa, the HRV field evoked the interest of very different actors. The media's illusio was triggered by the drama of honour killings, while the government's illusio contributed to its preference for a clearly defined problem. Both labels subsequently contributed to the emergence of the Dutch HRV field, making it possible for different key actors to join this new field. The label of *eerwraak* made the issue relevant to the media, while the policy definition of *eergerelateerd geweld* represented a first step in the development of theoretical unification within the emerging field.

5. Honour killings as field-configuring events

> ... discursive activity at a macro level can act to provide the building blocks for new institutional fields, but how these building blocks are used to construct a field depends upon local action and the strategies of local actors. (Lawrence & Phillips 2004:690)

With this quote Lawrence and Phillips (2004) direct attention to the micro-level activities that contribute to field emergence, while at the same time acknowledging the embeddedness of these activities within broader societal discourses. As such, in the following I first focus on the micro activities that contributed to the emergence of the issue of honour-related violence within the Dutch public discourse. In the subsequent chapter, I go on to describe the changes in macro-cultural discourses that enabled and constrained these activities.

This chapter therefore forms a next step towards answering the question of how the issue of honour-related violence emerged within the Dutch public discourse. In Chapter 4, I illustrated the emergence of the issue of honour-related violence by retracing the use of the labels *eerwraak* ("honour killing") and *eergerelateerd geweld* ("honour-related violence") within the Dutch media and political fields. The charts presented there provided an answer to the question of *when* the issue of honour-related violence first emerged within the Dutch public discourse, i.e. the beginning of the 21st century. Those charts also indicated that three years were of particular interest in the study of the issue's emergence: 1999, when a first increase in the use of the *eerwraak* label was visible, and 2003 and 2004, which showed a sharp rise in the use of the label within the media field. These were the years in which one or more murders or murder attempts took place, triggering a great deal of media attention and being labelled as honour killings.

In this chapter, the focus is therefore particularly on the activities that followed these actual and attempted honour killings. I argue that these incidents functioned as *field-configuring events*. Moreover, I provide an answer as to why these particular incidents functioned as *critical events*. Next, I present the key debates that followed these murders, viz. debates on 1.) the *applicability of the label* of "honour killing" and 2.) the *cultural basis for* these murders and attempted murders.

5.1 Analysing field-configuring events

According to Hoffman (1999:353), events such as murders can act as incentives for field emergence or field transformation. It is due to these types of events that fields "come alive" to perform sense-making and sense-giving work, thereby generating a perfect opportunity to study the *micro processes* involved in field construction (Wooten & Hoffman 2008:139).

Yet the actual and attempted murders of Kezban, Hassan, Zarife and Gül did more than merely disrupt the field and bring it alive. Within the emerging field their murders appear to have acted as *field-configuring events*, triggering a wide array of different activities that in turn influenced the configurations of the HRV field that emerged subsequently (see Part III).

The concept of field-configuring events was first developed by Meyer et al. in 2005. Their work focuses in particular on tradeshows and conferences as field-configuring events. According to these scholars, field-configuring events are

> [t]emporary social organizations such as tradeshows, professional gatherings, technology contests, and business ceremonies that encapsulate and shape the development of professions, technologies, markets, and industries (Meyer et al. 2005). They are the settings in which people from diverse organizations and with divers purposes assemble periodically, or on a one-time basis, to announce new products, develop industry standards, construct social networks, recognize accomplishments, share and interpret information, and transact businesses. (Lampel & Meyer 2008:1026)[43]

These types of *planned* field-configuring events were also visible within the emerging HRV field[44]. However, the field-configuring events that are the object of study in the present chapter are of a different type. The actual and attempted murders of Kezban, Hassan, Zarife and Gül are denoted here as *unplanned field-configuring events*: from a field perspective[45] at least, they were unplanned events with unanticipated consequences. This type of *unplanned field-configuring event* can therefore only be established in retrospect. Moreover, these incidents did not introduce a "new product" but rather a "new problem". Lastly, unlike with *planned* field-configuring events, the object of analysis is not the event itself, but rather the effects generated by the event.

Obviously, not all events have this type of field-configuring effect. While some murders went more or less unnoticed by the media, others turned into *critical events* that "focus sustained public attention and invite the collective definition or redefinition of social problems" (Hoffman & Ocasio 2001:414). In their work

---

43. This definition illustrates that these scholars focused on fields developing around new technologies and markets. Moreover, it shows that for them the object of analysis is the event itself – the tradeshow or business ceremony, for example – and not the event's subsequent ripple effects within the various populations that make up the emerging organizational field. Lastly, field-configuring events as meant in this definition are planned events, often organized by institutional entrepreneurs to push the emerging field in a particular direction (Meyer et al. 2005:467).

44. The parliamentary debates that I analyze in Chapter 8, for instance, could be described as *planned* field configuring events.

45. From the perpetrators' perspective, the incidents must have been planned events, as may be inferred from the fact that in three of the cases a gun was brought to the scene.

on critical events, Hoffman and Ocasio (2001) show that the amount of attention an event receives from field members depends on a number of aspects.

The first is how heated the debate is about the meaning attributed to the event. The second is whether the event triggers outside attention, outside attention here referring to attention from non-field members. The third is whether the event embodies a threat to the field's image. This threat may be formed by an "allocation of accountability" by outsiders. Where this accountability claim forms a threat to the field's reputation field members might be prompted to take action.

Lastly, Hoffman and Ocasio (2001) draw attention to a fourth characteristic of critical events. They argue that the amount of attention that an event receives from field members is affected by the field's *social structures of attention,* which they subdivide into three elements: a.) the status of the relevant actors or accountable party, b.) the congruity of the event with the field's "rules of the game"[46], and c.) the event's implication for the field's work practices.

These social structures of attention can be translated into Bourdieusian terminology. In Bourdieu's terms, status is determined by the actor's capital, which in turn determines the actor's possibilities to take position within the field. The rules of the game and the field's working practices correspond to Bourdieu's game metaphor work.

5.2 How honour killings become critical events

During the issue-emergence phase, four honour killings retrospectively became such critical events. The first murder that caught the attention of the broader public was the murder of Kezban Vural in June 1999. While walking down a street in Zwijndrecht Kezban, a 29-year-old woman of Turkish descent, was gunned down in broad daylight in the presence of her two children by her abusive ex-husband. The murder was initially framed by her close friend Nurdan Cakiroglu as an example of senseless violence and domestic violence. Later, however, she and others labelled Kezban's murder an honour killing.

This reframing took place after an attempted murder in December of that same year: the second critical event. This attempt was similarly committed in a public location, a school in Veghel[47], where a 17-year-old boy of Turkish-Kurdish descent walked into the computer science lab and shot five people. The victims – four students and a teacher – all survived this attack on their lives. Among them was the ex-boyfriend of the gunman's sister, Hassan Keskin. According to various

---

46. By "rules of the game" Hoffman and Ocasio (2001:425) mean the "formal and informal principles of action that guide decisionmakers in the industry".
47. Specifically, the *Regionaal Opleidings Centrum* (ROC) De Leijgraaf. ROCs are *Regional Training Centres* where students and adults can attend vocational training classes.

sources, the perpetrator's father was the mastermind behind this attempted honour killing. Although the incident was initially labelled a Columbine-type school shooting[48], the principal target's brother soon indicated that it was an attempted honour killing. This claim was subsequently backed up by Clementine van Eck, who shortly after the attempt defended her PhD thesis on honour killings within the Dutch-Turkish community.

The third incident that triggered a great deal of media attention occurred in Turkey, in the summer of 2003. After a series of ongoing arguments about her "traditional" upbringing, Zarife was gunned down by her father during a summer holiday with relatives in Turkey. This honour killing only became public knowledge in the Netherlands when Jaap Krikke, the director of her school, reported the news to the media. According to Krikke, his school regularly dealt with girls from migrant backgrounds who experienced severe conflicts with their parents, leading to abuse, suicide and now even murder. Zarife's death had convinced him to sound the alarm over the issue of honour-related violence.

Lastly, the murder of 32-year-old Gül in March 2004 formed what one MP described as an exclamation mark after the uproar that Zarife's murder had generated (Wolfsen, House of Representatives 64 64-41157, 7 April 2004). This murder showed some macabre similarities with Kezban's murder four years previously. Again, the murder was committed in broad daylight, again by an ex-husband. Both women had fled to a women's shelter and in both instances their ex-husbands had been able to trace them – in Gül's case to the fourth women's shelter to which she had fled. Amplifying the tragedy of her case, she was shot while walking back from the police station. According to representatives of women's shelter organizations this was the third time in ten months that they had been confronted with this type of violence. They now felt the need to raise the alarm, claiming that they were unable to guarantee the safety of the women staying in their shelters.

Why these murders became critical events

Above, I have briefly outlined the three murders and one attempted murder that were given the label of "honour killings" between 1999 and 2004. However, an analysis of the media coverage of these incidents reveals that some actors also referred to other cases of honour-related violence. Yet those cases of violence did not become critical events.

For example, an analysis of the media coverage of Kezban's murder (June 1999) reveals that she was not the only women to be murdered by an ex-husband during

---

48. In April 1999 two students killed twelve students and one teacher at a US high school in Columbine, Colorado. This shooting triggered extensive debate, including about gun availability in the US and school bullying.

that summer. Within two weeks two other Turkish women suffered the same fate (ANP 1999): one victim remained nameless and no additional information was provided about her death, while the second murder case generated slightly more media attention. Nevertheless, few articles mention the victim's name, Naciye Kurt. Moreover, only a single article explicitly described what befell her. In a large background article in national newspaper *De Telegraaf* (1999), a neighbour described how she had sounded the alarm after Naciye failed to pick up her son from school. A few hours later Naciye was found in her apartment, stabbed to death by her ex-husband in the presence of their 2-year-old daughter.

When Zarife's school director announced her murder, he also referred to two other instances of honour-related violence: the suicide of a Turkish pupil and the ostracizing of an Armenian girl by her family (*NRC Handelsblad* 2003). Both victims remained nameless.

Lastly, in Gül's case the women's shelter organizations that raised the alarm about the honour killings of women taking refuge in their shelters mentioned three honour killings within ten months' time. Nonetheless, the two other victims remained nameless and no other information was provided besides the locations of the murders: Venlo and Den Bosch (*Het Parool* 2004).

This gives rise to the question of why specifically the murders of Kezban, Zarife and Gül and the attempted murder of Hassan generated the resulting media attention and subsequently became critical events. This question is even more relevant when considered against the backdrop of a police report stating that the police registered between eleven and thirteen murders associated with honour-related violence in the years 2007, 2008 and 2009 (Janssen & Sanberg 2010:30). Assuming that no change occurred in the actual number of honour-related killings, it is safe to assume that on average the same number of murders occurred during the years under study.

A comparison of the four actual and attempted murder cases provides some clues to answer this question. First, with the exception of Zarife's murder, each of the incidents occurred at a *public location*, making them public knowledge.

Second, each of the cases carried the *dramatic features* necessary to generate media attention (Downs 1972). Kezban was murdered in broad daylight in the presence of her children. Moreover, it happened after she had left her abusive husband, had moved to a women's shelter and had reported her ex-husband at least ten times to the police for stalking. In the Veghel case the school location in combination with the "love story" that had triggered the shooting – the supposed relationship between the shooter's sister Yillez (aged 15) and Hassan (aged 19) – added sufficient drama for the media. Lastly, Zarife's young age (she was 18 at the time of the murder), combined with her struggle to escape her "traditional" upbringing, made for an appealing story for the media.

A third salient feature of these cases is that they all carried the connotation of *failing government agencies*. For example, like Kezban, Zarife had talked with the police before her murder. She had also spent time at a women's shelter before returning home for a family holiday in Turkey. In the Veghel case, both the shooter's family and the victim's family had been in contact with the police in the months leading up to the shooting: the first to report the abduction of their daughter, the second to file a complaint of harassment against the perpetrator's family.

This feature is most striking in Gül's murder. Gül had left her husband and taken refuge in a women's shelter with her children. Nevertheless, her husband had been able to trace her time and time again, forcing her to move to four different shelters. He ultimately traced her to Koog aan de Zaan, where she was shot more or less in front of the women's shelter. The women's shelter organizations later claimed that Gül expected that her husband would make an appearance sooner or later. They were often quoted as saying, "She knew that he would return and she knew that he would not be bringing her flowers" (Roel in *Leeuwarder Courant* 2004). This illustrates how helpless both Gül and the women's shelter organizations felt, being unable to prevent the inevitable.

Yet the final feature of these incidents, and the one that sets them apart, is that they were used by various actors to raise the alarm about this type of violence. An analysis of the media coverage shows that each case had its own *key instigator* to trigger a stream of articles about the event.

Table 1. Key instigators and their roles

Incident	Key instigator	Role
Kezban	Nurdan Cakiroglu (friend and social worker)	Sounded the alarm about gender violence
Hassan	Clementine van Eck (scholar)	Expert
Zarife	Jaap Krikke, (school director)	Blew the whistle about violence among migrant school populations
Gül	Women's shelters and *Federatie Opvang*, (umbrella organization for women's shelters)	Sounded the alarm and demanded action

In the following I provide further details about each of these key instigators.

Nurdan Cakiroglu, key instigator following Kezban's murder

In Kezban's case the most prominent actor to raise the alarm was Nurdan Cakiroglu, her close friend and a social worker. By making claims such as "Our friend Kezban has to be the final victim" and "Women need to be well-protected" (Cakiroglu in *Rotterdams Dagblad* 1999) Cakiroglu called attention to both violence against women and failing protection systems. Cakiroglu sought to draw attention to the problem of domestic violence in general. Asked about how culture or religion had influenced the murder, she initially explicitly denied any connection: "Our religion certainly does not allow men to treat their wives this way" (Cakiroglu in *De Dordtenaar* 1999). Later, however, the substance of her claims changed. She shifted her focus to violence within the Turkish community and the influence of the concept of honour on this type of violence.

Clementine van Eck, key instigator following the Veghel shooting

In the Veghel case, key actor Clementine van Eck claimed the role of expert to explain what the concept of *eerwraak* (honour killing) entailed. For example, in an article entitled "Honour-related violence is a cleansing ritual" she explained,

> It comes from a culture of shame and pride. In Turkey it is most common in villages in rural areas. We call it honour killing, but its actual name is honour cleansing. The perpetrator always goes about it in a strikingly calm way and always uses a pistol. Usually he stays at the crime scene or turns himself in to the police. The murder always takes place during daytime, in a public place with many bystanders, for example at a market. Another important characteristic of the ritual is that the perpetrator does not have any regrets. (Van Eck in Dubbelman 1999)

According to Van Eck, the Veghel shooting was therefore a classic example of an honour killing. Her opinion was quickly adopted by the media.

Jaap Krikke, key instigator following Zarife's murder

In Zarife's case, school director Jaap Krikke was the one to blow the whistle, seeking to call attention to the violence that he witnessed at his school. Moreover, he suspected that other schools experienced similar problems, but kept quiet about it. For instance, he stated,

> Supposedly it's a matter of family honour, but it does nothing to save the honour of a particular community. It's time that we draw attention to the problems surrounding the upbringing of migrant girls from orthodox homes. (Krikke in Mantel 2003)

His quote also illustrates a form of othering that is often found in claims made by both migrant and Dutch actors. By referring to "orthodox families", Krikke establishes a demarcation between integrated migrant families and those that cling to their religion. By doing so he implicitly uses religion to explain this type of violence.

Women's shelter organizations, key instigators following Gül's murder

Lastly, after Gül's murder women's shelter organizations and their umbrella *Federatie Opvang* (FO) sounded the alarm about their inability to keep their clients safe. Moreover, they expressed bewilderment about the lack of attention for, and action against, this type of violence. For example, in one of the first articles about Gül's murder, director Cocky Roel of the third women's shelter where Gül stayed stated,

> If someone is shot dead outside a disco, the incident is immediately followed by silent marches and a public outcry. Over the past year honour killings have already cost the lives of three innocent women. Last year it happened in Venlo and 's Hertogenbosch, and now in Koog aan de Zaan. I don't understand why so little is being said about it. (Roel in *Leeuwaarder Courant* 2004).

Like school director Krikke, she clearly felt that these honour killings were not receiving the attention that they deserved, neither politically nor otherwise.

The importance of key instigators

These quotes illustrate how different actors took centre stage following each of the incidents. Moreover, each actor performed a different role. Cakiroglu performed the role of agenda setter, first for domestic violence and later for honour-related violence. Van Eck's claims about the Veghel case focused on educating the broader public about the problem of honour-related violence. School director Jaap Krikke acted as a whistle-blower. Other actors, including politicians, quickly took over his claims and used Zarife's murder to call for action against this type of violence. These calls for action grew in volume after Gül's death, when women's shelter organizations made it clear that the existing measures to prevent violence were not adequate to handle honour-related violence.

These key actors not only were crucial as instigators of the attention for each incident, they also contributed to the *revival* of the attention given to these events within the media field at later moments. An analysis of the media coverage shows that the attention given to the actual and attempted murders fluctuated. The first articles always appeared shortly after the event became public knowledge. The amount of attention given to the incidents then generally declined after some days, only to flare up again once the cases were handled in court[49].

Nurdan Cakiroglu, for instance, was very successful in ensuring continued media focus on the problem of violence against women. She effectively dominated the news coverage of Kezban's murder and its aftermath. For example, she was in the media again to report on the fate of Kezban's children, who had been taken in by relatives in Turkey. She also actively intervened in the court case against Kezban's ex-husband when his lawyer sought to use the concept of hon-

---

49. Discussions about the applicability of the label of honour killing often took centre stage in the coverage of the various trials. The claims made during these trials are therefore presented in the following section.

our as a mitigating circumstance. In addition, she was actively involved in the efforts to develop a local safety network for victims of violence, and received two national awards in recognition of her work in that area. She later used the award money to set up *Stichting Kezban*, a foundation with the specific object of fighting violence against migrant women. This foundation later re-emerged as an actor in the media coverage relating to Zarife and Gül.

Another actor who became a recurring key actor in the media's coverage of the various murders was Clementine van Eck. She dominated the media coverage of the Veghel shooting and its aftermath. The media repeatedly quoted her as an expert in their coverage of the murders of Zarife and Gül. In Zarife's case, she also took on the role of agenda-setter, stating that honour-related violence had become a Dutch problem and was here to stay for at least another twenty years.

Jaap Krikke and the women shelter's organizations played less dominant parts in the aftermaths of the murders that they had brought to the media's attention. While they were crucial as instigators of the media's initial attention, they were swiftly joined by other actors in the discussions about the issue of honour killings. For instance, later media coverage of Zarife's murder was instigated primarily by Karima Ouchan, the new student counsellor at Zarife's school.

After Zarife's murder Krikke felt that someone was needed who possessed expert knowledge of the topic of honour-related violence, and he hired Ouchan as a student counsellor. Ouchan herself had suffered from honour-related violence and had written a book entitled *Nooit geschreven brief aan mijn vader*[50]. Krikke's move generated a considerable amount of media attention, as did Karima Ouchan herself. She later developed into a key actor within the emerging HRV field: first as a student counsellor, later as the coordinator of a large-scale pilot project to deal with honour-related violence at schools and ultimately as the coordinator of an honour-related violence project that was carried out by *Samenwerkingsverband Marokkaanse Nederlanders*[51], an umbrella organization for Moroccan NGOs.

Besides Ouchan, national politicians such as Ayaan Hirsi Ali (MP for VVD), Minister of Alien Affairs and Integration Rita Verdonk (VVD) and Minister of Justice Piet Hein Donner (CDA) also joined the discussions about honour-related violence. For example, in 2004 Minister Verdonk announced,

> I am very concerned about the rise in honour killings in our society. (…) Honour killings have recently acquired names in the Netherlands: Zarife, Gül and looking further back Kezban Vural. They represent an as yet unknown number of nameless women who live under duress, who are forced to flee or who are victims of violence. (…) The

---

50. Reysoo and Ouchan 2004, fourth edition. The title translates into English as "Never-written letter to my father".
51. In English: "Cooperative Association for Dutch people of Moroccan ethnicity".

key to eliminating honour killings is in your own community's hands. (...) Do not turn your face away, but identify them, report them and show your disapproval. We are talking about threatening a person's life. That is not honourable. (Verdonk in Heijmans 2004:3)

This quote was taken from a speech that Minister Verdonk held during the celebration of forty years of Turkish immigration into the Netherlands. During this speech she called on the Turkish community to act against honour killings, making reference to three honour killings: the murders of Zarife, Gül and Kezban. These women had clearly become *a point of reference* for various actors within the emerging HRV field.

In summary, while the described murders and attempted murder were not the only incidents between 1999 and 2004 that may be labelled honour killings, they stand out by a.) occurring in public locations, b.) carrying sufficient dramatic features to make them sufficiently interesting for the media to report, c.) being illustrative of failing government agencies and most importantly d.) provoking the interest of various actors who subsequently managed to air their concerns within the media field. These salient features are what turned these murders into critical events. The murders generated sustained public attention and invited actors to collectively work on defining the issue of honour-related violence.

These characteristics match the *critical event* features described at the beginning of this chapter. As the following sections show, these murders led to *fierce discussions* about their interpretation, revolving around two issues: the attribution of the label of honour killing and whether or not the murders had a cultural basis.

The second feature described by Hoffman and Ocasio (2001), triggering *outsider attention*, is also very much present in these events. Each successive shooting triggered the attention of another actor, starting with a friend, followed by a scholar, then a school director, women's shelter organizations and finally politicians. Moreover, as the key instigators of the media's attention for these incidents, these actors played a pivotal part in turning these murders into critical events.

The *attribution of accountably* feature described by Hoffman and Ocasio is also present in these incidents. As explained above, each event was illustrative of a failing government agency. Lastly, Hoffman and Ocasio argue that events become critical if they comply with the *social structures of attention* within a given field. In this case, the shootings complied with the media's social structures of attention and thus "the rules of the game" of the media field. Their public locations meant that the media was able to learn of them. Moreover, each incident carried the dramatic features necessary for triggering the media's attention. In addition, these murders also triggered the attention of actors who proved themselves able to comply with the rules of the game of the media field.

5.3 Discussion about the attribution of the "honour killing" label

Although these shootings were all labelled honour killings at some point, the attribution of this label caused discussion in all four cases. To illustrate these microlevel disputes, I analyse the media's representation of the court cases that followed the actual and attempted murders of Kezban, Hassan, Zarife and Gül.

In part, the disputes were generated by the legal repercussions of whether a murder was in fact deemed to be an honour killing: being labelled an honour killing automatically meant that it was premeditated murder. Moreover, attributing the label of honour killing also has implications for the role of the victim. In various cultural codes an honour killing is a legitimate act only if the victim acted dishonourably, for example through infidelity or loss of virginity before marriage. To some, labelling a murder an honour killing therefore implies that the victim did something to deserve the punishment. Lastly, in some quarters the label of honour killing was disputed on grounds that it led to stereotyping the Turkish community and to a demarcation between Dutch and Turkish violence.

The discussions about the attribution of the label of honour killing were fought either in the media or else in court with the media subsequently reporting. The opposing claims made by the various actors during these court cases evoked questions: "Was it or was it not an honour killing?" and "Who among the various actors has sufficient expertise to make this distinction?"[52] Yet the purpose of this section is not to formulate answers to these questions but rather to illustrate how the label of honour killing is a social construction and that the answers depend entirely on the actor's particular position. Moreover, the label was constructed by actors with their own reasons for defining a murder as an honour killing or as something else. The discussions presented below illustrate how these murders helped to crystalize what the problem of honour killings entailed. Part of the configuring effect of these murders, therefore, lies in their ability to generate this type of disputes.

The trial in the case of Gül's murder

Discussions about the attribution of the label of honour killing are nothing new. As noted in Chapter 4, the attribution of the label of honour killing was already challenged during the *Karaman* trial in 1990: the defendant's lawyer still sought to use culture as a defence, arguing that his client "was led to act this way out of his sense of duty to cleanse the family honour" (in Vermeulen 1990:2). However,

---

52. The actors involved in these disputes also wrestled with those questions. For example, during the court case about the Veghel shooting, the shooter claimed that the truth was that he had acted on his own. This claim caused the judge to comment ruefully, "That's precisely the difficulty: how can we know what the truth is with all these statements?" (Judge in Heijmans 2001b).

by 2004 the lawyer representing Gül's ex-husband Mustafa did everything in his power to remove any cultural connotation:

> Everyone is talking about the culture of violence in migrant circles, about the harmful influence of the Muslim faith on the actions of Muslims, but that did not play any part in this case. B.'s motives have no connection to any religious beliefs or cultural background whatsoever. (A. Moszkowicz in Soeteman 2004)

Moszkowicz had previously attempted to refute the claims made by women's shelter organizations and politicians categorizing Gül's death as an honour killing. In an article that appeared mere days after Gül's death he claimed that attributing the label was "premature" and "imprudent" (A. Moszkowicz in ANP 2004).

In a similar vein Ayhan Tonça, chair of the *Nederlands Overlegorgaan Turken*[53] and member of the Apeldoorn municipal council, announced that this was not a typical honour killing. "For it to be an honour killing, it must involve adultery or indecent behaviour. In principal a divorce is no reason to commit an honour killing" (Tonça in *De Stenor/Veluws Dagbald* 2004).

During the trial, the lawyer's claim was supported by other actors, including a psychologist and a psychiatrist. Both expressed the opinion that Gül's ex-husband suffered from a narcissistic personality disorder combined with an overblown ego. Moreover, the cultural expert in this case, Clementine van Eck, was also of the opinion that the murder was not an honour killing. According to Van Eck, Gül had done nothing dishonourable; she had not been unfaithful. All that she had done was leave her abusive husband. Both the Public Prosecution Service and the court adopted this line of reasoning and Mustafa was convicted of murder and sentenced to nine years in prison, plus hospital detention with compulsory psychiatric treatment.

However, Van Eck did not agree entirely with the court's verdict, as it made no allowance at all for the cultural context of the murder. Although it was not an honour killing, Van Eck felt that honour had in fact played a crucial role in the defendant's behaviour:

> His wife had left him because she was being systematically abused by him. He could not bear the fact that she had taken control of her own destiny and that of the children. This hurt his male pride. His prestige in his own community was at risk. (Van Eck in Santing 2004)

She therefore described this incident as a murder for wounded male pride. The 2005 report on the definition of honour-related violence retains this distinction between honour killing and murder for wounded pride, a *trotsmoord* (Ferwerda & Van Leiden 2005:26). However, that label never attracted much following.

---

53. In English: "Dutch Consultation Body for Turks".

The trial in the case of Kezban's murder

The discussions about the attribution of the label of honour killing in Gül's case are almost a mirror image of the discussions surrounding Kezban's murder. The former was immediately labelled as an honour killing by most actors and the label was only discarded during the trial. In Kezban's case the label was not attributed until shortly before the trial began in December 1999. Kezban's death was initially labelled as an act of senseless violence and domestic violence. However, the Veghel shooting on 7 December 1999, in combination with an article by the defendant's lawyer, led to Kezban's death being reframed in terms of an honour killing.

Urcun, the defendant's lawyer, seemingly had concerns about how a cultural defence would play out in court. He decided put it to the test in an article published in the widely read Turkish magazine *Ekin*. He posed the following question:

> Is what Erol [Kezban's ex-husband] did in fact wrong? Imagine a woman who tries to drive away her husband, puts her children to bed and visits other men with her girlfriends and parties until the small hours. (…) I want to use the cultural factors as the basis for my argument. (…) If I can substantiate it, I will win this case. (Urcun in Lange 1999)

The article drew furious responses from Kezban's relatives and friends, who felt that he had tainted the memory of their sister and friend. For instance, her brother Haci claimed,

> Kezban was my favourite sister. She had a nice character, everyone knows. She was sweet, helpful, good to her children. What possessed that man? (…) I know that his defence is his honour, Turkish culture and religion. But that makes absolutely no sense. A man should take care of his children, and then his wife. If a marriage breaks down, the honourable thing is to leave her alone and to continue to take proper care of the children! (Haci in Zijlstra 1999)

In this quote Haci emphasizes his sister's honourable behaviour, stressing that she was kind and loving and did nothing to justify an honour killing.

In a letter to the Public Prosecution Service, Cakiroglu also warned against Urcun's line of reasoning: "Nobody may kill in order to protect their family honour. A lawyer who studied in the Netherlands should know that he cannot make such dangerous statements" (Cakiroglu in *de Volkskrant* 1999).

Nederlands Centrum Buitenlanders[54] (NCB) also strongly protested against Urcun's position, arguing that the lawyer's article wrongly offered Turkish men an alibi. According to NCB director Ilhan Akel, Urcun "effectively publicly brands

---

54. In English: "Dutch Centre for Foreigners".

all women staying at a women's refuge[55] whores, which is hurtful, offensive and a bad signal" (Arkan in *NRC Handelsblad* 1999). NCB called on the Turkish community to change how husbands and wives resolved their conflicts[56].

In anticipation of the cultural defence, the Public Prosecution Service announced that the crime had taken place in the Netherlands and should therefore be judged according to Dutch standards. Ultimately, however, Urcun decided against using the cultural defence, arguing instead that his client had acted in a fit of temporary insanity and should be acquitted on that ground.

Still, the court sentenced the defendant to fifteen years in jail, plus hospital detention with compulsory psychiatric treatment. When handing down this sentence, which was more than the ten years sought by the Public Prosecution Service, the court explicitly held that the motive of violated honour could never justify any form of violence, let alone led to a reduced sentence.

The trial in the case of Zarife's murder

When Zarife was murdered in 2003, the incident was immediately labelled an honour killing and so termed by a wide array of actors. Despite some initial caution ("The motive was most likely an honour killing", *Utrechts Nieuwsblad* 2003), the titles of subsequent articles left no room for any doubt about the motive: "Turkish father in honour killing of daughter" (ANP 2003a), "Man kills daughter (18) for honour" (*NRC Handelsblad* 2003) and "School seeks public debate following honour killing of student" (ANP 2003b).

In later reports actors unanimously condemned this act of violence. Minister Verdonk stated that honour killings were "inadmissible" in the Netherlands and that "[h]onour killings need to be forcefully exorcized". She directly called on the Turkish community to take action: "We need to make it clear to the Turkish community in the Netherlands that this is unacceptable" (Verdonk in ANP 2003). Verdonk's claims again illustrate a form of delineation that is typical of the claims relating to these murders. This delineation and othering is discussed at greater length in the next chapter.

Another political actor who entered the emerging HRV field during this case was MP Ayaan Hirsi Ali (VVD). In an opinion article in national newspaper *NRC Handelsblad*, she linked Zarife's murder to the domestic violence discussion in the House of Representatives and called on the government to more adequately

---

55. Dutch *blijf-van-mijn-lijfhuizen* offer refuge to battered women. The name literally translates as "don't-touch-me house".
56. This call on the Turkish community also heralds a change in NCB's position. Immediately after Kezban's murder, the organization stressed that the murder of women by husbands or ex-husbands was not specifically a Turkish problem but a larger societal problem. Following the Veghel shooting, however, the organization acknowledged that women in the Turkish community were subject to a great deal of pressure and announced that Turkish men needed to change their attitude towards women.

tackle what she described as a culturally and religiously legitimized type of domestic violence. Her article concluded with the provocative question, "How many women must suffer Zarife's fate before the government starts to combat domestic violence effectively?" (Hirsi Ali 2003).

Significantly, the Turkish community also condemned Zarife's murder immediately. For example, spokesperson for *Samenwerkende Turkse Organisaties* (STO)[57] Zeki Arslan called the phenomenon of honour killing a "brainless" act (Arslan in De Fauwe 2003). The imam of Almelo's local mosque condemned this act of violence in one of his prayers. He proclaimed, "God has given life and God will also take it away. Nobody has the right to take away someone's life. What happened to Zarife is unacceptable" (Imam Makadder Arif Yuksel in De Fauwe 2003).

However, while condemning the act itself, the imam, the mosque's chairman and a local politician of Turkish descent questioned the honour motive. They argued that Zarife's murder was the act of a deranged individual and they warned against blaming the whole Turkish community for one man's actions: "How many Dutch children have been killed by their fathers in the past years? No brand should be put on Turkish people" (in De Fauwe 2003).

While not disputing the *honour killing* label, STO's chairman Arslan also developed a counter-argument. He wrote an opinion article in which he addressed Minister Verdonk's call to the Turkish community to take action. Over the past three years, he claimed, his organizations had already taken action, for example by organizing debates and inviting experts on the topic. Moreover, what was needed to combat the problem of honour-related violence was a "collective approach": cooperation between actors such as schools, the media and the government (Arslan 2003), rather than placing the burden on the shoulders of the Turkish community alone.

During the trial in Turkey, the defendant's lawyer Karabatan also claimed that Zarife's murder was an act of despair by a mentally sick man, not an honour killing. According to Karabatan, his client was made sick by all the rumours about Zarife's conduct, such as dating a married man and having affairs with both an Iranian and a Turkish man: "My client did not dare to show his face anywhere. His friends gave him the cold shoulder. He suffered from insomnia and his health deteriorated" (Karabatan in Ekiz 2003). He went on to argue that if his client had wanted to cleanse his honour he would have murdered Zarife in the Netherlands. "If it was an honour killing he would have killed Zarife among the people who had turned their backs to him, so that he could walk around with his head held high once more" (Karabatan in Ekiz 2003).

Ultimately, the father was convicted and sentenced to thirty years in prison. Whether the court viewed Zarife's death as an honour killing or as an act of des-

---

57. In English: "Cooperating Turkish Organizations".

pair, however, remains unclear, since no further clarification of its position was provided in the Dutch media.

The Veghel trials

While each of these murders generated a great deal of media attention, the media's representation of the disputes in the case of the Veghel shooting surpassed them all. During the court cases against the shooter Ali and his father Kerim, all manner of experts came forward, falling over each other to make their arguments. While some claimed that this was indeed an attempted honour killing, father and son as well as their relatives categorically denied this during the trials.

However, their claims were refuted, as immediately after the shooting Ali had given five detailed statements to the police, describing how Kerim had pressured him for months to take action against Hassan, the intended victim. He later retracted these statements, hired another lawyer and during the court cases took sole responsibility for the crime.

One of the first to explicitly label the Veghel shooting an attempted honour killing was Clementine van Eck. Immediately after the incident she was quoted in various articles, explaining what characterizes an honour killing. Van Eck later also testified against Ali and Kerim in court, and was criticized for doing so by Kerim's lawyer Knoops. He held the Public Prosecution Service at fault for building the case on an expert who had been quick to label the shooting an attempted honour killing despite not having all the facts at her disposal.

Knoops, in contrast, built Kerim's appeal (February 2001) on a report by a Professor Ozgen from Turkey. According to Ozgen, the shooting was not an attempted honour killing since a.) too much time that had passed between the alleged abduction of the daughter and the shooting: an honour killing would have had to take place immediately after the abduction; b.) given that the girl had voluntarily joined her boyfriend on a trip to Turkey, the moral code dictated that she should also have been punished; and c.) the family had already restored its honour by arranging an engagement for their daughter, and no further action was required.

Ozgen's claims were backed by the defendants' family. In an extensive interview that appeared a little while before Ali's trial (January 2001), his sister Yeliz and their mother Fatma told their story. Their main purpose in giving the interview seems to have been to clear Kerim, whose appeal was scheduled for shortly after Ali's court case. This intention is most explicit in Yeliz's final statement:

> Ali did it. He is my brother, but still he should be punished. Ali is no better than other people. But my father is being held for no reason and we will not stand for that. Everything is already messed up enough. (Yeliz in Heijmans 2001a)

According to them, Ali had acted on his own. Moreover, he had not tried to kill Hassan to cleanse the family's honour, but rather his act had been triggered by

Hassan's provocations. To support this claim, they announced that for them the problems between the families had ended after they had reported Hassan to the police: "Once Yeliz was home, we filed a report with the police and that was that. We never talked about an honour killing" (Fatma in Heijmans 2001a).

Yeliz also argued that her honour had not been shamed:

> If it had been about *namus*, the family's honour, like the reports say, then I would not have been sitting here, believe me. They simply kill the girl too then. Not only that, but my honour is still intact. I have a note here from my family doctor, who has examined me. (Yeliz in Heijmans 2001a)

The last part of Yeliz's statement refers to her virginity: according to the family doctor it was intact.

However, in both cases the Public Prosecution Service used the motive of *honour killing* as grounds for seeking long prison sentences. In the case against Kerim (May/June 2000), for example, the public prosecutor sought a twelve-year prison sentence, deeming Kerim to be the driving force behind the attempted honour killing and therefore ascribing him a very serious role in the shooting, even more so than Ali's. She supported her claim with a report by Ane Nauta, the inventor of the Dutch term *eerwraak*, who judged the Veghel shooting to indeed be an attempted honour killing.

Kerim's lawyer conversely sought acquittal. He argued reasonable doubt in connection with the father's role, stating that the only evidence against him lay in Ali's retracted statements. Kerim also defended himself by stating, "The honour killing story is neither here nor there. Honour killing plays no role anymore with modern Turks. I am not a conservative family dictator. The whole issue was off, once Yeliz was home again" (Kerim in De Vries 2000).

Ultimately the court found Kerim guilty and sentenced him to nine years in prison, holding that this severe sentence was necessary to guarantee "that standards were upheld properly." The sentence was subsequently confirmed on appeal: Kerim was again found guilty as the instigator of his son's act.

In the court case against Ali (in January 2001), the Public Prosecution Service once again followed the reasoning put forward by Van Eck and Nauta, claiming that the Veghel shooting was an attempted honour killing and demanding a prison sentence of eight years. The Public Prosecution Service rejected not only the family's statements and Ozgen's report, but also a report issued by psychiatric institute *Pieter Baan Centrum*, which found that Ali was a normal, intelligent boy who had acted out of rage and not because of cultural codes.

Ali's lawyer requested acquittal, referring to a second opinion report provided by Professor De Jong, a scholar of transcultural psychiatry. According to Professor De Jong, Ali was suffering from diminished capacity, being under extreme internalized cultural pressure, and therefore had not acted of his own volition. However, the court rejected the professor's line of reasoning, holding that Ali should have been able to resist his family's pressure, and sentenced him to five years in prison. It based this sentence on the following grounds:

> The court believes that the question of whether cultural background should result in an absence of punishment or in a more severe punishment in such cases only comes into play on an individual basis. D.[58] should and could have resisted the pressure put on him by his father and the Turkish community. (District Court of 's Hertogenbosch in ANP:2001)

This ruling created precedence in case law for the motive of honour as a mitigating circumstance in killings and attempted killings, establishing that this defence would not succeed. However, it also revealed that the motive of honour would similarly not lead to a harsher sentence.

In summary, while each of the shootings generated discussion about the attribution of the "honour killing" label, the intensity of the discussions varied. The Veghel case clearly generated the most intense debate on this subject. In part, this may be attributed to the fact that it involved two defendants, where the father's innocence or guilt depended on whether or not the shooting was found to be an honour killing. Moreover, more than the other cases the Veghel case became a case that educated the Dutch public on what *eerwraak* and honour killings entailed.

In addition, both the Kezban case and the Veghel case became judicial test cases, since the verdicts in these cases provided added clarity about the cultural argument as a mitigating circumstance. The court decisions can therefore be seen as the institutional legacy of these cases: in future, lawyers would know that a cultural line of defence would not result in greater leniency. Public prosecutors in turn would know that demanding a harsher sentence to serve as a deterrent would also not work[59].

The media's representation of these court cases also illustrates the amount of disagreement about the applicability of the label of honour killing and the great variety of actors that were involved in these disputes. The diagram below offers an overview of the contributing actors and their positions.

Clearly, classifying a murder as an honour killing presented a difficult and ambiguous task. In terms of Bourdieu et al. (1994), no *theoretical unification* existed in 2003/2004 that would have made it possible for actors to label a particular incident either as an honour killing or as murder. Moreover, depending on field position and habitus, actors used different arguments to substantiate their positions.

---

58. I.e. Ali. His surname was abbreviated to "D" for purposes of anonymity.
59. See also *Culture as defence. A fundamental-theoretical study into the scope and limits of cultural diversity in some doctrines of substantive criminal law* (Ten Voorde 2007).

Table 2. Actors and their claims about the attribution of the "honour killing" label

	Kezban	Hassan	Zarife	Gül
Key instigator	Cakiroglu: *honour killing, rejects cultural defence*	Van der Zee: *honour killing*	Krikke: *honour killing*	Women's shelter: *honour killing*
Defence lawyer	Urcun: *murder* but tests the cultural defence	Knoops: *murder*	*murder*	Moszkowicz: *murder*
Public Prosecution Service	*Rejects cultural defence*	*Honour killing*	*	*murder*
Experts		Van Eck: *honour killing* Professor Ozgen: *murder* Nauta: *honour killing* Pieter Baan Centrum: *murder* Professor De Jong: *honour killing*		Psychologist: *murder* Psychiatrist: *murder* Van Eck: *murder*
Court	*Rejects cultural defence*	*Honour killing*		*Murder*
Relatives	Victim's brother: *murder*, his sister did nothing dishonourable	Mother/wife and sister/daughter of the perpetrators: *murder*		
NGO	Nederlands Centrum Buitenlanders (NCB): *rejects cultural defence*		Samenwerkende Turkse Organisaties (STO): *honour killing*	Nederlands Overlegorgaan Turken (NOT): *murder* The victim had done nothing dishonourable
Politicians			Verdonk: *honour killing* Hirsi Ali: *honour killing*	

* Not all actors were quoted by the media in their coverage of the court cases. Consequently, some cells are left open.

For example, Kezban's family denied that her murder was an honour killing on grounds that their sister had done nothing dishonourable. Defence lawyers also denied that the murders were honour killings, though their motive was different.

While family members sought to uphold their loved one's honour, the lawyers hoped to eliminate the idea that the murders were premeditated. Interestingly, the various experts were particularly divided in the Veghel case. Depending on background – in anthropology, psychiatry or psychology – they claimed that the incident either did or did not constitute an attempted honour killing. Building on different scientific disciplines apparently led them to diverging conclusions.

Yet once the "honour killing" label was attributed to a murder it seemed to be attached permanently. For example, a 2007 article published shortly after the alleged honour killing of Zeynep Boral lists a series of honour killings to illustrate how "honour killings have become a Dutch problem" (Van der Zee 2007). This list included the cases of Kezban, Zarife and Gül, despite the fact that they had not been found to be honour killings in a court of law.

5.4 Disputes about the cultural background to honour killings

Besides disputes about the applicability of the label of honour killing, the shootings of Kezban, Hassan, Zarife and Gül generated a great deal of discussion about the cultural basis for these murders. The analyses that follow show that the acceptance of culture as an explanation for honour-related violence evolved over time.

Immediately after Kezban's murder, various actors (including Nurdan Cakiroglu) explicitly denied any connection between Kezban's cultural roots and her murder. For example, an anonymous letter left at the site of Kezban's murder site stated, "What happened here had nothing to do with religion or culture. He was a 100 percent idiot" (*Rotterdams Dagblad* 1999). During the commemoration service, only days after her murder, a mosque representative also stated, "It has to do with the man's background, how he perceives people, and not with culture" (*Rotterdams Dagblad* 1999). Social organization *Nederlands Centrum Buitenlanders* (NCB) also emphasized that this was "not a Turkish or cultural problem". Directing attention to the broader problem of domestic violence, it substantiated this claim by arguing that "[e]very year around 60 women are murdered by their partners or exes" (Akel in De Lange 1999).

In her commentary, Rene Römkes, a scholar specializing in domestic violence, uses the same type of reasoning:

> In certain cultures divorce constitutes a significant loss of standing and that might affect the use of violence. However, foreign research shows that violence against partners occurs in all cultures and is equally common across every layer of the population. (Römkes in De Visser 1999)

This statement emphasizes that domestic violence is a problem that is common to all cultures.

Despite these strong arguments denying a cultural explanation, the titles of other article show that the murder was quickly depicted as a problem that particularly concerned the Turkish community, implying a cultural explanation: "Turkish women often threatened after divorce" (De Visser 1999) and "Murders of Kezban Vural (29) and Naciye Kurt (30) terrify Turkish women" (*De Telegraaf* 1999).

Moreover, two months after Kezban's murder, Nurdan Cakiroglu started to change her earlier position of opposing any connection to culture. For instance, she claimed that many divorced Turkish women lived in fear as their ex-husbands had difficulty accepting the break-up (*De Telegraaf* 1999). In an article that appeared shortly after the Veghel shooting she clarified what had made her change her stance: "Time and again you hear on the news that another woman has been killed, or another woman's body has been found. That is terrifying. That shooting at the school in Veghel really tipped the scales. That family honour again" (Cakiroglu in Bosman 1999). Her change of position is also noticeable in her letter to the Public Prosecution Service, in which she claimed, "The killings in the name of honour must stop" (Cakiroglu in Bosman 1999).

Van Eck, in contrast, never hesitated to frame the Veghel shooting as related to cultural traditions: "It stems from a culture of shame and pride" (Van Eck in Dubbelman 1999). According to Van Eck honour killings are something entirely separate from the murder of a woman by a jealous Dutch ex-husband. "Every Turk immediately thinks of an honour killing if a woman commits adultery" (Van Eck in Jongerius 2000).

However, other actors in the Veghel case were more cautious about accepting a cultural explanation. In part, this position was inspired by a fear of forming an "undeserved image" of the Turkish community. *Palet*, Brabant's point of support for multicultural development, advised the Veghel municipal authorities to protect the local Turkish community from these stereotypes. How people act, Palet said, depends on how they cope with frustrations, not on their culture or nationality (Jongerius 2000). This position was immediately countered by Akel, representing the NCB, which by then had accepted honour-related violence as a Turkish problem. While seeking to avoid stigmatization, Akel also found that the problem was too serious to brush off lightly. He therefore criticized Palet for burying its head in the sand (Jongerius 2000).

Disputes about the influence of culture on honour killings also dominated the various trials. While lawyers initially sought to employ a cultural defence, claiming that the defendant's cultural background should be a mitigating circumstance, lawyers in later trials made every effort to remove any cultural connotations. After the Veghel trial they had learned that, if anything, a cultural defence would lead to a harsher sentence. Clearly, these lawyers' interests were different from Palet's. The lawyers used the cultural argument to obtain the lightest possible sentence for their clients. In contrast, Palet, an organization supporting the multicultural ideal, sought to keep this ideal intact by arguing that it was not culture but a crazed individual who had committed the crime. Nevertheless, by

2002 Palet had changed its stance and was organizing meetings to discuss the issue of domestic violence within migrant communities.

A similar change of position also emerges from an analysis of perspective of the women's shelters. While they later acted as agenda-setters following Gül's murder in 2004, in June 2002 Johan Gortworst of *Federatie Opvang* (FO)[60] stated, "Men hit women out of a sense of power, this has nothing to do with culture" (Gortworst in De Knegt 2002). He believed that the overrepresentation of migrant women in women's shelters was caused by smaller support networks, in combination with their battle for emancipation, which lagged behind relative to "native" Dutch women.

In a similar vein, at the commemoration one year after Kezban's murder, Mayor Corporaal of Zwijndrecht stated,

> One woman in nine experiences domestic violence. The Constitution says that every person's body is inviolate, but in practice we know that things are different. Most victims are women, women from a wide range of cultures. It is time for us to abandon old traditions and cultures. Times have changed. Current times demand equal rights for men and women. We should not shrug and accept Kezban's death, but actually get to work. (Corporaal in Vermeulen 2000)

Despite the heated discussions about Kezban's murder and the reframing of this murder as an honour killing by various actors, the mayor persisted in framing it as domestic violence and as violence against women.

In contrast, by 2002 various Turkish organizations had begun to fully embrace the cultural explanation. In the same article that quoted *Federatie Opvang*'s denial of any cultural connotation, *Inspraak Orgaan Turken in Nederland* (IOT) stated,

> Violence occurs in very many Turkish households. It is part of our culture. The relationship between man and woman, a region's customs and practices. From generation to generation, injustice has been met with violence. You cannot leave your cultural baggage at the border. You bring with you things that you learned at home, particularly in the confusing situation of migration, when you have to start over from nothing. (IOT in De Knegt 2002)

IOT clearly recognized that honour killings formed a serious problem within its community and hoped to break the taboo surrounding this topic. It therefore set about organizing meetings and conferences to discuss the issue of "traditional violence and honour killings".

IOT director Hatice Can-Engin understood that people might be afraid of stigmatization. Nevertheless, she goes on to state that "violence with migrant people often simply has a different background. Turkish girls need to preserve their virginity, women are more subordinate and have less freedom. We don't have to

---

60. *Federatie Opvang* is the umbrella for women's shelter organizations.

deny that" (Can-Engin in De Knegt 2002). She subsequently maintains that aid agencies were not yet properly equipped to tackle this distinct type of violence.

In summary, while a media analysis shows that activists, Turkish organizations and experts began to recognize honour killings and honour-related violence as a distinct social problem following Kezban's murder, and even more so after the Veghel shooting, government agencies were more cautious and subsequently hesitated to accept a cultural explanation of this type of violence. Instead, they framed it as domestic violence, being related to the power relationships between husbands and wives, or as acts of mentally sick individuals. However, this all changed after Zarife and Gül were murdered, when a school director and women's shelter organizations sounded the alarm on what they saw as the unspoken problem of honour killings and honour-related violence.

Bearing the above analysis in mind it is interesting to see that both the director of Zarife's school and the women's shelters stated that they were amazed by the silence surrounding this type of violence. The voices of the various Turkish organizations and activists that had already spoken out against this type of violence had evidently not reached them. Nor had they reached the politicians who started to raise the alarm after Zarife's and Gül's murders. For instance, after Zarife was murdered, Minister Verdonk promised the House of Representatives to ask IOT and other Islamic organizations to discuss this topic within their own communities, denying the work that these and other organizations had already done.

An analysis of the media's coverage of Zarife's and Gül's murders also reveals that by 2003 the cultural explanation of honour killings had become mainstream. Moreover, a further dimension had been added to the cultural explanation: the connection between this type of violence and Islam.

The actor who most prominently made this connection was Ayaan Hirsi Ali. Immediately after Zarife's murder she framed the incident as a culturally and religiously legitimized type of domestic violence (Hirsi Ali 2003). In partnership with filmmaker Theo van Gogh, she later made the film *Submission*, criticizing how women were portrayed in Islam. In an opinion article that appeared two months after the film's release, she explained her position:

> The essence of the matter is that most Muslim men do not view how they treat women as "oppression", "abuse" or "murder", but as a legitimate reply to those women's conduct. Muslim women know how things should be done. If they choose to act in a manner that is not in compliance with the rules, they will be punished. (Hirsi Ali 2004)

Some actors made the same connection, whether implicitly or explicitly. Zarife's murder, for instance, was depicted by some as stemming from Zarife's fights with her father about her "orthodox Islamic upbringing" (*NRC Handelsblad* 2003). Minister Verdonk also called on Islamic organizations to take action. In both instances, honour-related violence was implicitly framed as being connected to Islam.

In 2003, Sezei Aydogan, a psychologist working for an expertise centre on gender-related violence (*Transact*, later renamed *Movisie*), made a more explicit connection with Islam when he proclaimed that "[h]onour comes before religion. Honour killings are not directly connected to the Islam. Yet by stressing gender difference Islamic society does actually create the right climate for honour killings" (Aydogan in Bessems 2003).

Nevertheless, between 1999 and 2004 connecting this type of violence with Islam was more the exception than the rule[61]. In general, honour-related violence and honour killings were depicted as originating first from culture or nationality and second from gender differences and/or domestic violence.

The disputes outlined above about the cultural background to honour killings again illustrate how the shooting incidents had a field-configuring effect on the emerging Dutch HRV field. The shootings functioned as *crystallization points* for what honour killings entailed. The analysis reveals that these honour killings were first seen as a distinct social problem by Turkish-Dutch migrants and Turkish migrant organizations. It was only after the murders of Zarife and Gül that professional organizations such as schools and women's shelter organizations accepted the cultural explanation for these murders.

The evolving positions of actors in these disputes are illustrative of how honour killings were viewed in the Netherlands. At first, various actors tried to frame the murders as no different from domestic violence. However, as time passed, more and more actors started to view this type of violence as something distinct, a form of violence that had its own cultural basis.

The disputes about the cultural basis of honour killings had a two-sided effect. On the one hand, they added to the knowledge of what honour killings are while on the other the cultural explanation contributed to a demarcation process – between domestic violence and honour-related violence and by implication between what is Dutch and what is not. The disputes about the applicability of the label of honour killing and about the cultural basis of this type of violence are illustrative of how the public discourse on integration developed in the Netherlands between 1999 and 2004. These discourses are discussed at greater length in Chapter 6, as changes in the discourse can be linked to the evolving positions of actors in the disputes.

---

61. See Korteweg and Yurdakul (2009) for an analysis of the media's coverage of the topic of honour killings and honour-related violence in 2005.

5.5 How these events contributed to the emergence of a Dutch HRV field

In Hoffman's words (1999), disruptive events make fields come alive to do sense-making and sense-giving work. The disputes outlined above about the attribution of the label of honour killing and the cultural basis of the shootings illustrate that the actual and attempted murders of Kezban, Hassan, Zarife and Gül did in fact lead to this type of sense-making work.

The incidents, and in particular the court cases that followed, can be seen as *fields of struggle* (Bourdieu and Wacquant 1992:98-99, 101) in which actors came together to fight about the specific criteria for defining a murder as an honour killing. As such, these events and the subsequent court cases serve as *micro-level illustrations* of how the substance of a field's *issue* is disputed. Depending on their positions within the field and habitus, actors sought to push the definition of these murders in a particular direction. For instance, the defendants' lawyers all attempted to deny any instance of honour killing and looked for experts to substantiate this position. Conversely, in the Veghel case the Public Prosecution Service used experts to substantiate the point that the shooting was an attempted honour killing and demanded harsh sentences for father and son.

Moreover, the incidents did indeed function as *unplanned field-configuring events*. According to Meyer et al. (2005:1026) field-configuring events "encapsulate and shape" the development of a field. In this case, each shooting drew in yet another actor, enlarging the network of actors sharing information about the issue of honour-related violence. Moreover, the disputes about the label and the causes of this type of violence became *crystallization points* for the substance of the problem. As such, these disputes also contributed to the emergence of honour-related violence as a distinct social problem in need of its own policy approach.

The disputes also indicate that the label of honour killing referred to a very specific type of murder – so precise in fact that almost none of the incidents described matched the profile. This might plausibly have contributed to the state's need for a broader definition. Nevertheless, for the emergence of the issue the label *eerwraak* was pivotal. As explained in Chapter 4, it was the label *eerwraak* that triggered the media's illusio.

The foregoing not only shows the configuring function of the shootings. The incidents also reveal something about the workings of the media field. In order to become *critical events* (Hoffman & Ocasio 2001) the incidents needed to comply with the *social structures of attention* of the media field and so with the media's disposition. Moreover, only actors that knew how to *play the game* within this media field were able to air their concerns about honour killings. The key instigators clearly understood the dynamics of the media field and used the incidents to further their own respective agendas.

Lastly, the analysis presented above illustrates that actors were initially reluctant to label the murders as honour killings, instead seeking to frame them as "ordinary" domestic violence. However, with each new incident, the group of actors sounding the alarm about this type of violence grew. Moreover, their agreement about the interpretation of the incidents as a distinct type of violence also grew. Clearly, each shooting contributed to a growing sense of urgency that something needed to be done against this specific type of violence. The following chapter illustrates that these evolving positions echo changes in macro-cultural discourses that form the discursive backdrop to the various disputes.

6. Changing macro-cultural discourses

Lawrence and Phillips (2004) argue that micro-level activities such as those described in Chapter 5 are made possible through changes in macro-cultural discourses. These discourses, they say, form the building blocks for micro-level activities. As such, changes in macro-cultural discourses form the critical preconditions for the emergence of a new organizational field. I therefore now turn to those discourses that other scholars have linked to the emergence of the issue of honour-related violence.

According to various scholars the current attention for honour-related violence should be viewed in relation to changes in the discourses on multiculturalism, gender and nationalism (Dustin 2006; Pratt Ewing 2008; Phillips & Saharso 2008). For example, in their reflections on the increased attention for honour killings within the UK's public debate, Meetoo and Mirza (2007) state,

> (...) the increased focus on "honour" based crimes need to be seen within the current climate of Islamophobia. Fekete (2004) has written of the climate of claimed global threat to security by Islamic extremism. We are living in a time when it is not just a case of fear from 'outsiders' but also those within. Resident Muslim and Asian citizens within Western countries are now under the spotlight. The current discourse on "others" is about the threat that multicultural policies pose to core values, cultural homogeneity and social cohesion. To minimize the risk of threat we now have increased citizenship laws and security legislation, the introduction of compulsory language and civic tests for citizenship applicants, and codes of conduct for trustees of mosques. (Meetoo and Mirza 2007:194)

According to Meetoo and Mirza and other authors, discourses in the European Union (EU) on migrants changed significantly after 9/11. The later terrorist attacks in London and Madrid, and more recently in Paris and Brussels, have further heightened existing feelings of anxiety about the integration of migrants and more specifically of Muslims within "Western" societies. This has led to questions about the adequacy of multicultural policies and a quest for alternative integration policies (Bloemraad et al. 2008; Phillip and Saharso 2008; Vertovec and Wessendorf 2010).

The idea that the attention for honour-related violence should be seen in light of "othering" discourses, as they are known, can also be found in the work of Reimers (2007). In her study, she analysed how the honour killing of Fadime was described by the Swedish media⁶². According to Reimers, the way Fadime's death was framed was both an expression and a confirmation of the intersection of discourses on culture, gender, equality, social class and nationality. Within these discourses she identifies the construction of dichotomies between what is Swedish and what is not:

> (...) the press presupposes and establishes dichotomous notions of what is understood as typically Swedish and what is thought to signify migrants. It is also clear that "the Swedish" is constructed as being characterized by gender equality and opposition to male violence, while the non-Swedish is characterized by female subordination and the notion that male violence against women is legitimate and natural. (...) The media event of Fadime constitutes a discourse that induces preconceived notions of class, masculinity, and femininity, which together manufacture boundaries for a hegemonic notion of the Swedish. (Reimers 2007:249)

In a similar vein Korteweg and Yurdakul (2010) claim that the issue of honour-related violence has become politicized. They base this conclusion on their study of how honour-related violence has been framed within the Netherlands, Germany, Britain and Canada. For example, in relation to the Dutch case they conclude,

> (...) honour-related violence and honour killing were largely conceptualized as resulting from migrants' culturally specific gender relations. On the one hand, this opened the door to particular forms of stigmatization, which positioned gender equality as the hallmark to Western culture and gender inequality as the mark of the migrants who cannot and will not be assimilated. On the other hand, it also enabled an understanding of honour-related violence as a specific form of domestic violence within migrant communities. (Korteweg and Yurdakul 2010:12)

These quotes exemplify how different scholars have linked the issues of honour killings and honour-related violence to discourses on *multiculturalism, gender equality, citizenship, nationalism* and *Islamophobia*, and to concepts such as *othering, social cohesion* and *social imaginaries*.

In this section I therefore focus on these discourses and concepts, how they relate to each other and how they changed course during recent decades. However, the body of literature on these subjects is vast, and presenting a comprehensive review of the work on these discourses goes beyond the purpose of the present thesis⁶³. For purposes of this study, it is sufficient to understand how they

---

62. See also Wikan (2008) on this murder. In her book *In Honour of Fadime* social anthropologist Unni Wikan provides an inside perspective on the motives that drove Fadime's father to kill his daughter.
63. For a more comprehensive review of the concept of citizenship, I refer to Bloemraad et al. (2008). See Fox and Miller-Idriss (2008) for a review of nationalism, see Cohen et al. (1999) and Phillips and Saharso (2008) for their reviews of multiculturalism, and see Butler (2008) and others for reviews of how sexuality and gender have been framed within the EU.

changed and how this subsequently opened up the discursive space needed for the emergence of the issue honour-related violence within the Dutch public debate. The following description should therefore be regarded as a broad sketch of these developments.

6.1 Multiculturalism and gender-inequality

Europe

Whether as policy or a description of society, multiculturalism was widespread in Europe until the late 1990s. Within its rhetoric, diversity was perceived as intrinsically positive and respect for different cultural and religious practices was deemed desirable (Dustin 2006:3-4). Since then, however, a disenchantment has emerged with the ideals of multiculturalism, and diversity is increasingly regarded as a problem rather than a resource. Moreover, multiculturalism is now blamed for failures of economic and social integration by migrants. Following the recent series of terrorist attacks multiculturalism is now also seen as a hindrance to the political integration of (particularly) Muslim migrants (Phillips and Saharso 2008:291-292).

As such, multiculturalism is perceived as a threat to social cohesion within Europe. It is said to encourage divided loyalties, and critics fear that "without a primary loyalty to the nation-state, the civic, political, and even moral community of a country will fragment" (Bloemraad et al. 2008:160). As Dobbernack (2010:149) phrases it, the criticism of multiculturalism is that "it allegedly fosters separatism rather than uniting different segments of the population (...)." According to Scuzzarello (2008:6), one reaction to the alleged failure of multicultural policies has been to return to assimilationist approaches, which are then used as a means to generate and/or support social cohesion within countries[64].

Within the current trend away from multiculturalism, the rights of women have come to play a prominent role (Phillips and Saharso 2008:292, Ghorashi 2010). In part, this can be attributed to Okin's ground-breaking paper, in which she asks the question, "Is Multiculturalism bad for women?" (Okin 1999). Okin's work shows that respect for other cultures may lead to cultural relativism and so to acceptance of practices, such as forced marriages, that are at odds with universal human rights (Okin 1999:17; see also Bloemraad et al. 2008:161; Langvasbråten 2008:33,35; Abu-Lughod 2002). Okin (1999:12) argues that multiculturalism is gender-blind, in the sense that it represents migrant communities as homogenous, showing no awareness of their internal stratifications. In other words, Okin

---

64. For a more detailed review of multiculturalism and assimilation approaches to the management of immigration and diversity, see Rodríguez-García (2010).

blames multiculturalism for its preferential treatment of group rights over gender rights[65].

Okin and other feminists have drawn a powerful connection from gender equality discourse to discourses on multiculturalism. In the words of Phillips and Saharso (2008:294), this connection has been made so strongly that now "it is hard to imagine a sustained discussion of multiculturalism that now proceeds without *any* reference to gender or sexual violence."

However, juxtaposing gender equality and multiculturalism has its flaws. According to Langvasbråten (2008:35-36) contrasting gender equality and multiculturalism is not a fruitful path. Firstly, the author finds that both lines of reasoning carry similar drawbacks, both are liable to an essentialist view of culture. In this view, how people differ culturally is used as a means to explain the wide array of human behaviour. She refers to this essentialist representation of culture as a "package" view of culture: culture is viewed as "a neatly wrapped parcel, sealed off from each other, possessing sharply defined edges or contours, and having distinctive contents that differ from those of other 'cultural packages'" (Narayan 2000:1084). Secondly, Langvasbråten (2008:36) draws attention to the fact that both traditions "rest on claims for greater equality (women and cultural minorities), and should therefore be seen not as competing, but as related parts in an overlapping equality project."

Be this as it may, the intertwining discourses on multiculturalism and gender equality have led to the creation of a new "site of controversy". Langvasbråten explains this concept as follows:

> Although the questions framed and discussed specifically as multicultural ones vary across time and place, the notion of gender equality has developed into a "site" of controversy in several countries; the status of women in minority communities is frequently called to attention in the media, within politics, and in feminist academic discourse on multiculturalism. (Langvasbråten 2008:33)

In turn, these sites of controversy have led to the development of an "explicitly minority group related, gender equality agenda" (Siim and Skjeie 2008:323). At the heart of this agenda are policies for combating honour-related violence, genital mutilation and forced marriage.

While the aim of these policies is to warrant women's individual rights, Siim and Skjeie (2008:323) critically note that some of the measures presented in fact limit women's individual rights rather than enhancing them. They argue that this

---

65. Okin's work has been heavily criticized by some, see for instance the work of Gilman (1999), Lutz (2002) and Saharso (2002). Be it as it may, her work has drawn a powerful connection between gender equality discourse and discourses on multiculturalism.

becomes particularly apparent when restrictions on religious clothing are presented as necessary for countering gender hierarchies within Islam[66].

The Netherlands

In the Netherlands similar discursive changes have been described by scholars such as Roggeband and Verloo (2007), Ghorashi (2006, 2010) and Prins and Saharso (2010). For example, Roggeband and Verloo (2007) argue that the attention for honour-related violence can be interpreted as a consequence of the gendering of Dutch integration policies, as well as the focus on ethnicity within Dutch emancipation policies. Political and public debates that focus on migrants and their integration and on honour-related violence as a symbol of their failing integration, "create and reproduce social dichotomies and oppositions between Dutch and 'others', between men and women, and between traditional (Muslim) and modern ('Western') cultures" (Roggeband & Verloo 2007, pp. 286). In their 2016 paper Roggeband and Lettinga also argue that, while migrant women's organizations and female migrant politicians have acted as agenda-setters on issues such as violence and discrimination, these issues were later co-opted by (predominantly) right-wing politicians who problematized the "deviant" culture of minorities and proposed policies that further excluded them and paternalized them rather than improving their situation.

In her work Ghorashi (2006, 2010), in addition, points out the historical embeddedness of the Dutch approach to migrants. She firstly connects the way migrants are approached in the Netherlands with the Dutch *pillarization tradition*[67]. According to Ghorashi,

> [the] essentialist approach to culture is, in a way, embedded in the pillarization habitus, with its assumption that difference is surrounded by 'thick' boundaries. This has led to the creation of cultural contrast, which make it virtually impossible to consider the individual migrant as separate from his or her cultural or ethnic category. (Ghorashi 2010:78)

This *essentialist perspective on culture* contributed to the construction of migrants as cultural "others". Moreover, this construction was, according to Ghorashi (2010:78), amplified by a second feature of the Dutch approach: the *deficit approach*. In this approach, migrants are seen as a target group that require special

---

66. See Lettinga (2011) for a detailed discussion of how the headscarf debates were played out in three EU countries: the Netherlands, France and Germany.
67. This typical Dutch tradition was developed in the Netherlands after the Second World War and refers to the construction of pillars along lines of religious denomination and political ideology. Until the 1960s the various pillars served as safety nets for their members. However, the emergence of the welfare state, in combination with processes of secularization and individualization of society, made the existence of pillars unnecessary and unwanted (Ghorashi 2010: 77-78).

attention in order to help them out of their disadvantaged position, as they were perceived as not having "the required skills to become active participants in Dutch society" (Ghorashi 2010:78, see also Eijberts and Ghorashi 2017). According to Ghorashi (2010:79) this view on migrants reflects the Dutch welfare state's habit of always focussing on "liberating" those in the "socially disadvantaged position". Besides,

> [t]he often-unintended result of this urge for equality, combined with the routine like character of the entire system of welfare organizations, has been that even active and capable people have often been too easily reduced to helpless creatures. (Ghorashi 2010:79)

This combination of perspectives, coined by Ghorashi (2006) as *categorical thinking*, subsequently contributed to 1.) the use of "cultural differences" as the sole explanation for honour-related violence and 2.) a representation of the victims of honour-related violence as helpless agents. Moreover, according to Ghorashi (2010:75) this combination of perspectives on migrants had the consequence (albeit an unintended one) that "the border between the Dutch as 'emancipated self' and the Islamic migrants as the 'unemancipated other'" was reinforced instead of diminished.

Prins and Saharso (2010), lastly, establish that anti-Islam sentiment and criticism of the multicultural ideal had emerged in the Netherlands long before 9/11. In her 2002 analysis of the Dutch public discourse on multiculturalism Prins shows that the integration of migrants and specifically Muslims was problematized by Frits Bolkestein, leader of Dutch conservative liberal party VVD, as far back as 1991. Yet it was an essay by publicist Paul Scheffer in 2000 that marked a true turning point in the Dutch public discourse. The essay's title was "The multicultural drama" and in it Scheffer argued that

> the Dutch mistakenly held on to their trusted strategy of peaceful coexistence through deliberation and compromise. In doing so they ignored the fundamental differences between the new situation and the earlier days of the pillarized society. At the time, Scheffer argued, fewer sources of solidarity existed, while Islam, with its refusal to accept the separation of church and state, could not be compared to modernized Christianity; lastly, young immigrant people were increasingly harbouring feelings of frustration and resentment. Lessons in Dutch language, culture and history should be taken much more seriously. Only then would the immigrant population gain a clear understanding of the basic values of Dutch society. (Prins 2002:370)

According to Prins (2002), both Bolkestein and Scheffer utilized a new type of genre within Dutch discourses on multiculturalism: *new realism*. This genre of new realism, as Prins explains, refers not so much to a new way of describing Dutch society, a new *content*, as to a new way of conveying information about society, a new *tone*. Nevertheless, as their later analysis of this type of genre reveals, this new tone also led to a change in content[68] (Prins 2002:365), with the new tone enabling new realists to say things that previously could not have been said.

Prins and Saharso (2010:74-75) describe five elements that characterized this new genre. First, actors utilizing this genre presented themselves as people speaking candidly about the problems of the time, as people who dared to face the facts, who were finally speaking the truth and left no room for taboos. This contrasts with earlier times, when problems such as the integration of migrants were bottled up. Second, the new realists presented themselves as spokespersons for ordinary people, by which they meant "native" Dutch people. These "ordinary people" were then portrayed as the ultimate realists, being the ones dealing with the real problems of society in their everyday lives, unhindered by politically correct ideas. Third, actors utilizing the genre of new realism presented realism as a characteristic feature of the Dutch national identity, which embraces frank and straightforward communication. Fourth, utilizing this genre intrinsically involved a resistance to the supposed relativism of the political left. In the words of Prins (2002:369), "New realists feel that it is high time to break the power of the progressive elite that dominates the public realm with its politically correct sensibilities regarding fascism, racism and intolerance."

In her 2010 work Prins, in partnership with Saharso, ultimately added a fifth element to this genre: its gender focus. Like Ghorashi (2003) they argued that new realists, often referred to gender and sexuality issues such as headscarves, forced marriage, female genital mutilation, honour killings and homophobia in order to support their criticism of the multicultural ideal (Prins and Saharso 2010:75).

Based on their analysis of Dutch multicultural discourses these scholars conclude that the genre of new realism continued to flourish within the Dutch political field after 9/11, with political actors such as Pim Fortuyn, Ayaan Hirsi Ali, Rita Verdonk and more recently Geert Wilders as its representatives (Prins and Saharso 2010). Pim Fortuyn, the leader of the right-wing populist party *Leefbaar Nederland*, in fact introduced a radicalized type of the new realism genre, which Prins labels *hyperrealism*. Within this genre

> [f]rankness was no longer practiced for the sake of truth, but for its own sake. References to reality and the facts had become mere indicators of the strong personality of the speaker, proof that a "real leader" was now on the scene. (Prins 2002:376)

A subsequent development within the genre of new realism was its increasing focus on gender issues, which was particularly highlighted by Ayaan Hirsi Ali, MP for VVD and a Dutchwoman of Somali descent, who combined this focus with a fierce criticism of Islam. As Prins and Saharso (2010:80) put it, "Hirsi Ali

---

68. Prins (2002:363) refers to the performative power of discourse.

showed the same guts as her new realist predecessors in attacking Islam and the 'left church', and putting issues of gender and sexuality squarely on the public agenda." Lastly, Prins and Saharso (2010:86) claim that by 2010, with Wilders as its most outspoken member, new realism has become a mainstream genre within Dutch public discourses on migrants, immigration and their integration.

Based on this description, it is tempting to explain the emergence of the issue of honour-related violence within societal discourses solely by the increased attention for gender equality within multiculturalism. However, scholars working on what is commonly termed the "crisis of multiculturalism" relate this crisis to changing discourses on nationalism, citizenship and social cohesion. In the following section, I therefore examine these discourses in greater depth.

6.2 Social cohesion, national imaginaries and the creation of the other

In a world with increasing forms of supranational governance (for example the EU and the UN), blooming global capitalism and expanding flows of transnational migration, concepts such as nationalism and citizenship are regarded by some as redundant. Rather than being citizens within a single nation state, people are expected to become cosmopolitan. People would then see themselves as "world citizens" and national borders would supposedly disappear (Fox and Miller-Idriss 2008:536; Bloemraad et al. 2008:154,164-169; Vieten 2007). Yet while physical boundaries between states are perhaps blurring, *symbolic boundaries* are being raised in their place (Vieten 2007:9). Nationalism continues to flourish (Fox and Miller-Idriss 2008:536), and "nation states continue to hold substantial power over the formal rules and rights of citizenship" (Bloemraad et al. 2008:154).

However, these developments have led to concerns about *social cohesion* within nation states. Traditionally, social cohesion has been associated with concepts such as integration, harmony, social order and stability. However, according to Dobbernack (2010:146), at present cohesion can best be regarded as a *social imaginary*. Drawing on the work of Taylor, Castoriadis and Laclau, he defines imaginaries as images that

> provide horizons against which background understandings of society and, notably, social problems become available. Moreover, they reflect an aspiration to fullness that might explain the way in which new accounts of social relations capture the imagination of a public and/or of policy actors. (Dobbernack 2010:153)

Within these imaginaries, societies are redescribed as "essentially harmonious" and "non-conflictual" (ibid.:147). As such, this type of imaginary does not match the notion of cultural differences. Moreover, it seemingly creates new boundaries between those who fit the picture presented by the imaginary (the imagined community) and those who do not (Vieten 2007:7). Moreover, social problems within these imaginaries become *boundary markers*, essentially forming new borders.

The idea of a social imaginary can be reconciled with the *nationalism* project, which Fox and Miller-Idriss (2008) describe as follows:

> Nationalism is the project to make the political unit, the state (or polity) congruent with the cultural unit, the nation. (…) Through the promotion of standardized languages, national (and nationalist) educational curricula, military conscription and taxation – and more nefarious methods of war, forced assimilation, expulsion and extermination – the nation, or people, are made one with their nation. Nationalism recast the mosaic of diverse peoples within the boundaries of the state (or polity) into a uniform and unified national whole (…). (Fox and Miller-Idriss 2008:536-537)

To rephrase this, nationalism[69] provides the social imaginary for the aspired social cohesion (Dobbernack 2010) and raises the symbolic boundaries described by Vieten (2007).

Citizenship is subsequently used as a means to control these new borders (Vieten 2007:34-37). According to Bloemraad et al. (2008:154) *citizenship* can be defined as "a form of membership in a political and geographic community." This membership can then be subdivided into four dimensions: legal status, rights, participation (political and other forms) and a sense of belonging. Increasingly within the current context, aspiring citizens are required to subscribe to their adoptive country's social imaginary in order to acquire legal status as a citizen. Mepschen et al. (2010) therefore describe this development as the "culturalization of citizenship"[70]. Moreover, migrants are increasingly asked to assimilate into this national imaginary in order be accepted as members of the imagined community.

For example, within the context of its citizenship test, the Netherlands presents itself as a nation in which sexual freedom is a core value. Applicants for immigration are therefore asked to look at a picture of two men kissing and asked if they are willing to live in a country where this is seen as an expression of personal liberty[71]. Butler (2008), who presents this example in her work, queries

> whether such freedoms (…) are being instrumentalized to establish a specific cultural grounding, secular in a particular sense, that functions as a prerequisite for admission into the polity as an acceptable immigrant. (…) In this instance, a set of cultural norms are being articulated that are considered preconditions of citizenship. (…) And so a

---

69. Fox and Miller-Idriss (2008) perceive nationalism as a social construction that is both produced and reproduced in everyday life. It reveals itself in formal symbols, rituals and policy discourse, but also in people's everyday talk and choices.

70. See also Lewis (2006:90-91) and Schinkel (2010).

71. For a more comprehensive analysis of the Dutch civic integration test, see Van der Haar et al. (2010). Their paper shows how an image of "Dutch-ness" is created in the film that would-be migrants are required to watch in preparation of their language and civic integration test. An analysis of the German "Muslim test" can be found in the work of Pratt Ewing (2008:181), who makes a connection between the "Muslim test" and Germany's national imaginary with "its constitution of discursive subjects as gendered citizens through the process of abjection of an other".

certain paradox ensues in which the coerced adoption of certain cultural norms becomes a requisite for entry into a polity that defines itself as the avatar of freedom. (Butler 2008:3)

Clearly, Butler's reflection is a critical one. She argues that we live in an age of *sexual politics*, an age in which sexual freedom is seen as a key ingredient of Europe's social imaginary. Protection of this "privileged site of radical freedom" is then used as a means to draw boundaries between the "modern", "free" Europe and the "putative orthodoxies associated with new immigrant communities" (Butler 2008:2).

Besides, or perhaps related to, this key aspect of Europe's national imaginary, a strong discourse on gender equality has emerged. As Korteweg and Yurdakul (2010:12) find, gender equality is now positioned as a "hallmark of Western culture." However, similar to Butler's criticism of sexual politics, Phillips and Saharso (2008) state,

> The endorsement of gender equality as a defining feature of European polities is, at one level, very much to be welcomed. When, however, the rights of women figure as a marker of a modern liberal society, one of the key things differentiating such societies from 'traditional', non-western, illiberal ones, this encourages a stereotypical contrast between western and non-western values, and represents (all) migrants as less likely than those long established in Europe to accept equality of the sexes. (Phillips and Saharso 2008:295)

In addition to the foregoing criticism of gender equality as a marker of difference, Dustin (2006:13) notes that by claiming gender equality as a core value Europe supports the "unfounded assumption that white European women have achieved equality and the task is now to bring women from minorities up to their level", while at the same time concealing the "levels of gender inequality and violence against women that persist in every European country." Moreover, it not only conceals the persisting gender inequalities within Europe, it also homogenizes both the EU community and the migrant community, additionally concealing the internal variations that can be found within both[72].

A common theme in these criticisms is the use of gender equality and sexual freedom as boundary markers, contributing to the development of dichotomies between the modern and the traditional, between the established and the outsiders, between inclusion and exclusion.

Both nationalism and citizenship contain an inherent tension between inclusion and exclusion. Nationalism, for example, can be studied as "a site for material and symbolic struggles over the definition of national inclusion and exclusion"

---

72. For example, see Pascall and Lewis (2004) and Verloo (2007) for an explanation of the differences between EU countries and for an in-depth analysis of persisting gender inequalities within those countries.

(Fox and Miller-Idriss 2008:536), while citizenship always entails exclusionary aspects: it determines who has the right to participate in a society and who does not. As Bloemraad et al. (2008:155) establish, "Notions of belonging inherently have exclusionary tendencies; some must fall outside the community in order for a 'we' to exist (Bosniak 2001: 156)." The authors go on to note that such exclusions are often justified by the need for social cohesion.

These developments have therefore been linked to the rise of discourses on the "*other*", where the other becomes a "symbolic point of reference", depicting the boundaries that are being drawn around countries' national imaginaries (Vieten 2007:8). In the post-9/11 era, Muslims have become these symbolic points of reference, perceived as the "threatening Other" (Vieten 2007:6)[73]. The rise of these discourses on otherness and their connection with national boundaries is eloquently summarized by Vieten (2007:37):

> As the numbers of illegalized people are rising steadily, the ideological tension of legal and symbolic boundaries has emerged as a new contested discursive ground. Hence, it is the symbolic boundary that matters in which Otherness, as a collective signifier of uncanny and "dangerous" abnormality, is defined as the outside of the internationally enclosed civil order.

Within contemporary discourses on the "other", the figure of "migrant women", particularly veiled women, has become the key symbol of the "non-European" (Lewis 2006:93). Strong stereotypes have been connected to this figure[74].

According to Pratt Ewing (2008:1-2) migrant women, and specifically Muslim women, are stereotypically portrayed as "victims of male brutality who must be rescued from traditional, oppressive male morality, which is imagined as a total control over female bodies and action." As such, practices such as honour killings and debates about banning headscarves are at the heart of European othering discourses. They form the axiomatic signifiers of otherness.

6.3 How the changes in macro-cultural discourses contributed to the emergence of a Dutch HRV field

The foregoing illustrates how the increased attention for honour-related violence should be seen in light of the changing and mutually connected macro-cultural discourses on multiculturalism, gender equality, nationalism, citizenship and so-

---

73. According to authors such as Pratt Ewing (2008:3), Abu-Lughod (2002:784-785) and Narayan (2000:2083-1084) the origin of these othering discourses can be traced back to colonial times and what Said (1978) describes as the Orientalist discourse in which "the Muslim stands as other in a discourse that cast the Orient as the antithesis of the West and its Enlightenment values" (Pratt Ewing 2008:3).

74. As Phillips and Saharso (2008:292) say, "the critique of minority cultures and religions is played out largely on the bodies of young women."

cial cohesion. In short, the links between gender issues and multicultural discourses led to disenchantment with the multicultural ideal, which in turn made it possible to criticize culture-linked forms of violence. Moreover, these gender issues were subsequently "hijacked" as a means of reinforcing the symbolic boundaries of the imagined communities that states began to foster to further new forms of social cohesion after being confronted with diminishing physical boundaries.

These changes can be related to the micro-level disputes about the honour killings and attempted honour killings of Kezban, Hassan, Zarife and Gül that were presented in the previous chapter. In particular the disputes about the cultural basis of this type of murder echo the changes in the macro-cultural discourses.

The media analysis presented in Chapter 5 shows that Turkish organizations, activists, academics and other experts were the first to recognize honour killings and honour-related violence as a distinct social problem. Government agencies, in contrast, were more reluctant to do the same and so hesitated to accept a cultural explanation for this type of violence. For instance, as late as 2002 Johan Gortworst of the umbrella organization for women's shelter organizations announced that "[m]en hit women out of a sense of power, this has nothing to do with culture" (Gortworst in De Knegt 2002). It was only after Gül's murder, when women's shelter organizations were directly confronted with this type of violence, that they started to sound the alarm about this type of violence. Moreover, the umbrella for women's shelter organizations later became an important actor within the emerging Dutch HRV field.

Similarly, it was only after the murders of Zarife and Gül in 2003/2004 that national politicians such as Ayaan Hirsi Ali and Rita Verdonk entered the emerging HRV field. Their entry into the field coincided with the disenchantment with the multicultural ideal described above. The fact that others such as Okin (1999) had begun to criticize the multicultural ideal made it possible for these Dutch politicians to do the same. Moreover, they did so by utilizing a new type of genre within the Dutch public discourse, which Prins (2002) labelled *hyperrealism* and which uses frankness for no other reason than for its own sake.

This analysis substantiates Lawrence and Phillips' proposition that changes in macro-cultural discourses form a critical precondition for field emergence (2004:690). The changes in the macro-cultural discourses on multiculturalism and gender equality made it possible for actors to criticize culture-linked types of violence, while changing discourses on nationalism, citizenship and social cohesion created a climate where such criticism was welcomed as a means of enforcing moral boundaries between what is and what should not become Dutch.

7. The moral panic driving the attention for honour killings

> It doesn't belong, we don't know it, it is – or rather, until recently it was – entirely alien to us. There's no entry for "honour killing" in our dictionary. That harsh combination is in fact so contradictory that we don't utilize it. Honour is showing someone respect. Honour is keeping a promise. You can have a sense of honour, you can restore lost honour. We promise something on our honour. We honour a person's memory. (…) But honour killing? I'd rather not allow the term to enter our language forever. (*Haagsche Courant* 2004)

This quote illustrates how boundaries are drawn when the topic of honour killings is discussed in the Dutch media. In this case, the author contrasts the label of honour killing (*eerwraak*) with existing Dutch words and sayings in which the concept of honour has a positive connotation. By doing so he creates a boundary between what *is* Dutch and what should *not become* Dutch.

This form of boundary-drawing appears not only in opinion articles such as that quoted above. Comments about the murders of Kezban, Zarife and Gül and the attempted murder of Hassan contain a wide variety of othering and boundary-drawing statements. For instance, during court cases the public prosecutor claimed that harsh sentences were needed to maintain clear moral boundaries. At political gatherings Minister Verdonk stated that honour killings had to be exorcized from the Netherlands.

In Chapter 6 I connected these boundary-drawing processes to changes in the macro-cultural discourses on multiculturalism, gender equality, nationalism, citizenship and social cohesion. In this chapter, I further build on this idea and introduce the concept of *moral panic* as a means to understand the boundary-drawing processes I have identified within the emerging HRV field.

The concept of moral panic additionally helps to explain the widespread public, political and scholarly attention that honour-related violence and honour killings were given in the Netherlands in 2007. The concept of moral panic helps explain why domestic violence against migrant women became reconceptualized as honour-related violence at that particular moment in time. Finally, the concept of moral panic functions as a bridge between the micro processes described in Chapter 5 and the macro processes described in Chapter 6.

7.1 Amplifying issue attention: the moral panic concept

The general argument behind the moral panic concept is that the attention given to a particular problem does not correlate to the problem's "objective" severity. Rather, the attention given to a social problem indicates worry about broader societal changes and challenges. The social problem subsequently becomes a *boundary object* along which good versus bad is discussed.

The concept of *moral panic* was developed by criminologists in the 1970s[75]. Theorists studying moral panics focus on the construction of deviant individuals, known as *folk devils*, who are seen as threat to society. These folk devils are consequently treated with hostility by society at large; they are "collectively designated as the enemy of respectable, law-abiding society" (Goode and Ben-Yehuda 1994:157). Goode and Ben-Yehuda describe the concept as follows:

> These historical episodes represent explosions of fear and concern at a particular time and place about a specific perceived threat. In each case, a specific agent was widely felt to be responsible for the threat; in each case, a sober assessment of the evidence concerning the nature of the supposed threat forces the observer to the conclusion that the fear and concern were, in all likelihood, exaggerated or misplaced. Sociologists refer to such episodes as moral panics. They arise as a consequence of specific social forces and dynamics. They arise because, as with all sociological phenomena, threats are culturally and politically constructed, a product of the human imagination. (Goode and Ben-Yehuda 1994:150-151)

According to Goode and Ben-Yehuda (1994:157) a moral panic refers to a process of stereotyping in which some individuals – villains – are presented as folk devils and others as folk heroes. Moral panics subsequently contribute to processes of dichotomization between "them" and "us". Together these processes lead to the development of a "morality play of evil versus good". An example of this morality play can be found in the moral panic about witchcraft that swept through Europe in the Middle Ages. During this time up to half a million people, most of the women, were killed for supposedly having "consorted with the devil" (Goode and Ben-Yehuda 1994:150). In this instance, the moral panic had a demonstrable folk devil.

However, as Critcher (2003:2) eloquently describes, the moral panic concept should be viewed as a Weberian ideal type, in that it functions as a yardstick

---

[75]. The first to introduce this concept was Stanley Cohen with his 1972 Ph.D. thesis on Mods and Rockers. His thesis emerged out of his amazement about the large-scale attention given to relatively innocent riots in the coastal resort of Clacton and the ensuing policy actions. The work of Hall et al. (1978) is subsequently pinpointed as an important addition to Cohen's work. In their work on the moral panic about street muggers in London they specifically focus on the roles of the media and the state in creating this panic (Critcher 2003:9-16, Garland 2008: 9-10).

against which actual examples of moral panics can be measured[76]. Not all actual moral panics satisfy each of the requirements of the moral panic model[77]. For example, in his study of the moral panic over *senseless violence*[78] Schinkel (2008:737) concludes that this panic was able to develop without a clear-cut folk devil. On the contrary, according to the author, this missing feature might even have contributed to a sustained moral panic, as "nothing incites fear as an invisible or at least not clearly identifiable threat."

Another characteristic of the moral panic concept is that the concern about a problem is disproportionate to the nature of the threat. This *disproportionality* criterion can be satisfied in various ways. For instance, it is satisfied if the figures quoted for the number of victims, costs, etcetera are grossly exaggerated, or if the available evidence suggests that the problem might not even exist. The attention given to a particular problem is also qualified as disproportionate if it outweighs the attention for another problem that is as severe as, or even more severe than, the problem causing the moral panic. Lastly, this criterion is met if a particular problem receives more attention at one moment in time than it had received during previous times, without a corresponding increase in the problem's "objective" seriousness (Goode and Ben-Yehuda 1994:158).

Contrary to how it is sometimes presented, the moral panic concept does not merely point out that the actors involved might be exaggerating the severity of the problem (Critcher 2003:143). Nor is it the same as a media hype, which is more superficial in nature. Crucial to the moral panic concept is the *symbolic function* of the problem generating all the attention (Garland 2008:11, 21; Young 2009:4; Bovenkerk et al. 2009:58-59). Theorists on moral panics are, consequently, not only interested in how a particular problem was constructed through a moral panic, they are also very much interested in what the problematized issue represents. According to these theorists, claims about a particular issue or group are often symbolic underlying anxieties about major structural and cultural value

---

76. See the work of Garland (2008:13-14) for a detailed discussion of the various shapes and sizes that moral panics can take.

77. Critcher positions himself in opposition to what he terms Goode and Ben-Yehuda's *attributional model* (1994). In this model, instances missing one of the requirements for a moral panic are not categorized as moral panic (Critcher 2003:25). Critcher contrasts the attributional model with a *processual model* of moral panics, which is based on the works of Cohen (1972) and Hall et al (1978), In this model the focus is not so much on the attributes that make a moral panic into a moral panic, but on the central processes in a moral panic. This process can be divided into seven stages: emergence, media inventory, moral entrepreneurs, experts, coping and resolution, fade-away and legacy (Critcher 2003: 17-19). The seven stages that are part of the processual model roughly correspond to the stages described by Blumer (1971:304) in the career of a social problem.

78. The label of *senseless violence* stems from the Dutch term *zinloos geweld*. In English this type of violence is often referred to as *random violence*, meaning "apparently random instances of violence in the public sphere that do not take place for the sake of some extrinsic motive such as, in the case of robbery, financial gain" (Schinkel 2008:735).

changes (Young 2005:102, Garland 2008:14). Theorists on moral panics therefore explicitly focus on these underlying anxieties:

> You cannot have a moral panic unless there is something out there morally to panic about, although it may not be the actual object of fear but a displacement of another fear or, more frequently, a mystification of the true threat of the actual object of dismay. The text of panic is, therefore, a transposition of fear – the very disproportionality and excess of language, the venom of the stereotype signifies that something other than direct reporting is up. (Young 2005:102)

One scholar who explicitly connects the current attention for honour killings to the concept of moral panic is Katherine Pratt Ewing (2008). Applying the moral panic concept, she presents the honour killing of a Turkish woman, Hatum Sürücü, in Berlin in 2005 as representing anxieties about Turkish men as "dangerous others", who form a threat to Germany's social order by refusing to integrate (Pratt Ewing 2008:154, 178). By doing so she also identifies a clear folk devil. According to Pratt Ewing, Turkish Muslim men were marginalized, stigmatized and represented as the "alien other" within public discourses on this murder (Pratt Ewing 2008:153). Lastly, Pratt Ewing's analysis shows that this moral panic did indeed serve as a "morality play of evil versus good" (Goode and Ben-Yehuda 1994:157). The following quote illustrates how this scenario played out in the German media:

> This particular flurry of media production – a paroxysm in a discourse in which immigrants serve as a focal point for the country's ills and a threat to the democratic principles that are the foundation of the German state – is the sort of event that periodically constitutes the Turkish minority vis-à-vis the German nation and crystallizes public understandings of Germany's Turkish and Muslim minorities. The discussion of honour killing in public fields and in the press display facets of German self-understanding that draw on the concepts of equality, freedom, and human rights. At the heart of these discussions is a juxtaposition of an idealized, hegemonic German masculinity and the stigmatized masculinity of the Turk who refuses to integrate. (Pratt Ewing 2008:154)

By contrasting what is German (equality, freedom and human rights) with what is not, this quote also illustrates how a morality play also serves as a way to create (or recreate) a nation state's actual or imaginary boundaries. As Goode and Ben-Yehuda (1994:169) note, "With the eruption of a given moral panic, the battle lines are redrawn, moral universes are reaffirmed, deviants are paraded before upright citizens and denounced, and society's boundaries are solidified"[79].

---

79. See also the work of Young (2009) on the connection between the moral panic concept and the concept of Othering: "A moral panic is a moral disturbance centering on claims that direct interests have been violated – an act of othering sometimes expressed in terms of demonization, sometimes with humanitarian undertones that are grossly disproportionate to the event or the activities of the individuals concerned" (Young 2009:13).

Two further elements characterize a moral panic. First, a moral panic presupposes a degree of *consensus* about the severity of the threat. Nonetheless, moral panics come in a range of different shapes and sizes, and the proportion of the population that perceives the threat to be real and serious may therefore vary (Goode and Ben-Yehuda 1994:158). Garland (2008:17) notes that the current rise in publicly accessible media means that the "consensual expression of concern [is] much more unusual" as the diversity of information channels provides easy access to counterclaims.

Second, moral panics are *volatile*. A moral panic flares up quickly as a result of factors such as exaggerated numbers, but also dies down relatively soon. However, this does not mean that moral panics are necessarily without historical or structural antecedents, since a specific issue can give rise to multiple different moral panics. Moreover, its volatile nature does not prevent a moral panic from leaving a cultural and/or institutional legacy (Goode and Ben-Yehuda 1994:158, Garland 2008:15-16). For example, Schinkel (2008:738) introduces the concept *institutionalization of anxiety* to describe the effects of the moral panic in response to senseless violence. According to Schinkel, this institutionalization processes may even extend the lifespan of the moral panic that led to these processes in the first place.

7.2 Honour killings, moral panic and the emergence of an issue-based field

The foregoing introduces the various elements that together constitute a moral panic. In this section I investigate whether these elements can also be found in the attention given to the issue of honour killings in the Netherlands.

"Folk devils": the deviant other

One of the key elements of a moral panic is the presence of a folk devil, the deviant other. The deviant other is represented as evil and contrasted with the good (Goode and Ben-Yehuda 1994:157). The media's representation of the shootings of Kezban, Hassan, Zarife and Gül includes this same good-versus-evil divide. The evil, the folk devil, is given shape in the male perpetrators, while the good is reflected in the female victims.

The lives of Kezban, Zarife and Gül, perhaps stereotyped, were repeatedly narrated in interviews with their relatives, friends and neighbours, and through claims made by agencies such as women's shelter organizations and schools. We know their ages, their education, in which shelters they stayed, the fact that they were modest, good mothers, well educated, etcetera. Moreover, the female victims were portrayed predominantly as emancipated women who, through their education and their struggles against their traditional upbringing or the traditional gender division in their marriages, sought to escape their cultural heritage. In these accounts, each of the female victims is represented as aiming to become one of "us".

The focus on female victims is also illustrated by the fact that when referring to the murders various actors repeatedly mentioned the victims' names if they were female: Kezban, Zarife and Gül. This contrasts with the only case in which the principal victim was male, which was referenced by the location of the shooting: Veghel. Moreover, very little information at all emerged about Hassan's background.

The names of folk devils, the perpetrators, were also provided: Erol (Kezban's ex-husband) Ali and Kerim (son and father in the Veghel shooting), Ozkan (Zarife's father) and Mustafa (Gül's ex-husband). However, most of these names only became public knowledge during the trails. Moreover, the life stories of the individuals were not given in the media's representation of the incidents.

With more and more actors joining the disputes about the honour killings, the perceived deviant other also changed over time: from traditional/conservative Turkish men to Turkish men in general. The first to clearly identify a deviant other were Turkish actors, for example Nurdan Cakiroglu and Turkish migrant organizations. For instance, in 2000 Cakiroglu claimed,

> Not just migrant women are abused by their husbands, but Dutch women also. (…) In *traditional* [Turkish] families, however, the man is clearly in charge. It's perceived as less unusual if he hits his wife occasionally, as long as he doesn't go too far. (Cakiroglu in De Wit 2000; italics by NVB)

She goes on to add that these men need to learn that "this is not tolerated in the Netherlands". This quote contributes to the production (or reproduction) of two dichotomies: that between Dutch and Turkish violence and that between modern and traditional Turks. Moreover, her final addition also helps to enforce of a boundary of what should be accepted in the Netherlands.

Turkish consultation group *Inspraak Orgaan Turken in Nederland* (IOT) also applied the "traditional" label. However, rather than labelling specific individuals as traditional, it labelled honour-related violence and honour killings as a traditional form of violence. The following quote by IOT director Can-Engin illustrates this *traditional* versus *modern* dichotomy:

> (…) we cannot go back to a *primitive society* where people take the law into their own hands. If a woman is hit, her brothers should not arrive at the door with guns. In a *modern society* people settle their conflicts in court. (Can-Engin in De Knegt 2002; italics by NVB)

In a similar vein, director Zeki Arslan of Turkish umbrella organization *Samenwerkende Turkse Organisaties* (STO) claimed that "[u]nfortunately the traditional way of thinking is still alive and well" (Arslan in Steinmetz 2004).

Yet other actors did not make this distinction between modern and traditional Turkish men. According to Van Eck all Turkish men are potential offenders. Her quote, "[e]very Turk immediately thinks of an honour killing if a woman commits adultery" (Van Eck in Jongerius 2000) exemplifies this point. Later claims, for example Minister Verdonk's call to the Turkish community as a whole to tackle the problem of honour killings, show that the distinction that cultural insiders made was lost as other actors entered the emerging field of honour-related violence.

Disproportionality

A second key element of a moral panic is the disproportionality of the attention that the issue receives. An examination of the attention given to honour-related violence reveals that the various forms of disproportionality described by Goode and Ben-Yehuda (1994:158) are all present.

First, the disproportionality of attention is illustrated by the fact that the problem had always existed, but had only recently triggered much attention. As the quote at the top of Part II illustrates, this was certainly the case with honour-related violence. According to the social worker quoted, this type of violence was not new; however, it was only recently that is had been labelled as honour-related violence.

Second, the disproportionality of attention is also apparent from the exaggerated numbers in this case. When the attention for this type of violence first emerged, no clear numbers were available for the frequency of honour killings. Not until in 2010 did the police announce definite figures for occurrences of honour killings in the Netherlands each year (Jansen and Sanberg 2010). Nonetheless, after Gül's murder, women's shelter organizations sent a letter to Parliament claiming that every year a hundred women were at risk of being murdered in the name of honour (House of Representatives 49-3170, 10 February 2005).

Third and last, the element of disproportionality can be seen in the overrepresentation of the problem honour-related violence at the expense of the attention for domestic violence. In the Netherlands domestic violence is the most commonly occurring form of violence. In 2006, for instance, a third of all murders and manslaughters in the country were traced back to fatal domestic violence. This translates as 49 victims of fatal domestic violence (Nieuwenhuis & Ferwerda 2010:19). Other years show similar figures: 45 in 2009, 44 in 2010 and 52 in 2011 (Ferwerda & Hardeman 2013:31). Precise data about occurrences of honour killings in those years are also available: 13 in 2009, 11 in 2010 and 7 in 2011 (Jansen and Sanbergen 2010; Jansen and Sanbergen 2013). While these figures show that honour killings are a serious problem in the Netherlands, they also illustrate that the victims of fatal domestic violence outnumber the victims of honour killings by three or four times. Despite this, to date no moral panic has emerged about fatal domestic violence.

Consensus about the severity of the issue

As a third element, according to Goode and Ben-Yehuda (1994), a moral panic also presupposes a degree of consensus about the severity of the threat. The analysis presented in Chapter 5 shows that the consensus about honour killings as a Dutch problem grew with each successive incident. Moreover, with each successive incident new actors joined the emerging HRV field. The first key actors to sound the alarm were migrants and migrant organizations. They were then joined by scholars, notably Van Eck, a school director, women's shelter organizations and ultimately national politicians such as Ayaan Hirsi Ali and Rita Verdonk. These actors declared unanimously that the honour killings needed to stop and could not be tolerated in the Netherlands.

Volatility of the issue

The fourth characteristic of moral panics (Goode & Ben-Yehuda 1994:158) is that they flare up quickly but also fade away soon. The moral panic about honour killings started slowly, however. While Kezban's murder triggered the attention of some actors, it was only after Gül was shot that a full-blown moral panic about the honour killings of migrant women developed. The anxiety about this type of murder then grew with each successive shooting. Moreover, actors sounding the alarm after Gül's murder, notably Minister Verdonk, referred to Kezban's murder as a means of substantiating their claim that honour killings were a serious problem.

The issue's symbolic function

The final and most crucial element of a moral panic is the *symbolic function* of the problem generating the attention. According to scholars on moral panics, the claims made about a particular issue represent the society's underlying anxieties (Young 2005:102, Garland 2008:14).

In the previous chapter I already argued that the sudden focus on honour killings should be seen in light of changing macro-cultural discourses on multiculturalism, gender equality, nationalism, citizenship and social cohesion. The changes in the macro-cultural discourses on multiculturalism and gender equality described there made it possible for actors to criticize this type of violence. However, the underlying anxieties about social cohesion within nation states formed the feeding ground for the widespread attention for culture-linked forms of violence such as honour-related violence. Moreover, the changing discourses on nationalism, citizenship and social cohesion created a climate in which such criticism was welcomed as a means of enforcing moral boundaries.

7.3 How the moral panic about honour killings contributed to the emergence of a Dutch HRV field

In the previous chapters I presented the actors, actions and processes that contributed to the emergence of the issue of honour-related violence. Firstly, the development of the labels *eerwraak* and *eergerelateerd geweld* made it possible for actors to discuss the issue of honour-related violence. Secondly, several of the "honour killings" (actual and attempted) acquired a field-configuring function through their ability to 1.) trigger the attention of a diverse group of actors and 2.) trigger disputes about the substance of these crimes. Thirdly, changes in the dominant discourses on multiculturalism, gender equality, nationalism and social cohesion created the necessary space to see these crimes as something distinct from and unrelated to "ordinary" domestic violence. It is due the combination of these processes that over the past two decades domestic violence against migrant women has become reconceptualized as violence in the name of honour.

Nevertheless, these processes alone cannot explain why the issue of honour-related violence gained so much momentum at the dawn of the 21st century. The concept of moral panic is essential for understanding the widespread and organizational focus on this issue. This *objectified structure*, to use Bourdieu's term, makes it possible to understand how the issue gained such momentum and why the issue's emergence also led to the emergence of an issue-based field. In addition to changes in the macro-cultural discourses and the micro-level disputes about honour killings, the underlying anxieties about national identity and social cohesion within the Netherlands contributed significantly to the emergence of a Dutch HRV field.

Theoretical implications

I argued in Part I that Bourdieu's work does not offer much information about how fields come into being. I therefore based my analysis of the processes that contribute to these first stages of issue and field emergence primarily on the work of institutionalists such as Lawrence and Phillips (2004), Grodal (2007), Mayer et al. (2005), Hoffman (1999) and Hoffman and Ocasio (2001). Their work has been pivotal to making sense of the empirical reality confronting me in my study of the issue's emergence. Yet the concept of moral panic offers a very useful addition to the work of these institutionalists, contributing to a better understanding of why the emergence of the issue of honour-related violence subsequently led to the emergence of the Dutch HRV field.

Based on this research the following premise may be formulated: not all issues that emerge in the public discourse subsequently lead to the emergence of an issue-based organizational field. For an issue-based organizational field to emerge, a combination of processes is required: changing macro-cultural discourses, micro-level activity about the issue *and* a moral panic about the severity of the issue. These multi-layered processes are what bring new issue-based organizational fields into being.

As this premise is based purely on the present research, further study into the emergence of issue-based fields is necessary to establish whether a moral panic about a particular issue is indeed a critical precondition for the emergence of an issue-based organizational field.

Part III
State practices and emerging field configurations

Introduction

> Words have become truth, the other residents of the women's refuge in Zaanstad wrote in the newspaper obituary. Any murder is horrifying, but to my party the murder of Ms Gül is all the more cruel and bitter, coming so soon after our debate on domestic violence and honour killings and so putting an exclamation mark, as it were, behind everything that was discussed then about how serious this phenomenon is. For now, my party sees Ms Gül's death as a symbol for all the victims of what are presumably a million instances of domestic violence every year. It is less safe inside than outside [a refuge, NVB].
> Sadly Ms Gül was not the first women who fled her home and paid with her life. It is also difficult to understand how on earth this happened. She had first talked to the police at the end of last year. Was this case on a pile marked "Take another look today" or not? She lived in various refuges. How did the murderer find out the address? Could it have been prevented? Did the murderer have help from anyone? If she had been someone important things would have been very different, chair of the National Platform against Racism and Discrimination Ms Borst recently claimed in *NRC Handelsblad*. She even suggested that this case might involve discrimination.
> That is why my party proposes an investigation to get to the bottom of this case, and a number similar cases.
> (Wolfsen, House of Representatives 64-41157, 7 April 2004)

This quote was spoken by Aleid Wolfsen, a member of Dutch labour party *Partij van de Arbeid* (PvdA), during a parliamentary debate that followed the murder of Gül on 11 March 2004. According to Wolfsen Gül's murder not only illustrated the seriousness of the issue of violence against women, it also brought to the fore the inadequacy of the Dutch support and police system.

The quote is illustrative of how the issue of honour killings, after having taken centre stage within the media field in 2004, had now also become a key issue within political debates. The following chart supports this idea[80]. The blue line in the chart illustrates how the label of honour killing (*eerwraak*) rose to an attention peak in parliament in 2005.

The chart additionally shows that the label of honour-related violence (the red line) gained even more attention in the subsequent years. I therefore first shift my focus from the media field to the political field. In the subsequent chapters I then discuss the emerging configurations of the Dutch HRV field.

---

80. This diagram was first presented in Chapter 4.

Figure 5. Occurrences of the labels of honour-related violence *and* honour killing *("eerwraak") in Dutch parliament, 1996-2010*[81]

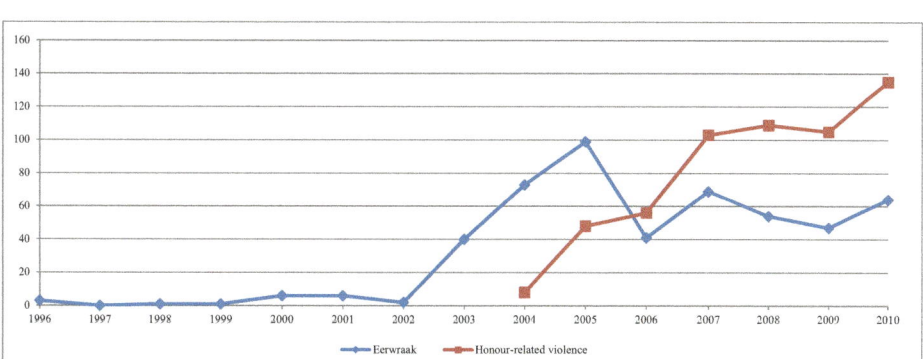

This shift in focus is inspired not only by the empirical data presented above. According to scholars such as Bourdieu (1994, 1996), Clegg (2010) and Grodal (2007), states play a crucial role in determining a field's structures. For instance, according to Bourdieu states are able to push forward specific organizational and mental structures that not only define a field's makeup, but also contribute to the reaffirmation of the state's own domination within that field (Bourdieu et al. 1994:4). Like Bourdieu, Clegg (2010) draws attention to the state's powerful position within fields and criticizes institutionalists for their lack of attention to this specific actor. Grodal (2007) also draws attention to the state's financial resources. Grodal's research into the emergence of a nanotechnology field shows that the government's adaptation of the label of nanotechnology and its subsequent relocation of resources to this field was pivotal for its emergence.

This gives rise to questions about the state's role in this particular case: Did the Dutch state indeed play a pivotal role in the emergence of a Dutch HRV field? And if so, how did it contribute to the emergence of this field? Moreover, did its power reach as far as Bourdieu presupposes? These and related questions are explored and answered in Part III by first describing the debates that took place in parliament after Gül's murder (Chapter 8) and then describing the emerging configurations of the Dutch HRV field (Chapters 9, 10 and 11). First, however, I address Bourdieu's work on state power in greater detail, as this is one of the domains in which institutional theory could benefit from his insights.

---

81. Numbers are based on an analysis of "official announcements" by the Dutch national government using the search engine Overheid.nl, 30 March 2011.

Bourdieu on state power

According to Bourdieu et al. (1994) one of the key powers of the state lies in its ability to present particular ways of acting as "natural" that are anything but natural. As they describe it, "one of the major powers of the state is to produce and impose (especially through school systems) categories of thought that we spontaneously apply to all things of the social world – including the state itself" (Bourdieu et al. 1994:1).

These *categories of thought* also include the issues that become labelled as social problems. According to Bourdieu *social problems* are issues that a society, at some point, takes to be "legitimate, worthy of being debated, or being made public and sometimes officialised, and in a sense, *guaranteed by the state* (Bourdieu & Wacquant 1992:236). In other words, social problems are socially constructed. Their emergence, in addition, offers some insight into the *zeitgeist* at that particular moment in time: they are only "debated" if they fit the spirit of the age. Moreover, Bourdieu argues that both states and social scientists play an important role in their production. His critical description states that states are "great producers of 'social problems' that social science does little more than ratify whenever it takes them over as 'sociological' problems" (Bourdieu et al. 1994:2).[82]

Therefore, Bourdieu advises scholars considering the workings of the state to take a position of "*hyperbolic doubt*", given that "when it comes to the state, one never doubts enough" (Bourdieu et al. 1994:1). He subsequently urges scholars to

> retrace the history of the emergence of these problems, of their progressive constitution, i.e., of the collective work, oftentimes accomplished through competition and struggle that proved necessary to make such and such issue to be known and recognized (...) as legitimate problems, problems that are avowable, publishable, public, official. (Bourdieu & Wacquant 1992:238)

By retracing the history of the emergence of a problem, instead of blindly reifying the issues that states define as social problems, scholars can uncover how states exert their power and define what is normal and what is not and therefore what is a problem and is not.

Bourdieu goes on to define "state" as an "ensemble of fields that are the site of struggles" (Bourdieu & Wacquant 1994:111). Consequently, "the state" as such does not exist. In contrast, states are formed by

> an ensemble of administrative or bureaucratic fields (...) within which agents and categories of agents, governmental and non-governmental, struggle over this peculiar form of authority consisting of the power to *rule* via legislation, regulations, administrative measures (...). (Bourdieu & Wacquant 1992:111)

---

82. Chapter 3 offers a more comprehensives reflection on Bourdieu's criticism of the social sciences and on how my research seeks to counter this criticism.

By breaking up the state into separate bureaucratic fields, which in turn are formed by different agents, it becomes possible to study the struggles, and thus the micro dynamics, that contributed to the emergence of a particular social problem[83].

On what basis are states then able to exert the power to define social problems? According to Bourdieu, states typically have access to various types of capital that together form the foundation of their power. These *types of capitals* are the capital of physical force, economic capital, information capital and symbolic capital. This accumulation of types of capital subsequently makes it possible for a state to become the holder of a *meta-capital* or *statis capital*. This meta-capital in turn enables states to exercise power over other fields and thus over the actors and species of capital within those fields. As a consequence states are able to define the *field of power* within other fields (Bourdieu et al. 1994: 4-5).

The *capital of physical force* is the capital for which states are traditionally known: on the one hand states protect their borders through military forces and on the other hand states maintain their internal order through the deployment of the police. However, this concentration of physical force is only possible if a state has access to *economic capital*, which is traditionally realised by developing an efficient tax system.

The concentration of economic capital is paralleled by a concentration of *information capital*. As the following quote illustrates, the scope of this type of capital is vast:

> Through classification systems (especially according to sex and age) inscribed in law, through bureaucratic procedures, educational structures and social rituals (...), the state molds *mental structures* and imposes common principles of vision and division (...) And it thereby contributes to the construction of what is commonly designated as national identity (...). (Bourdieu et al. 1994:7-8)

In this manner, Bourdieu argues, states utilize their informational capital to advance cultural and linguistic unification (i.e. *theoretical unification*) within their borders, which in turn contributes to the development of a national identity[84].

Lastly, states have access to the *symbolic capital of authority*: states can only hold the other types of capital (physical, economic and informational) as long as they are perceived as the legitimate source of authority. According to Bourdieu et al. (1994:8-12), over time states have objectified this symbolic capital by becoming bureaucracies that form a source of authority in many different domains. Moreover, their authority over these domains is mostly left unquestioned as citizens

---

83. While I agree with Bourdieu on this point, I still use the label of "state" for maximum readability. Bourdieu does the same in his own work, apparently for the same reasons.
84. See also Chapter 6 on "national identity" and nationalism.

have, again over time, integrated the existing social and cultural order into their habitus, a process that Bourdieu terms *doxic submission* (Bourdieu et al. 1994:14).

As such, Bourdieu continues, states are not only powerful because they have access to many types of capital, they are also powerful because their position of authority has become normalized within their society. The following quote comprehensively summarizes Bourdieu's position on state power:

> If the state is able to exert symbolic violence, it is because it incarnates itself simultaneously in objectivity, in the form of specific organizational structures and mechanisms, and in subjectivity in the form of mental structures and categories of perception and thought. By realizing itself in social structures and in the mental structures adapted to them, the instituted institution makes us forget that it issues out of a long series of acts of institution (in the active sense) and hence has all the appearances of the natural. (Bourdieu et al. 1994:4)

Nevertheless, as Bourdieu also establishes with this quote, the doxic submission did not come about without struggle. Elsewhere he explains this as follows: "What appears to us today as self-evident, as beneath consciousness and choice, has quite often been the stake of struggles and instituted only as the result of dogged confrontations between dominant and dominated groups" (Bourdieu et al. 1994:15).

It is for this reason that he calls on scholars to study the genesis of the state, of state practices and of social problems. More specifically, he calls on scholars to study what he describes as the *bureaucratic microcosm* and the position that the *agents of the state* take within this microcosm (Bourdieu et al. 1994:16).

Bearing in mind Bourdieu's caution about the state's power, it seems vital to reconstruct how the state contributed to the emerging configurations of the Dutch HRV field. Therefore, instead of taking the state's definition of honour-related violence for granted, I reconstruct how this definition came into being within the political field. The same principle is also applied to the proposed measures, such as the interministerial programme to combat honour-related violence. An analysis of the micro dynamics that preceded the state's action reveals the state's power – or, as Bourdieu et al. (1994:4) put it, "by bringing back into view the conflicts and confrontations of the early beginnings and therefore all the discarded possibilities, it retrieves the possibility that things could have been (and still can be) otherwise."

Part III: outline

One last step needs to be taken before I turn at last to the results of the study that formed the starting point for this thesis. In the chapter that follows I describe the political debates that followed Gül's murder. In 2006 these debates eventually led to the announcement of a large-scale interministerial programme to combat honour-related violence by the then Minister of Alien Affairs and Integration, Rita Verdonk (VVD). As the data presented in Chapters 9, 10 and 11 shows, that programme proved to be pivotal for the emergence of a Dutch HRV field.

Chapter 8 therefore serves multiple purposes. It bridges the time that passed between the emergence of the issue in public discourse (1990-2004) and the initial research period (2007-2008). Moreover, the description that it offers of the field dynamics within the political field reveals some of the micro dynamics that contributed to the emergence of the HRV field. Lastly, through the examination of the state's role in the formation of the Dutch HRV field, it becomes possible to assess, ultimately, to what extent the state was able to impose its mental and organizational structures on the emerging configurations of the HRV field.

In the subsequent chapters I then present the data that led me to believe that an HRV field may indeed be said to have emerged. Those chapters answer empirical questions such as, What actors play key roles in the field of honour-related violence and on what basis do they come by these positions? What do the actors involved understand the term "honour-related violence" to mean? Lastly, an analysis is performed of how the various actors organize themselves in relation to this problem.

The answers to these and related questions form an outline for sketching the emerging field configurations of the Dutch HRV field. Data on the key actors and their roles, for instance, provides input about the types of *capital* that are deemed to be important within the emerging field. Moreover, information on how the label of honour-related violence is utilized provides input about the *doxa* developed within the field. Information on how actors perceive the problem of honour-related violence also provides input about the *habitus* guiding the actors' interpretations of reality. Lastly, the answers to questions on how actors view one another provide input for analysing how actors are positioned according to their capital.

8. The political field as a field of struggle

During a parliamentary debate held almost one year after Gül's murder (10 February 2005), various MPs showed a clear discontent with the measures that had been taken by the Members of Cabinet so far. Those MPs felt that the Dutch state was "missing in action" when it came to tackling honour-related violence in the Netherlands. Nebahat Albayrak (PvdA), for instance, argued,

> The minister's letter of 4 November [2004] sets out what measures she will use to tackle honour killings. Those measures fall completely short of the mark. The problems surrounding honour killings are so great that much more stringent measures must be taken. (…) [T]he government's letters show little sense of urgency that it is in fact embarrassing that this government dared to send entirely inadequate letters to the House. (House of Representatives 28 345 / 29 203, no. 38:3)

Other MPs expressed similar complaints during this parliamentary debate. For example, Margot Kraneveldt (LPF) stated that the Minister for Alien Affairs and Integration displayed a "staggering lack of decisiveness" (House of Representatives 2004-2005, 28 345 / 29 203, no. 38:5). Others joined Albayrak in complaining about the lack of urgency (House of Representatives 2004-2005, 28 345 / 29 203, no. 38). The sections that follow further address the parliamentary debates between MPs and the responsible Members of Cabinet on the issue of honour-related violence in order to establish whether the state was indeed "missing in action".

Analysing the interaction between the MPs and the ministers reveals the political field's dynamics and *field of struggle*. Moreover, an analysis of the substance of these debates brings into view: 1.) the discussion about the appropriate problem definition and problem solutions, 2.) the actors that were deemed to be crucial to the implementation of these solutions and 3.) various demarcation processes. In Bourdieu's terms these issues relate successively to the emerging doxa of the field, the actors that determine the HRV field and the field's boundaries.

For purposes of the present study, the political field is viewed as one of the bureaucratic fields that together make up the state. The political field is subsequently viewed as an organizational field which is formed by various actors whose positions in respect of each other are determined by the value of their capital within this particular field. I particularly focus on the "front stage" actors: MPs in the House of Representatives and Members of Cabinet, whose interactions can be traced by studying official parliamentary documents[85]. However, their contributions to the field are influenced by other bureaucratic fields such as those formed by lobby organizations and civil servants. Those fields are not included in this analysis, though, as their input is difficult to trace by analysing official documents. Nevertheless, where relevant I elaborate on how other fields, for example the media field, informed the content of the political field.

8.1 Field-configuring events within the political field

Similar to the media field, the political field has its own field-configuring events, albeit of a completely different nature. Here, the *planned field-configuring events* are formed by the parliamentary debates following a particular event or letter sent to parliament by one of the Members of Cabinet. These events take place within a highly structured field that follows its own set of rules, which structure how the main actors within this field – MPs, ministers and state secretaries – communicate with each other. For instance, the rules dictate how parliamentary debates are held: the MPs are first given a fixed number of minutes to pose their questions, then the relevant minster gives his or her initial response, next the MPs are given the opportunity to ask follow-up questions and lastly the minister speaks again (Tweede Kamer 2015a: website).

Besides these formal communication rules, MPs may also use a number of instruments to call ministers and state secretaries to account, for example asking questions during Question Time, proposing motions or launching a parliamentary inquiry. Members of parliament who perceive a particular policy issue to be very important may also assign it "*priority project status*". However, this is not a very common procedure. Moreover, this status is granted only if certain conditions are met. For example, it must involve a significant financial interest and a link must be drawn between the policy issue and major consequences for society or the state. Granting a policy issue priority project status also has consequences for the minister involved, who is subsequently obliged to provide parliament with extensive financial and other information. As a result, in the past this status has been given predominantly to infrastructure projects such as the construction of railway lines (Tweede Kamer 2016: website).

In the following I describe how, within this highly structured field, the issue of honour-related violence was played out between the MPs and the Members of Cabinet. This analysis focuses on the key moments of interaction: the parliamentary debates that followed a particular event or letter sent to parliament. The table groups these letters and debates into larger clusters, each of which incorporates

---

85. Dutch parliament is made up of two houses: the House of Representatives (*Tweede Kamer*) and the Senate (*Eerste Kamer*).

the letters that were discussed during a parliamentary debate and the follow-up debates. The table also shows what instruments were utilized by MPs to steer the government in a specific direction.

Table 3. Letters and parliamentary debates on honour-related violence, 2004-2006

Cluster	Date	Type of event	Parliamentary instrument
1.	10 March 2004	Parliamentary debate on the emancipation and integration of ethnic minorities, with the Minister of Social Affairs and Employment (De Geus) and the Minister of Alien Affairs and Integration (Verdonk).	
	11 March 2004	Parliamentary debate on domestic violence, with the Minister of Justice (Donner), the Minister of Social Affairs and Employment (De Geus) and the Minister of Alien Affairs and Integration (Verdonk).	
	11 March 2004	Murder of Gül.	
	16 March 2004	Follow-up debate on the emancipation and integration of ethnic minorities, with the Minister of Alien Affairs and Integration (Verdonk).	Five motions are proposed, three of which specifically concern honour-related violence.
	7 April 2004	Follow-up debate on domestic violence, with the Minister of Justice (Donner).	Nine motions are proposed, one of which particularly concerns honour-related violence.
	21 April 2004	Letter from the Minister of Justice (Donner) on the proposed motions during the follow-up debate on domestic violence on 7 April.	
2.	27 September 2004	Letter of deferral from the Minister of Alien Affairs and Integration (Verdonk), acting in part on behalf of the Minister of Justice (Donner).	
	1 November 2004	Letter announcing two studies and a pilot into police registration from the Minister of Alien Affairs and Integration (Verdonk), acting in part on behalf of the Minister of Justice (Donner).	

Cluster	Date	Type of event	Parliamentary instrument
	6 December 2004	Letter containing an update on the domestic violence approach in 2004 from the Minister of Justice (Donner), acting in part on behalf of the Minister of Alien Affairs and Integration (Verdonk), the Minister of the Interior and Kingdom Relations (Remkes), the Minister of Social Affairs and Employment (De Geus) and the State Secretary for Health, Welfare and Sport (Roos-van Dorp).	
	10 February 2005	Parliamentary debate with the Minister of Alien Affairs and Integration (Verdonk) and the Minister of Justice (Donner), to discuss the letters of 1 November 2004 and 6 December 2004.	
	10 February 2005	Emergency debate with the Minister of Justice (Donner) and the Minister of Alien Affairs and Integration (Verdonk) in response to the warning from *Federatie Opvang*[86] that around a hundred women are not safe in their shelters.	Five motions are proposed.
	9 March 2005	Follow-up debate to the debate on 10 February with the Minister of Alien Affairs and Integration (Verdonk) and the Minister of Justice (Donner).	Five motions are proposed.
3.	3 March 2005	Letter from the Minister of Justice (Donner) and the Minister of Alien Affairs and Integration (Verdonk) providing written answers to questions posed during the emergency debate on 10 February 2005[87].	
	6 June 2005	Letter from the Minister of Alien Affairs and Integration (Verdonk), acting in part on behalf of Minister of Justice (Donner), the Minister of the Interior and Kingdom Relations (Remkes), the Minister of Social Affairs and Employment (De Geus) and the State Secretary for Health, Welfare and Sport (Roos-van Dorp), accompanied by two research reports and the first results of the police registrations pilot.	

---

86. *Federatie Opvang* is the umbrella organization for women's shelters.
87. The reason why this letter is included in this particular cluster is that its contents were discussed during the parliamentary debate on 29 June 2005.

Cluster	Date	Type of event	Parliamentary instrument
	29 June 2005	Parliamentary debate with the Minister of Alien Affairs and Integration (Verdonk) and the Minister of Justice (Donner), to discuss the letters of 3 March 2005 and 6 June 2005.	Two MPs (for VVD and PvdA) propose giving honour-related violence priority project status.
	23 November 2005	Letter from the Presidium[88] declaring that the Standing Committee on Government Spending[89] has issued a positive opinion on assigning priority project status to honour-related violence.	
	6 December 2005	Vote on giving honour-related violence priority project status.	The majority of MPs vote to give honour-related violence priority project status.
4.	14 February 2006	Letter from the Minister of Alien Affairs and Integration (Verdonk) about the pilot for police registrations.	
	28 March 2006	Letter presenting the organizational outline for the priority project on honour-related violence, sent by the Minister of Alien Affairs and Integration (Verdonk), acting in part on behalf of Minister of Justice (Donner), the Minister of the Interior and Kingdom Relations (Remkes), the Minister of Social Affairs and Employment (De Geus) and the Minister of Health, Welfare and Sport (Hoogervorst).	

---

88. The Presidium is formed by the Speaker of the House of Representatives and the Deputy Speakers. The Presidium is responsible for handling the day-to-day affairs of the House of Representatives (Tweede Kamer 2015b:website).

89. At the time, the Committee on Government Spending (*Commissie voor Rijksuitgaven*) was a standing committee that assisted other standing committees of the House of Representatives. It specialized in information about governmental budget accountability and the procedures involved in giving policy issues "priority project" status. On 22 September 2015 the Standing Committee on Finances took over these tasks (Tweede Kamer 2015c:website).

Cluster	Date	Type of event	Parliamentary instrument
	4 April 2006	Parliamentary debate with the Minister of Alien Affairs and Integration (Verdonk) and the Minister of Justice (Donner), to discuss the letters of 14 February 2005 and 28 March 2005.	MPs ask the Minister of Alien Affairs and Integration to put forward an alternative for the priority project status.
5.	19 April 2006	Letter from the Minister of Alien Affairs and Integration (Verdonk) about the possibilities for granting residency permits to victims of honour-related violence.	
	16 May 2006	Letter from the Minister of Alien Affairs and Integration (Verdonk), presenting the outline of an interministerial programme to combat honour-related violence.	
	23 May 2006	Parliamentary debate with the Minister of Alien Affairs and Integration (Verdonk), to discuss the letters of 19 April 2006 and 16 May 2006.	
	29 June 2006	Recommendation by the Presidium to lift the priority project status of honour-related violence.	The priority project status is lifted.

These debates took place during the Balkenende II government (27 May 2003-29 June 2006). This Cabinet was formed by a coalition consisting of the *Christen Democratisch Appèl* (CDA), the *Volkspartij voor Vrijheid en Democratie* (VVD) and the *Politieke Partij Democraten* (D66). This is relevant here, as during the debates the government came under criticism from not only the opposition, but also MPs representing the coalition parties.

Moreover, these debates took place at a time when the populist right-wing parties were gaining ground in Dutch politics. Those parties played an important role in pushing immigration and integration issues. The analysis by Roggeband and Verloo (2007), for instance, shows that while left-wing parties had been advocating more attention for the position of migrant women, it was the right-wing parties that determined the direction of these policies: a focus on culture change. Moreover, they identify MP Ayaan Hirsi Ali and Minister Rita Verdonk as being among the most outspoken right-wing representatives. They subsequently conclude that it is remarkable how "some political actors who have never been strong advocates of gender equality before now use the argument of gender equality to reassert national identity and place more restrictive demands upon migrants and resident minorities" (Roggeband and Verloo 2007:272). (See also Chapter 6 for a more extensive review of the spirit of the age within Dutch politics.)

Below I provide brief descriptions for each of the clusters listed. My particular focus is on the instruments that were utilized by MPs and on the government's subsequent response. This reveals the "struggles" that contributed to the social construction of honour-related violence as a social problem.

8.2 Accelerating the honour-related violence debate: Gül's murder

The first cluster of MP-Cabinet interactions on the issue of honour-related violence is formed by the parliamentary debates preceding and following Gül's murder in March 2004. While Gül's murder functioned as a catalyst for the attention given to honour-related violence in parliament, the issue was not a new one within the political field.

The issue of honour-related violence had already surfaced during two parliamentary debates that took place shortly before Gül's murder. The first debate was held on 10 March 2004 and focused on the *emancipation and integration* of women and girls from ethnic minorities, which fell under the responsibility of Rita Verdonk (VVD) as Minister of Alien Affairs and Integration and Aart Jan de Geus (CDA) as Minister of Social Affairs and Employment. The issue resurfaced the next day, this time during a debate on Dutch policy on *domestic violence*, which fell under the responsibility of those same ministers and Piet Hein Donner (CDA) as Minister of Justice.

However, in both these debates honour-related violence – mostly referred to by the label of *eerwraak* or as culture-linked violence – only played a minor role. For instance, during the debate on domestic violence the MPs' focus was on advancing the measures against domestic violence. While domestic violence was high on the political agenda in 2004, this had not always been the case. As recently as in 2002 the national government had presented a coherent plan of action against this type of action, entitled *Privé geweld, publieke zaak* ("private violence, a public matter"). A number of MPs felt that a great deal of work yet remained to be done – for example, arranging for a nationwide network of Advice and Support Centres for Domestic Violence (*Advies en Steunpunten Huiselijk Geweld*) to be set up (House of Representatives 28 345, no.9).

In a similar vein, the debate on the emancipation and integration of migrant women primarily focused on advancing their participation in Dutch society, particularly by helping them to find jobs. However, the connection with culture-linked violence was drawn more openly during this debate. The MP who made this connection most explicitly was Ayaan Hirsi Ali (VVD). During this debate she stated,

> The greatest obstacle to emancipating and integrating women from ethnic minorities is culture-legitimized violence committed by male relatives and the hushing-up by female relatives – the social gossip culture, so to speak. (...) Of concern are that culture and those expressions of faith that, through coercion and force, restrict the freedom and safety of individuals, in particular women. (House of Representatives 29 203, no 9:2)

Hirsi Ali argued that culture-linked violence stood in the way of migrant women's emancipation. Others too, while not making this connection quite so explicitly, expressed their concerns about this type of violence. While not completely invisible, therefore, the issue of honour-related violence was not at the heart of the debates on domestic violence and migrant women's emancipation.

However, after Gül's murder honour killings became the key issue during the two follow-up debates. Moreover, her murder not only united members from very different political parties in their rejection of this type of violence, it also seemingly brought together two policy arenas: domestic violence and the emancipation and integration of migrant women.

The first follow-up debate was held on 16 March 2004, just five days after Gül's murder, and the first to take the floor was Hirsi Ali. She opened her contribution with the following statement:

> Mr Chairman. During the general debate about the outlines of the plan of action to integrate and emancipate women from ethnic minorities, my party supported the Cabinet's plans to take measures in terms of education and employment. However, we also made it clear that the greatest obstacle to emancipating and integrating a considerable portion of the women from ethnic minorities is what is termed culture-legitimized violence. When I asked, on behalf of the VVD party, for a specific programme for protecting these women, the Minister for Alien Affairs proposed waiting for the general debate on domestic violence, which was scheduled to take place the following day.
>
> During that general debate I was given no promises, nor any answers to my questions. Sadly, the VVD party was tragically proven right last Friday by the murder of Gül, 32 years of age, a mother of three. She was murdered outside the women's refuge in Zaanstad, on grounds of honour. The refuge has been cleared, because relatives of her husband, the murderer, said literally that the job would only complete once they have also got the children. As such, my party wishes to repeat the importance of the safety of these women. As long as these women are threatened with violence by their relatives and friends, their integration and emancipation will fail. That is why the VVD party wishes to submit three motions. We urgently call on the Minister for Immigration and Integration, in her role as coordinator, to expedite the implementation of this motion. (House of Representatives 58-3840, 16 March 2004)

Hirsi Ali's statement supports the analysis that Gül's murder functioned as a catalyst for the attention given to honour-related violence in Dutch politics. Her death prompted Hirsi Ali to bringing forward three motions, which in turn forced the government to take action against honour killings.

The manner of Gül's murder also led MPs to focus on specific issues and solutions, which subsequently informed the substance of the later interministerial programme to combat honour-related violence. For instance, the fact that Gül's husband had been able to trace her and her children to a women's shelter – a place where women were supposed to be safe – led MPs to appeal for 1.) the development of more refuges and 2.) better coordination between women's shelters and the police. Moreover, the fact that the husband's family was involved in finding Gül led to repeated appeals for the Public Prosecution Service to bring the entire family to justice.

During the two follow-up debates four motions were brought before the assembly that specifically focused on honour-related violence. In the end, three of those motions proved to be pivotal for the development of an interministerial programme to combat honour-related violence, and Hirsi Ali was involved in each of them. The first was a motion by Wolfsen (PvdA) and Hirsi Ali (VVD), in which they called for a general inquiry into Gül's murder and for her case to be compared with previous instances of honour killings (submitted during the debate on 7 April). The second was a motion by Hirsi Ali (VVD), Stuurman (PvdA) and Bakker (D66), in which they called for a national register of honour killings (submitted during the debate on 16 March). The third was a motion by Hirsi Ali (VVD) and Bakker (D66), calling for a specific programme to protect women (submitted during the debate on 16 March).

Only two weeks after the second follow-up debate, the Minister of Justice (Donner) sent a letter to parliament, in which he indicated that he supported the motion by Wolfsen and Hirsi Ali. Nonetheless, he asked them to put off this motion: together with the Minister of Alien Affairs and Integration (Verdonk) and the Minister of Health, Welfare and Sports (Hoogervorst), he was developing a series of initiatives that addressed the precise issues raised in Hirsi Ali's motions (House of Representatives 28 345, no.19).

This analysis of the first cluster of interactions between MPs and ministers illustrates how Gül's murder became politicized within the political field. It was subsequently used by politicians, including Hirsi Ali, to further their own agendas on the emancipation of migrant women. Moreover, the field dynamics described here illustrate how strongly both left-wing and right-wing MPs felt about the issue. No disagreement was expressed about the severity of the problem or the need for action. Nor did any discussions emerge about how this issue differed from domestic violence; from the start, honour-related violence was perceived as distinct, in need of its own solution.

Various MPs subsequently used one of their most powerful instruments, motions, to urge the Cabinet to take action. Nevertheless, as the next cluster of interactions illustrates, the MPs were not satisfied with the steps taken by the ministers: their quest for action clearly collided with the Cabinet's quest for a more thorough understanding of the issue at hand.

8.3 Developing a better understanding of the problem: two studies and a pilot

The second cluster of MP-Cabinet interactions on the issue of honour-related violence comprises the debates that followed a letter from the Minister of Alien Affairs and Integration in November 2004. In that letter Minister Verdonk set out the Cabinet's course of action, which was aimed at gaining a better understanding of the nature and extent of the problem of honour-related violence.

The subsequent debates were also influenced by the *Federatie Opvang* (FO), the umbrella organization for women's shelters. According to FO, women's shelters were harbouring around a hundred women whose safety they could not guarantee in light of the threat of honour-related violence. Together with its warning, FO again pointed out the apparent inadequacy of the Dutch system to cope with this type of violence. As explained in Part II, each of the analysed shootings shared an element of failure by government institutes (see Chapter 5). FO's claim took this view further, while also supporting the idea that honour-related violence was distinct from domestic violence and therefore needed its own solution.

In the following I briefly describe the substance of Minister Verdonk's first "plan of action", after which I describe the field dynamics that can be observed during the debates that it triggered. According to Verdonk the first step in the battle against honour-related violence lay in gaining a better understanding of the nature and extent of the problem. She therefore commissioned various studies. First, she asked independent research group *COT*, an institute for Safety and Crisis Management, to conduct a case study covering twenty cases of honour-related violence, including Gül's murder. The focus of this study was on identifying possible problem areas in the cooperation between organizations dealing with honour-related violence (Wolfsen and Hirsi Ali's motion). Next, a pilot study was launched in two police districts, to identify 1.) how to organize registration of cases of honour-related violence within the police and 2.) how to prevent honour killings (motion presented by Hirsi Ali et al.). Last, Verdonk announced that she was commissioning a project to establish a "working definition" of the label of *eerwraak*, the Dutch word for honour killings, in order to improve practitioners' knowledge of honour-related violence (House of Representatives 29 203, no. 15).

As the following chapters show, the actions that she announced impacted the emerging HRV field. For instance, one of the police districts that conducted the pilot study became a key actor within the emerging HRV field. The agency that was set up in that police district would later become the *Landelijk Expertise Centrum eergerelateerd geweld* (LEC), the National Expertise Centre on honour-related violence. Moreover, the researchers who were commissioned to develop the working definition, Ferwerda and Van Leiden, concluded that the label of *eerwraak* was inadequate. They then went on to develop the label of honour-related violence, which encompasses a much broader range of types of violence. As the definition now also included more subtle forms of violence, more actors were able to see roles for themselves in combatting honour-related violence (see Chapter 4 and Chapter 9 for further details about this definition).

Minister Verdonk's letter of 1 November (House of Representatives 29 203, no.15:4) goes on to describe how the results of the studies and the pilot would serve as input for measures that would help bring about 1.) recognition and acknowledgment of honour killings, 2.) protection of victims, 3.) cooperation between relevant organizations and 4.) investigation into and prosecution of perpetrators. She then expressed the "ambition" to present a detailed set of measures early in 2006. Verdonk's intention with those measures was to give shape to Hirsi Ali and Bakker's motion about developing a specific programme to protect women (House of Representatives 29 203, no. 15).

It interesting that Verdonk was the Minister who sent this letter. She explicitly elaborates on the fact that she would act as the minister coordinating the various efforts. According to Verdonk, honour killings occur predominantly among members of migrant communities, and as she was responsible for relationships and communications with migrant communities she was the appropriate minister to coordinate the Dutch approach on honour-related violence (Verdonk, House of Representatives 29 203, no. 15:2). In this way, honour-related violence was framed as a migrant problem and therefore an integration issue, rather than a domestic violence issue. This point is confirmed by the following quote by Verdonk: "The phenomenon of honour killing is wholly incompatible with the Cabinet's desire to promote the integration and self-reliance of minorities and encourage the emancipation of women and girls from minorities" (House of Representatives 29 203, no. 15:2).

During the debates that followed Verdonk's letter and a letter from Donner, the Minister of Justice (House of Representatives 28345 nr. 26), the MPs were unanimous in their response: they all expressed their disappointment with the Cabinet. The MPs felt that the Cabinet did not share their sense of urgency as it only wanted to present tangible measures in 2006. Hirsi Ali in fact went so far as to propose filing a "motion of misgivings" against the Minister of Justice[90]. She felt that her third motion, asking for a protection programme for women, would not be realized at all. According to Hirsi Ali, this showed that the Minister of Justice was taking the seriousness and extent of the issue of honour-killings too lightly (House of Representatives 28 345 / 29 203, no. 38:17).

---

90. A "motion of misgivings" (*motie van treurnis*) is a tool that MPs can use to express their disappointment about a minister's actions (or lack thereof). Unlike a "vote of censure" (*motie van afkeuring*), a motion of misgivings does not imply a lack of confidence in the minister's capabilities and therefore has no consequences for the minister. As such, these motions primarily serve a symbolic function.

The sense of urgency among MPs was amplified by FO's recent warning about the safety of some hundred women in their shelters. This claim reignited the *moral panic* about honour killings that already existed within the media field. During the emergency debate (10 February 2005) that subsequently took place within the political field, Albayrak (PvdA) referred to several recent honour-killings to substantiate her argument that there was "no time to waste":

> How can we live with the idea that it is a matter of time? That it is inevitable that another woman will be murdered, here in the Netherlands, for her family's honour? The government is doing everything that it can to combat honour killings, but for now it is unfortunately busy trying to understand what we are talking about, and in particular what the extent of the problem is and whether it is big enough to warrant harsh measures. We should not expect this reflection to bear fruit until 2006. Measures will take even longer. My conclusion is that this is unacceptable and bitter. The government's thoughts should focus on adequate measures to combat honour killings. A case study, as announced. Pilot projects, like in The Hague. These could certainly be useful in preventing the phenomenon of honour killings. Honour killings are already occurring in the Netherlands as we speak. Kezban, Gül, Serife and Schyman have already been murdered! Others will follow. That is why we need action now. (House of Representatives 49-3170, 10 February 2005:1).

This quote clearly illustrates Albayrak's frustration with the government's slow pace in developing adequate measures against honour-related violence. It also reveals her discontent with the government's strategy of first gaining a better understanding of the nature and extent of the problem.

Albayrak subsequently filed three motions during this debate. The first motion, which she filed together with other opposition parties (green party GroenLinks, Christian party CU and socialist party SP), requested the government to develop more refuges. In her second motion she asked the government to define domestic violence and honour-related violence as distinct grounds for asylum (motion filed together with GroenLinks and SP). Lastly, again together with GroenLinks (Naïma Azough) and SP (Fenna Vergeer), she filed a motion requesting the government to arrange for municipalities to provide shelter to persons in need.

In addition Mirjam Sterk (CDA), Lousewies van der Laan (D66), Hirsi Ali (VVD) and Bas van der Vlies (SGP) filed a motion in which they urged the government, together with FO and the relevant municipal authorities, to take measures to ensure that every threatened woman was given proper shelter. They also asked the government to inform parliament as soon as possible about these measures. Azough (GL) also filed a motion in which she asked the government to ensure that threatened women were offered long-term assistance by both professionals and volunteers.

During the follow-up debate, which took place on 9 March 2005, Albayrak again filed a number of motions. In the first, which she filed together with Kraneveldt (LPF) and Azough (GL), she asked the government to develop an "instruction"⁹¹ for the Public Prosecution Service stipulating that persons who are presumed to be involved in cases of honour-related violence would not be exempt from prosecution. A second motion that was filed by Azough, Albayrak and Kraneveldt urged the government to subsidize organizations that encouraged a debate about honour-related violence within migrant communities.

Albayrak, MP on behalf of the labour party PvdA, so became one of the main driving forces behind the state's response to honour-related violence. While the ministers involved, Verdonk and Donner, initially advised against the motions described above, the substance of a later letter (6 June 2005) showed that they had taken on board many of the requests. Nevertheless, as the description of the following cluster of interactions reveals, this was not enough to satisfy Albayrak and Hirsi Ali. They still felt that the government's approach to honour-related violence lacked coherence and speed, and therefore demanded that honour-related violence be assigned "priority project status".

8.4 Assigning honour-related violence "priority project status"

The third cluster of MP-Cabinet interactions on honour-related violence is formed by the debates that followed a letter (6 June 2005) in which Minister Verdonk of Alien Affairs and Integration presented the results of the studies and the pilot that had been announced in the preceding cluster.

The MPs' tone during this parliamentary debate was very different from their tone in the previous debate. This time various MPs complimented the government on its course of action. In particular, they expressed their satisfaction with the results of the case study and the police pilot. Albayrak (PvdA), for instance, stated that she was "pleased with the steps that have been taken since the previous debate" and later added that the case study conducted into twenty honour killings was a "masterful move" (House of Representatives 28345 and 29 203, no. 40:2-3).

Contributing to this new tone was the fact that in her letter Minister Verdonk had addressed many of the issues previously raised, either via motions or via MPs' contributions to parliamentary debates. For instance, she promised to expand the scope of the Public Prosecution Service's instruction on domestic violence to include information about honour-related violence (motion by Albayrak et al.). Moreover, she explained to parliament that a protocol would be developed that stipulated that the police, the Public Prosecution Service and women's shelter organizations must coordinate their efforts. She also explicitly referred to Azough's motion and promised that more funding would be provided for mi-

---

91. The technical Dutch policy term is "*aanwijzing*", which refers to a formal instruction to the police and the Public Prosecution Service. An *aanwijzing* sets out general principles for the police and prosecutors to follow with regard to a particular issue.

grant organizations to work on bringing about a change in mentality within their communities.

Based on the results of the police pilot, the case study and the various measures that were already in place, Verdonk subsequently concluded, "It is neither necessary nor appropriate to develop a special infrastructure to tackle honour-related violence" (House of Representatives 29 203 and 28 345, no. 25:9).

The government's strategy to first develop a better understanding of the nature and extent of the problem appeared to have worked, as it tempered the MPs' quest for tangible measures. Vergeer (SP), for instance, concluded that the minister had incorporated many of the issues raised during previous debates (House of Representatives 28 345 and 29 203, no. 40:5). Despite these compliments, however, various issues remained to trouble the MPs during these debates. The working definition that was presented, for instance, gave rise to some discussion.

According to Verdonk the goal of the definition was to function as a framework for both practitioners and policy development, and to function as a tool for developing more expertise on this issue (House of Representatives 29 203, no.5:2). The definition that was developed to meet these goals was this:

> Honour-related violence means any form of physical or mental violence perpetrated from within a collective mentality, in response to a breach of honour (or the threat of such a breach) concerning a man or woman and therefore his or her family, where the outside world is or might become aware of the breach. (Ferwerda and Van Leiden 2005:25)

As such, the definition now referred to a broader spectrum of types of violence, included both female and male victims, and did not refer to Islam as its underpinning. This aligned the definition with comments made by various MPs during previous parliamentary debates, for example the debate on 10 February 2005. During this debate Albayrak had stated, "The best definition of *eerwraak* [is] culture-related violence (…), as *eerwraak* is not limited to murder alone. It also includes abuse and confinement, while moreover men may just as easily become victims" (House of Representatives 28 345 and 29 203, no. 38:3). Azough stated that "it is unfortunately a widespread phenomenon that is not limited to countries and cultures where Islam dominates" (House of Representatives 28 345 and 29 203, no. 38:6).

Nonetheless, while many MPs referred to honour killings as culture-linked violence, the definition does not make any mention of the word "culture". Moreover, as Albayrak remarked, the new definition was in fact more limited in scope. During the parliamentary debate on 29 June 2005 she stated that firstly focusing on the collective aspect of this type of violence and secondly adding the sentence "where the outside world is or might become aware of the breach" now made it more difficult to prove this type of violence (House of Representatives 28 345 and 29 203, no. 40:3).

In his response, Minister of Justice Donner explained that the new definition was not a "precise criminal-law definition". Moreover, he explained why he was not in favour of such a criminal-law definition: "In practice, the problem would to a certain extent be swept under the rug again: asserting, proving and convicting for honour-related violence would be possible in significantly fewer cases than occur in practice" (House of Representatives 28 345 and 29 203, no. 40:11).

Besides the definition, the results of the case study – particularly the conclusion that the Dutch approach lacked "administrative control" – led to some critical questions. Two MPs remained particularly critical about the government's course of action. During the second part of the parliamentary debate Hirsi Ali (VVD) and Albayrak (PvdA) jointly proposed to assign honour-related violence *"priority project status"*. This was a bold step, since priority project status had previously never been given to this type of issue. In her contribution Albayrak explained this step as follows:

> Nevertheless, a risk remains that the right things are not being done and that matters are not moving fast enough. Changes in behaviour are needed. Conceiving a set of instruments is one thing, but it is primarily a matter of authority, trust and how to bring about a change in mentality. The Cabinet rules and the House oversees, yet on this issue it is not enough to simply exercise the House's standard duties of oversight. Too much is at stake, too much is happening. The VVD and PvdA parties therefore wish to ask the House to designate everything concerning honour-related violence as a priority project. This will allow matters such as *eerwraak*, wife abandonment, child abduction and repudiation to be dealt with as a whole. The more intensive reporting will enable the House to ensure both this connection and the implementation of the measures in the constituent areas of registration, protection, investigation, prosecution and trial. The House may not run the risk that years later all the money and energy that has been put into it proves to have not yielded a solution. (House of Representatives 28 345 and 29 203, no. 40:12).

With this step Albayrak and Hirsi Ali brought a powerful instrument to bear. Their intention was to ensure that related problems such as honour killings, wife abandonment, child abduction and repudiation were tackled in conjunction. They also wished to make certain that the government would maintain its focus on honour-related violence and keep parliament properly informed about its actions.

Assigning a policy issue this priority project status requires support from other MPs. Moreover, priority project status may only be assigned to a policy issue if the Committee on Government Spending expresses a favourable opinion. However, the initial responses during the debate were not encouraging. MPs representing the coalition parties in particular were taken by surprise by this step. For instance, Van der Laan (D66) stated,

> seeking major problem status [is] not nothing (..). The ministers have to make additional reports. This takes time that cannot be spent attempting to actually resolve the

problem. It is also surprising that Ms Hirsi Ali first expresses her confidence in the government, and then presents a motion, together with Ms Albayrak, that nevertheless involves extraordinarily strict oversight of the ministers. (House of Representatives 28 345 and 29 203, no. 40: 13).

Sterk (CDA) supported this by arguing that the victims of honour killings did not need more paperwork. She added that the available manpower and resources should rather be spent on actually combatting honour crimes (House of Representatives 28 345 and 29 203, no. 40:13).

Nonetheless, in November 2005 the Committee on Government Spending advised in favour of assigning priority project status to honour-related violence (House of Representatives 30 388, no. 1). When the MPs were subsequently asked to vote on the matter, the majority did indeed vote in favour, including VVD and D66 (House of Representatives 30-2064, 6 December 2005). The Cabinet was then left with no other option than to develop a special infrastructure for honour-related violence, something which it had previously explicitly advised against.

The MP-Cabinet interactions observed here show that the government's strategy to first acquire a better understanding of the nature and extent of the problem worked to a degree. Despite the initial frustration among MPs about the government's lack of urgency in developing adequate measures, they were satisfied with the results of the studies and the pilot. However, in contrast to the government's appreciation of the results, parliament felt that those results gave reason to set up a specific infrastructure to tackle honour-related violence. As such, the priority project status was another step in framing honour-related violence as a distinct social problem, in need of its own problem solution.

8.5 Questioning the priority project's adequacy

> Today we are talking about the Honour-Related Violence priority project that was supposed to be launched today. Of course you are entirely free to organize your input as you see fit, but a priority project is subject to various formal requirements that must be satisfied. I believe that we should consider carefully whether we should continue with its launch, and if so how. (House of Representatives 30 388, no.4:1).

These words from the Chairwoman of the House set the tone for the parliamentary debate that followed the letter outlining the priority project: she openly questioned the attribution of the priority project status. This was in fact the central point of discussion in the fourth cluster of MP-Cabinet interactions.

In March 2006 Minister Verdonk sent a letter to parliament in which she presented the general outline of the honour-related violence project (House of Representatives 30 388, no.3). That letter focused on three elements.

Firstly, it focused on the project's organizational structure: besides setting up a programme office and an interministerial steering group, a panel of experts would be formed to help with the project.

Secondly, she explained to parliament how she planned to present the information about the project's progress. On the subject of financial data she informed parliament that it would be impossible to present a coherent overview, for a variety of reasons. One of those reasons was that organizations such as the police would be required to set up alternative budget statements, as their current statements did not include specific information on activities connected to honour-related violence. Most crucially, however, Verdonk informed parliament that the scope of any priority project was limited to activities falling under the direct responsibility of the central government. This meant that activities that were undertaken by municipal authorities or women's shelter organizations, for instance, fell beyond the scope of the project.

Lastly, she informed parliament about three subprojects that she wished to develop: a project entitled "social prevention", which focused on bringing about a change in mentality within migrant communities, a project aimed at protecting potential victims and a project that focused on the criminal prosecution aspects.

In contrast to previous letters, this was somewhat procedural in nature, focusing on the technicalities of priority projects. This came as a disappointment to some MPs. During the subsequent debate Khadija Arib (PvdA)[92], for instance, stated that she was disappointed with the letter's content, as it completely lost sight of the victims:

> When I was reading the documents I almost lost track. It seems as if the priority project has become a goal in and of itself. A priority project is a means, not an end. In all those papers that the minister sent to the House on the subject the problem that actually matters has become more or less invisible. The women about whom this matter ultimately revolves, the women who are unable to arrange their own protection, have been lost from sight. And it is not only women that this concerns, but also men. (…) The group about whom this matter ultimately revolves have become invisible. (House of Representatives 30 388, no. 4: 2-3).

Arib's statement triggered some critical responses from other MPs. Sterk (CDA), for example, commented that this was the result of PvdA's wish to grant honour-related violence priority project status. She subsequently challenged Arib to put forward an alternative.

This interaction is illustrative of the substance of this debate: MPs started challenging each other, rather than the minister, about a proper solution to the problem. Following further critical comments about the usefulness of the priority

---

92. Arib had replaced Albayrak as spokesperson for the PvdA.

project instrument, Hirsi Ali launched a passionate defence of its added value. She explained,

> When I was introduced to the House, I was told that a priority project is a thing that the government fears greatly. It is starting to work, that fear of the priority project. Setting up the priority project has already resulted in a steering committee with a procurator general, chaired by none less than the director general of law enforcement. This means that the fear of the priority project is starting to have effect on the government. I still refuse to abandon that status, as those strict protocols are necessary. (…) If we want to compel the Cabinet to provide information about its policy, we will have to use every means at our disposal. All the motions that we have presented to date have been left unimplemented, or only partly. Now we see how fast this priority project is working. Therefore, I would like to urge my colleagues to support it after all. (House of Representatives 30 388, no. 4:9)

This quote illustrates Hirsi Ali's informed choice of using the priority project instrument to steer the government in a particular direction. It demonstrates her satisfaction with its effect so far.

Nevertheless, when at the end of that same debate Minister Verdonk offered to put forward an alternative that properly reflected the objectives of the priority project but did not have the same practical drawbacks, all MPs – including Hirsi Ali – agreed that this would be a good idea. The debate therefore ended with Verdonk's promise to quickly present an alternative solution for tackling honour-related violence. This solution in presented in the next section.

8.6 Presenting the interministerial programme

The fifth cluster of MP-Cabinet interactions on the issue of honour-related violence consists chiefly of an extensive letter from the Minister of Alien Affairs and Integration in May 2006. In her letter Verdonk presented the interministerial programme on honour-related violence as an alternative to the priority project (House of Representatives 30 388, no. 6). The subsequent parliamentary debate led to a unanimous decision to end the priority project on honour-related violence.

In her letter Verdonk presented what she called a *"programme-based approach"* to honour-related violence. The aim of the programme was to obtain a better understanding of the problem of honour-related violence and to intensify the government's approach (House of Representatives 30 3888, no. 6:3). The programme was developed around the idea that policy should be built on a solid *knowledge base*. This meant that more information was needed about, for instance, what behaviours could be defined as honour-related violence and what instruments could be used to prevent honour-related violence. According to Verdonk, the definition developed by Ferwerda and Van Leiden (2005) would always function as the point of departure for answering these and other questions. This confirmed the central role of this definition within the programme and thus within the Dutch HRV field.

A second key element of the programme was to advance the *collaborative efforts* between the relevant local and national actors, for example the police and women's shelters, but also between schools, youth protection organizations, social workers and migrant organizations. The programme would encompass various initiatives to enhance these efforts, for example developing a protocol. Moreover, as municipal authorities were responsible for monitoring the administrative aspects of safety issues, the programme would also help them to develop of a reliable knowledge base and local infrastructure to encourage and facilitate the necessary coordination. Rotterdam was selected to function as a pilot, while two other municipalities would be encouraged to develop similar pilots (House of Representatives 30 388, no. 6:6-7).

The three subprojects that had been part of the priority project – the prevention, protection and prosecution projects – were also incorporated into this programme. For the *social prevention project* Minister Verdonk gave particular focus to the role of migrant organizations. She felt that those organizations could function as intermediaries between migrant communities and the administration. She therefore hoped to encourage the umbrella organizations for migrant organizations to develop a long-term programme to bring about a change in mentality within migrant communities.

Minister Verdonk's letter also directed attention to the crucial role that schools could play in identifying and discussing honour-related violence. She addressed two existing initiatives in particular: *Verdwaalde gezichten* ("lost faces"), an organization that encouraged discussion about the issue of honour-related violence in the classroom, and theatre group *DOX*, which used a play to trigger discussions about this type of violence at schools. In addition Verdonk planned to launch a *school pilot*, aimed at acquiring further information about the nature of honour-related violence and how schools could contribute to identifying this type of violence at an early stage.

For the *protection project*, Verdonk indicated that the interministerial programme would build on existing domestic violence initiatives such as the *Drempels weg* ("removing thresholds") project, which aimed to enhance the safety and accessibility of shelters. Moreover, the programme would also include a study into the necessity of additional refuges and the need for a shelter for minors. Verdonk also promised that victims lacking official resident status would not be barred from help from the shelters. To this end, the Immigration Service appointed several of its people to provide women's shelter organizations and other organizations with the necessary information.

Lastly, for the *prosecution project* she underlined the success of the police pilot in the The Hague region, and promised that the registration method developed would be rolled out on the national level. Moreover, she repeated her promise to develop an instruction about honour-related violence for the Public Prosecution Service.

Verdonk ended her letter with an explanation of how she hoped to inform parliament about the programme's progress. These progress reports would revolve chiefly around an *integrated approach* to honour-related violence. As a result, the focus would not be on state policy alone, but also on the local initiatives. As such, the programme offered a broader approach to honour-related violence than the priority project approach had.

This summary of the highlights of Minister Verdonk's letter illustrates the consequences of this "integrated approach": the interministerial programme now covered a wide range of different initiatives, measures, policies and organizations.

During the parliamentary debate that followed this letter, Verdonk was lauded for this new approach. Various MPs also explicitly acknowledged that the priority project status was not the appropriate instrument for tackling honour-related violence. Ursie Lambrechts (D66), for instance, announced that honour-related violence failed to meet the standard for a priority project (House of Representatives 30 388, no. 7:2). Arib (PvdA) also admitted that the status of priority project was not necessary to guarantee the victims' safety. However, while she supported the minister's course of action, she challenged her to put forward more concrete measures in her next report (House of Representatives 30 388, no. 7:2). Sterk (CDA) also supported the idea of an interministerial programme, underlining the need to involve all the relevant organizations, particularly minority organizations. She too challenged the minister to present more tangible measures in the short term (House of Representatives 30 388, no. 7:3).

Despite some critical comments, therefore, all the MPs agreed that ending the priority project on honour-related violence was the appropriate step. Nevertheless, this does not imply that Albayrak and Hirsi Ali had failed in their attempt to convince the government to take more action. On the contrary: while they may not have succeeded in maintaining the priority project status, their initiative led to the development of a distinct interministerial programme[93]. Moreover, as is explained in the chapters that follow, the government's integral approach to honour-related violence strongly contributed to the development of the Dutch HRV field, as did the government's annual contribution of €2.6 million to this programme (House of Representatives 3- 388, no.9:7).

---

93. Neither Hirsi Ali nor Albayrak spoke on behalf of their parties during this final debate. Albayrak had been replaced by Arib and Hirsi Ali by Frans Weekers. One can only wonder what might have happened if they had both been present at the time.

8.7 How these state practices contributed to the emergence of a Dutch HRV field

The question of how the state practices described contributed to the emergence of a Dutch HRV field can only be answered properly after the following chapters. Only then is it possible to assess whether the state was indeed able to impose its organizational and mental structures on the emerging field. Nevertheless, the analysis above already sheds light on how the problem of honour-related violence became "officialized" by the state.

According to Bourdieu social problems are issues that at a certain point are perceived as being worthy of being debated, both by society at large and by the state. Bourdieu then goes on to describe states as "great producers of 'social problems'", which they create by officializing them, legitimizing them. (Bourdieu and Wacquant 1992:236, Bourdieu et al. 1994:2). The development of both the working definition and the interministerial programme should be seen in that light. Together they contributed to the construction of honour-related violence as a social problem, classified as being distinct from domestic violence.

As such, both these actions also functioned as a critical precondition for the emergence of the HRV field: a state will only allocate funds to tackle a problem if it is perceived as a legitimate problem. Moreover, both the legitimization of the problem and the allocation of funds will boost other actors' interest in the problem, which in turn might cause the emerging HRV field to expand. In the following chapters I provide further substantiation for this proposition.

In his work, Bourdieu also points out the crucial role of social scientists in the construction of social problems (Bourdieu et al. 19994:2). This case study illustrates that the Dutch state did indeed use two independent research groups, COT and Bureau Beke, to ratify honour-related violence as a distinct social problem. The first research group conducted a case study of twenty cases of honour-related violence and the second developed a definition of the problem. In this manner both research groups had a significant impact on the emerging HRV field – the latter by introducing a definition of honour-related violence that opened up the HRV field to other actors and the former by pinpointing some of the current bottlenecks in the cooperation between organizations dealing with honour-related violence. These bottlenecks were subsequently tackled by the interministerial programme, which strongly influenced the emerging field configurations.

This case study therefore also illustrates how much influence research groups and scholars can have on the emerging configurations of an organizational fields. The access that scholars have to informational capital would later also place them in a position of power within the emerging HRV field. This is addressed at greater length in Chapter 9; here, it is sufficient to note that the experts' key position within the emerging HRV field and the field's preference for academic knowledge over migrants' knowledge can be traced back to the early beginnings of the field's development, i.e. to the moment that the state made its first efforts to officialize honour-related violence as a distinct social problem. [94]

Finally, Bourdieu also finds that the construction of social problems is often accompanied by considerable struggles (Bourdieu et al. 1994:1). The debates described illustrate that this was also the case with the problem of honour-related violence. In the following section I explain this point further by analysing the power dynamics within the Dutch political field. I also summarize the final outcome of the analysed debates, making it possible to subsequently assess the state's power to define the configurations of the Dutch HRV field. Lastly, I describe the relationship between the political field and other fields.

Power dynamics within the political field

As explained at the start of this chapter, the political field is a highly structured field. For instance, the positions of the MPs and the Members of Cabinet within this field are clearly defined. Moreover, the interactions between these actors follow strict rules, for example with regard to speaking time during parliamentary debates. The instruments available to MPs are also clear-cut. Nevertheless, something new occurred during the observed struggles: priority project status was attributed to an *issue*. This was a new development, this status previously having only given to infrastructural projects.

During the first debates MPs sought to promote certain solutions to the problem by filing motions. However, when those motions did not yield the expected success, a more powerful tool was brought into play: priority project status. In response to the MPs' actions, the government initially attempted to push back by using a tested method: commissioning a series of studies and a pilot. Nonetheless, when priority project status was attributed to honour-related violence, this left the government with little room to manoeuvre. Yet by elaborating on the limitations of the priority project status, the government was able to push back successfully, causing the priority project status to be lifted. Nonetheless, the temporary attribution of this status was one of the factors behind the development of a large-scale interministerial programme to combat honour-related violence.

What then prompted this new course of action within this highly structured field? In part, it may be explained by the inexperience of Hirsi Ali, one of the MPs proposing the use of this instrument. In her contribution she explicitly referred to her introduction to the House of Representatives: "When I was introduced to the House, I was told that a priority project is a thing that the govern-

---

94. As such, the present case study substantiates Bourdieu's et al. (1994) proposition that scholars sometimes do "little more than ratify" the sociological problems presented to them by the state. By tracing the origins of honour-related violence as a distinct social problem, I hope to have escaped this fallacy. See Chapter 3 for more information on my own position as a scholar within the HRV field.

ment fears greatly." Her inexperience perhaps contributed to the fact that she did not comply fully with the *rules* of this field, given that priority project status, although a formal instrument, was generally not assigned to issues.

In addition, the instrument's use illustrates the growing understanding that an integrated plan of action was needed to properly tackle honour-related violence. While the motions asked for an array of separate measures, varying from refuges to subsidies for migrant organizations, the priority project status called for a more integrated approach. Likewise, it was the understanding that a more integrated approach was needed that led to the priority project being replaced by an interministerial programme.

Finally, the use of this instrument also underlines the sense of urgency that MPs felt with regard to tackling honour-related violence. Confronted with a moral panic about honour killing, various MPs felt compelled to reach for extraordinary measures, in this case the application of priority project status to an issue.

The foregoing analysis highlights how Bourdieu's theory of practice can help to make sense of field activity. Like Bourdieu (1977) I see an actor's action as the result of a combination of factors: the situation confronting the actor, his historically developed dispositions (i.e. habitus), his position within a certain field (i.e. his capital) and the field's logic (See Figure 1, Chapter 2.). In this case, the utilization of the priority project status is the result of 1.) an MP's habitus which was not yet fully aligned with the political field's logic, 2.) the political field's logic in which MPs can make use of powerful instruments, and 3.) being confronted with a new situation, namely a moral panic about a new and unusual type of violence.

The results of the political debates

As becomes apparent in the following chapters, what happened within the political field impacted the emerging configurations of the Dutch HRV field. A number of factors come into play here: the development of the definition of honour-related violence, the proposed solution to the problem, the actors accredited with roles in tackling honour-related violence and the state's financial contribution.

Firstly, the foregoing analysis highlights how the state purposefully developed a new definition of honour-related violence. This definition not only encompassed other types of violence next to honour killings, it also set honour-related violence apart from domestic violence. The state actively contributed to the classification of honour-related violence as a distinct social problem and demarcated it from domestic violence. With this in mind, Chapter 10 explores whether other actors within the emerging HRV field in fact subscribed to this definition. In the words of Bourdieu, I will investigate the emergence of theoretical unification within the HRV field (Bourdieu et al. 1994).

Secondly, the debates resulted in the development of an interministerial programme to combat honour-related violence. That programme consisted of various distinctive elements: 1.) an *integrated approach* to the problem, 2.) a focus on developing a reliable *knowledge base*, 3.) a focus on *collaborative effort* and 4.) a focus on three particular domains: *prevention, protection* and *prosecution*. In the following chapters I explore whether those elements can be identified within the emerging configurations of the Dutch HRV field.

Lastly, during the analysed debates various organizations came to the fore as key actors. The following organizations were deemed particularly crucial to tackling honour-related violence: the police (the Multi-Ethnic Policing ("MEP") Unit in particular), women's shelters (FO in particular), the Public Prosecution Service, schools, municipal authorities and migrant organizations. In part, their key roles can be related to elements of the honour-related violence programme. For instance, migrant organizations were perceived as actors that could help bring about a change in mentality within their communities. In the following I therefore explore whether the organizations that were perceived as key actors within the political field did in fact come to occupy key positions within the emerging HRV field. Exploring the positioning of the various actors makes it possible to assess whether the state was indeed able to define the *field of power* within the Dutch HRV field.

How the political field relates to other fields

Part II described how the issue of honour-related violence emerged within the media field. Four *unplanned* field-configuring events occurred that were crucial to the issue's emergence within the media field: the murders and attempted murders of Kezban, Hassan, Zarife and Gül. In a similar vein, the parliamentary debates may be seen planned field-configuring events within the political field. Yet their contributions are very different. While the murders strongly contributed to the *issue's emergence* in the public discourse, the debates helped to *officialize* honour-related violence as a distinct social problem. As such, the debates that took place within the political field may be viewed as a new step in the emergence of the Dutch HRV field.

However, the debates and the moral panic that emerged within the media field also influenced the debates that subsequently developed within the political field. The analysis of the parliamentary debates brings to the fore that MPs regularly referred to the murders of Kezban, Zarife and Gül to motivate their actions. For instance, Albayrak made explicit reference to the murders before proposing various motions (Albayrak, House of Representatives 49-3170, 10 February 2005:1). As elected representatives the MPs' habitus is directed towards dealing with the issues that concern their society. They subsequently picked up on the moral panic that developed within the media field in connection with the issue of honour killings and transferred that issue to the political field, resulting in extraordinary measures against this type of violence.

Besides the media field, the political field is also *influenced by* and *of influence on* the macro-cultural discourses presented in Chapter 6. Both Bourdieu and scholars working on the concept of moral panic address how the emergence of a social problem and/or a moral panic is connected to the spirit of that time. Using the analysis presented in Chapter 6, this *Zeitgeist* can be summarized as follows: it is an era in which the intertwinement between gender issues and multicultural discourses led to disenchantment with the multicultural ideal, which in turn made it possible to criticize culture-linked forms of violence. In addition, evolving discourses about nationalism, citizenship and social cohesion created a climate in which such criticism was welcomed as a means to enforce moral boundaries between what is Dutch and what should not become Dutch.

By officializing honour-related violence as a distinct social problem, the state also contributed to these boundary-drawing processes. The parliamentary debates described in this chapter show that both MPs and ministers drew a boundary between migrants' types of violence (e.g. honour-related violence) and Dutch types of violence (e.g. domestic violence). As a consequence, honour-related violence was framed as an integration issue rather than as a domestic violence issue. This also meant that honour-related violence became a factor that migrants needed to overcome in order to "become" Dutch. This line of reasoning is explicitly visible in Hirsi Ali's contributions, for instance where she claims that culture-linked violence is the largest obstacle to the integration of migrant women (House of Representatives 29 203, no. 9:2).

Concluding remarks

The foregoing illustrates how the debates within one field might have consequences for what occurs in other fields. In this case the moral panic that emerged within the media field led to heightened activity about the issue of honour-related violence within the political field and to the extraordinary measures used to combat it. This heightened activity within the political field in turn facilitated the emergence of a new issue-based field, as it resulted in the classification of honour-related violence as a distinct social problem.

It also illustrates the interaction between the occurrences in the political field and changes in the dominant macro-cultural discourses. The existing macro-cultural discourses on nationalism, citizenship and social cohesion prompted the definition of honour-related violence as a distinct social problem, while the decision to define honour-related violence as a distinct social problem in turn reaffirmed the existing boundary-drawing processes.

Lastly, the preceding analysis confirms Bourdieu's claim that the study of the *genesis of social problems* can bring back into view "the discarded possibilities, it retrieves the possibility that things could have been (and still van be) otherwise" (Bourdieu et al. 1994:4). In this case, the analysis reveals that honour-related violence could have been framed as a form of domestic violence and the problem might then have been tackled using existing organizational structures rather than through the development of a new issue-based field. Yet the spirit of the time and two persistent MPs motivated the state to define honour-related violence as a distinct social problem, one that needed its own solution.

9. Key actors and their capital

One of the dichotomies that Bourdieu seeks to break by means of his *theory of practice* is the micro-macro dichotomy (Bourdieu 1977). He does so by offering a theoretical framework – habitus, field and capital – that combines multiple levels of analyses. Moreover, his work illustrates how occurrences at the micro level impact the macro level and vice versa.

In this thesis I do the same, for instance by illustrating how changes in the macro-cultural discourses on multiculturalism and gender equality created the critical preconditions for the emergence of the issue of honour-related violence within the media field (see Part II). In this chapter I again change the level of analysis, from the micro level of the political field (Chapter 8) to the meso level of the HRV field. As a consequence, in the present chapter *actors* denote not individual persons, but a particular type of sector, for example, the educational sector, the media or the state.

Each of these actors in turn could be studied as a field in its own right: a field that consists of a large group of organizations. However, the scope of this research does not allow for a thorough investigation of each of the organizations that together comprise actors within the HRV field. Nevertheless, in this chapter I consider some of the individual organizations that represent these actors as a means of illustrating what type of organizations together form a single actor within the HRV field.

In the following I first describe what actors could be denoted as key actors within the emerging HRV field. In Chapter 10 I compare the formal definition of honour-related violence with the *definitions-in-use* within the HRV field. Lastly, Chapter 11 describes how the actors were positioned in respect of each other within this emerging field. This reveals the emerging field configurations of the Dutch HRV field, i.e. the relevant types of capital, the field's emerging doxa and the field's emerging structures.

It is important to bear in mind that these chapters present a "snap shot" of the Dutch HRV field. This chapter therefore describes which actors were the most visible at that particular moment in time and how they, at that time, defined the problem. Obviously, since then the field has developed and possibly collapsed again[95].

---

95. In his work on issue-based fields, Hoffman (1999:352) directs attention to the fact that these fields might not be in use all the time, as their lifespans might coincide with the issue's attention cycle.

Moreover, the following is not meant as an evaluation of the interministerial programme against honour-related violence, which only ended in 2010. Nevertheless, this chapter carries elements of an evaluation, since it is the aim of this chapter to "evaluate" how the described micro dynamics within the media and political fields contributed to the emerging field configurations. Moreover, by using Bourdieu's triad of habitus, field and capital to describe these field configurations I "evaluate" whether his work does indeed offer institutional theory an adequate *theory of action*.

9.1 Key actors and their roles within the emerging HRV field

Based on the results of the study that was conducted in 2007-2008, a number of actors can be denoted as "*key actors*" within the emerging HRV field: the police, women's shelters, municipal authorities, Support Centres for Domestic Violence, the Youth Care Agencies, the state, educational institutions, migrant organizations, citizens' initiatives, the media and the "subject-matter experts". These actors are denoted as key actors based on the number of mentions that they received as relevant partners by interviewees and in policy documents and other documentation. Moreover, these are the actors that organized and/or were present at meetings on the issue of honour-related violence.

In addition, the research results indicated that these actors acquired their prominent position by combining multiple *roles* that are perceived as crucial within the emerging HRV field, for example the expert role or the financier role. Notably, these roles also offer information about the *types of capital* that were deemed to be valuable within the emerging HRV field. In this section I therefore further elaborate on who could be denoted as key actors and on what grounds they gained that position.

The following "*roles*" came to the fore as key roles within the emerging Dutch HRV field: 1) the "agenda-setter role", 2) the "expert role", 3) the "bridge-building role", 4) the "financier role" and 5) the "regular-function role".

The *agenda-setter role* is fulfilled by actors who continuously demand attention for the issue of honour-related violence. This role is both claimed by and attributed to actors such as politicians, the media, citizens' initiatives, migrant organizations and women's shelters.

The *expert* role was ascribed to and/or claimed by various actors within the HRV field. Practitioners such as the police, for instance, claim this role on the basis of their "*practical experience*", gained through their day-to-day dealings with victims. Others claim this role on the basis of their "*member experience*", gained as members of a migrant community. In general, however, this role is attributed to scholars who have conducted research into what is often described as a "complex" phenomenon of honour-related violence. Within the HRV field these experts are termed *materiedeskundigen,* which can be translated as "subject-matter experts".

The *bridge-builder role* is primarily attributed to and claimed by migrant organizations. They are regarded as a bridge between the policies developed and the migrant communities. The Support Centres for Domestic Violence (*Advies en Steunpunten Huiselijk Geweld,* or "ASHGs") and the Youth Care Agencies (*Bureaus Jeugdzorg*) also fulfil a bridging role, albeit a different one: they function as intermediaries between victims and the organizations providing assistance.

The *financier role* was also found to be significant within the field of honour-related violence. The role of financier may be fulfilled by the central government (ministries), the interministerial programme to combat honour-related violence and municipal authorities.

The *regular-function role*, lastly, refers to the roles that actors fulfil based on their regular tasks, such as the powers of investigation that the police have and the assistance that is provided by women's shelters. Consequently these are tasks that these actors also fulfil in other fields. Crucially, however, this involves tasks that are deemed to be of particular relevance by other actors in the battle against honour-related violence. The table below summarizes the key actors and their roles.

Table 4. Key actors and their roles

	Agenda setter	Expert	Bridge builder	Financier	Regular function
Police	(X)	X			X
Women's shelters	(X)	(X)			X
Municipal authorities		(X)		X	X
Support Centres for Domestic Violence			X		X
Youth Care Agencies			X		X
State	X			X	X
Education sector		(X)	X		
Migrant organizations	X	X	X		
Media	X	X			X
Subject-matter experts	X	X			X
Citizens' initiatives	X	X			

Notably, in practice the roles identified are not always fulfilled by an actor. Some actors are given a key position by other actors even though they do not, or at least not yet, fulfil that role. In contrast, some actors also claim a particular role as their own while other actors do not acknowledge that role. Moreover, it is possible that a particular role is fulfilled only by a small number of representatives of an actor (in the table above this is denoted by a bracketed "X"). For instance, not all schools functioned as experts within the emerging HRV field. However, the schools that were part of a specific honour-related violence pilot did in fact fulfil this function. The same holds true for the Multi-Ethnic Policing ("MEP") Unit of the police, the Rotterdam municipal authorities and *Federatie Opvang* (FO).

Furthermore, some actors appear to be missing from this table, including the Public Prosecution Service, social workers in general, the Child Care and Protection Board (*Raad voor de Kinderbescherming*), after-care services, provincial authorities etc. Although all these actors were mentioned by interviewees or in policy documents as partners in collaborative efforts, further analysis shows that they occupied less central positions within the field of honour-related violence at that moment in time. While these actors encounter honour-related violence in their regular work, they neither fulfilled nor were ascribed roles that marked them as key actors. They were not bridge builders such as the Support Centres for Domestic Violence and the Youth Care Agencies, nor were they perceived to be relevant financiers in the way that municipal authorities and ministries were. Moreover, they were not regarded as agenda setters and had not developed into experts within the field of honour-related violence. For purposes of this study, I therefore focus on those actors that can be denoted as key actors, given that their key positions provide information about the types of capital that were deemed to be of particular relevance within the emerging HRV field.

The foregoing illustrates that the configurations of the Dutch HRV field were indeed emerging by 2007-2008. Based on the interviews conducted, the policy documents and other documentation and the observations performed, it is possible to determine who were the most prominent actors at that time and on what grounds they obtained their key positions. Nonetheless, the above also illustrates that the field was still under construction. Some actors claimed roles that were not acknowledged by others, while other actors did not take on the roles that were attributed to them. Clearly, by 2007-2008 some struggles still remained in terms of the field's organizational structure. This point is discussed at greater length in the following sections, where I describe the various roles in more detail.

9.2 The agenda setters

The following actors were pinpointed by field representatives as having functioned as agenda setters within the HRV field: the police, women's shelters, the state, migrant organizations, the media, subject-matter experts and citizens' initiatives. For some of these actors, the agenda-setter role was part of their regular work: the media and politicians, for example. For others, this was a role that they assumed within this specific field: *Federatie Opvang* (FO), the police's MEP Unit and certain citizens' initiatives such as the *Kezban Foundation* and *Verdwaalde Gezichten*.

Interestingly, some of the actors that functioned as agenda setters within the media field and/or within the political field were also named as agenda setters in the 2007-2008 study. By sounding the alarm after Gül's murder, for instance, women's shelters functioned as *key instigators* of the media's attention for honour killings. Later, the umbrella organization for women's shelters FO sounded the alarm about the safety of a hundred women in their shelters, triggering an emergency debate in the House of Representatives. By 2007-2008 they were still agenda setters, this time by demanding the development of specialized shelters for minors. Two pilot projects were subsequently set up in Friesland and Tilburg to provide assistance to underage victims of honour-related violence.

Another interesting example is the *Kezban Foundation,* a citizens' initiative set up by Nurdan Cakiroglu[96]. Within the media field Nurdan Cakiroglu functioned as a key instigator of the media's attention for honour killings after her friend's murder in 1999. In 2007-2008 her foundation was still active, having set itself the following goal:

> The Kezban Foundation seeks to bring about discussions about violence within non-native circles by providing information; increasing accessibility to and the vigilance of care services for foreign women; being alert to policy implemented by the government for domestic violence; and championing the interests of migrant women and girls. (Stichting Kezban 2008: website)

By 2008 the *Kezban Foundation* had extended its focus from sounding the alarm on the issue of honour killings to functioning as an expert within the HRV field.

Some migrant organizations, and most notably various umbrella organizations for migrant organizations, also explicitly laid claim to the role of actors putting honour-related violence on the political and public agenda. However, they did not feel acknowledged in this role: in the public debates political actors, for example Minister Verdonk and MPs Hirsi Ali and Albayrak, were often quoted as the agenda setters. Moreover, migrant organizations felt misrepresented as only acting against honour-related violence when forced to do so by the state. In contrast, migrant organizations saw themselves as "problem owners" who had actively voiced their concerns about honour-related violence long before the political attention first began in 2005[97].

The misrecognition of migrant organizations as agenda setters is illustrative of one of the key struggles within the emerging HRV field: the position of migrants and migrant organizations within this field. Migrant organizations wished to be

---

96. See Chapter 5 for more information about Kezban's murder and the role that Nurdan Cakiroglu played as agenda setter for honour killings within the media field.

97. Their claim is substantiated by the results of the media analysis presented in Chapter 5.

accepted as full and equal partners in combatting honour-related violence. Other actors, however, only acknowledged their role as mentality changers.

Clearly, the role of agenda setter is crucial for emerging issue-based fields such as the HRV field. Without people and/or organizations to sound the alarm about a particular issue, it is impossible for an issue-based field to emerge. The above also illustrates that actors that sound the alarm within the media field and/or the political field often later become key actors within the issue-based field that subsequently emerges. In this case this holds true for actors such as women's shelters, the police (particularly the MEP Unit), migrant organizations and their umbrellas and citizens' initiatives such as the *Kezban Foundation*. The positioning of actors within the emerging HRV field therefore also features a historical component.

9.3 The experts

A wide variety of actors claimed the role of expert within the emerging HRV field. This includes the police, women's shelters, municipal authorities, schools, migrant organizations, the media, subject-matter experts and citizens' initiatives. The expert role also generated a great deal of discussion about legitimate sources of knowledge and thus the relevant type of information capital. Three types of knowledge can be distinguished within the emerging field: *expert knowledge*, *practical knowledge* and *member knowledge*.

Within the emerging HRV field the role of expert is ascribed principally to *subject-matter experts*. The term "subject-matter expert" refers to both individual actors such as scholars[98] as well as the many knowledge and advisory organizations active within the HRV field[99]. At some point during the conversations, almost every interviewee referred to people or organizations that they believed possessed a great deal of expert knowledge about this topic. The following quote is illustrative of how interviewees referred to the expertise of these subject-matter experts:

> (…) [A]nyway, my knowledge is increasing by the day (…) though I really don't want to say that I'm an expert in the field of honour-related violence. I was hired as a project leader to set up the information point, to ensure that the right knowledge and skills are obtained but I am not an expert on the Arab world or the Turks or a Middle East specialist, you know. (Project leader at a women's shelter)

---

98. Names that are mentioned include Ane Nauta, Rob Ermers, Clementine van Eck, Ibrahim Yerden, Erdal Gezik, Janine Janssen and Renate van der Zee.
99. This involves organizations such as MOVISIE, TransAct, COT, Beke Advice and Support Group, FORUM, Inflecto and the Verwey Jonker Institute.

However, some interviewees also challenged this key position of the subject-matter experts. The following quote from a representative of a migrant organization exemplifies the criticism:

> It [honour-related violence] is clearly surrounded by a hype and then you see all the experts suddenly appear. I don't think I'm an expert, there are no experts; the only experts are the people themselves. They can tell you something about the subject themselves (…)

According to this interviewee the real experts were the members of the communities involved, being the ones with member knowledge of the problem. The distinction between expert knowledge and member knowledge is another example of the struggle that migrant organizations faced in obtaining a key position within the emerging HRV field.

Within the emerging HRV field other actors claimed the expert role based on their practical knowledge. These were typically actors that took part in one of the *pilots* that were set up within the framework of the honour-related violence programme. A particular case in point is the *Multi-Ethnic Policing* (MEP) Unit. This unit took part in the pilot study that was commissioned by Minister Verdonk in response to a motion filed by MP Hirsi Ali (House of Representatives 29 203, no. 15). During the parliamentary debates that followed MPs regularly referred to the MEP Unit as a crucial actor in the fight against honour-related violence.

By 2008 the MEP Unit was functioning as the back office for all Dutch police regions. It therefore changed its name to "National Expertise Centre on honour-related violence" *(Landelijk Expertise Centrum eergeraleteerd geweld*, or "LEC" for short). Moreover, the results of the 2007-2008 study indicated that for many interviewees, including non-police, the LEC was the first point of contact for questions regarding honour-related violence. The LEC's key position was also enhanced by its affiliation with some of the key subject-matter experts in the field, including Clementine van Eck and Rob Ermers.

The pilot "Honour-related violence in and around schools" was also set up within the framework of the interministerial programme. This pilot took place at two ROCs (regional training centres): *Albeda College* in Rotterdam and *ROC van Twente*. The latter was Zarife's old school in Almelo. Within the HRV field both the pilot schools and *Stichting Verdwaalde Gezichten* ("the Lost Faces Foundation, a citizens' initiative)[100] subsequently functioned as experts on the issue of honour-related violence within the educational sector.

---

100. Zarife's and Gül's murders inspired two Dutch-Turkish women to set up *Verdwaalde Gezichten*. The foundation's aim was to educate young people through a study curriculum called Black Tulip. In 2007 this educational programme was recognized by the Dutch Ministry of Education, Culture and Science through a "best practice award" and received additional funding to continue its work (*Verdwaalde Gezichten* 2010: website).

Nonetheless, in practice the media also functioned as an expert within the educational sector. Two Master's degree students demonstrated that the media was the primary source of information for both teachers and those providing assistance at a ROC and a university (Kiewit 2008, de Kruijff 2010). While the media's expert role in other fields was not studied, it is plausible that the media played a similar role there too.

Lastly, the pilot municipality of Rotterdam played an special role within the emerging HRV field; Rotterdam was perceived as the expert with regard to the *municipal approach* to fighting honour-related violence. Rotterdam devoted particular effort to developing an effective network of partnerships, using the Dutch term *"ketensamenwerking"*, between the organizations that were involved in helping victims of honour-related violence. The concept of *ketensamenwerking* was one of the main organizing principals within the emerging HRV field. It is discussed in further detail in Chapter 11.

This explanation of the "expert" role highlights a number of points. Firstly, knowledge was perceived as a valuable commodity within the HRV field. This is interesting given that the state's focus was also very much on building a solid *knowledge base*. The state's appreciation of knowledge seems to have transferred to the emerging HRV field's doxa. Subsequently, one of the key struggles within the emerging HRV field concerned debates about what type of informational capital represents the relevant type of knowledge: practical knowledge, member knowledge or scholarly knowledge.

These types of knowledge can be related to various species of informational capital that are distinguished by Bourdieu (Bourdieu and Wacquant 1992:119). Both member knowledge and practical knowledge pertain to *embodied informational capital*: knowledge which through processes of socialization is engraved on an actor's *habitus*. Scholarly knowledge, in addition, also refers to both *objectified informational capital* – the ability to use and develop books and instruments – and *institutionalized informational capital*, or the educational credentials that determine an actor's status. Chapter 10 further explores what type of informational capital most strongly informed the definitions-in-use within the emerging field.

The above also illustrates that being involved in a pilot initiated by the state can bring an actor into a position of power. By taking part in a pilot, actors develop a degree of expertise. In addition, it also contributes to the actor's visibility within the political field, which might subsequently lead MPs to actively support a specific actor, as was the case with the MEP Unit.

9.4 The bridge builders

Within the emerging HRV field the role of bridge builder was primarily claimed by and/or attributed to migrant organizations, Support Centres for Domestic Violence, Youth Care Agencies and schools. The bridge-builder role is substantiated in two ways. Some actors are expected to build a bridge between government policy and the "target demographic", i.e. the communities in which honour-related violence occurs. Most interviewees explicitly attributed this role to migrant organizations. At the same time, the role of bridge builder was also attributed to actors functioning as bridges between the victims of honour-related violence and the organizations providing assistance. This role was fulfilled by the Support Centres for Domestic Violence, the Youth Care Agencies and schools.

The Support Centres for Domestic Violence were regarded by many as fulfilling a *front office* function: victims of honour-related violence could go there for assistance, concerned neighbours could obtain information and other actors, such as schools and the police, could report their honour-related violence cases to these organizations. The fact that honour-related violence can also involve minors, both as primary victims and as the children of victims, contributed to the fact that both the Youth Care Agencies and schools were also perceived to be key actors within the field of honour-related violence.

However, despite being described by many field representatives as bridge builders, the Youth Care Agencies did not fulfil this role in practice. For instance, in 2007-2008 no policy documents were available in which the Youth Care Agencies presented a coherent course of action to combat honour-related violence. Moreover, in contrast to other fields, for example education or women's shelters, no pilots or conferences were organized that were aimed at enhancing the Agencies' knowledge of honour-related violence. This makes the Youth Care Agencies an interesting case within the emerging HRV field: they were the only actor to which a key position was ascribed by others but that did not then assume that position in practice.

In contrast, umbrella organizations for migrant organizations considered themselves to be official policy partners of the government. In 2006 their sense of problem ownership also led four of those umbrella organizations to write a letter to Minister Verdonk, offering their help in combatting honour-related violence. Within the framework of the social prevention project they developed a policy programme of their own, called "*On the right side of honour*". Through this programme migrant organizations sought to bring about a *double change of mentality* within their grassroots. On the one hand, they hoped to change the mentality that led to honour-related violence; on the other hand, they sought to change the negative attitude towards support agencies such as women's shelters.

To these umbrella organizations, being accepted as a policy partner was therefore an important point of dispute, as is illustrated by the following quote:

> We have pointed out: If you [the Honour-Related Violence Programme] hope to achieve something, if we hope to achieve something, then it [honour-related violence] must be seen as a problem for society at large. We must be seen as a full and equal partner: the migrant organizations are the problem owners.

This quote also illustrates the migrant organizations' awareness of their potential position of power. The state needed them to bridge the divide with migrant communities. It was this position of power that afforded migrant organizations the opportunity to claim a policy-partner position within the emerging HRV field.

The foregoing furthermore illustrates that social capital was perceived as a valuable type of capital within the emerging HRV field. Migrant organizations subsequently sought to capitalize on their strong position as bridge builders. However, the quote presented above illustrates that they did not feel that they were recognized as full and equal members of the HRV field. This point is addressed in Chapter 11, where I describe how the key actors were positioned in respect of each other.

In addition, this section demonstrates that a regular function, in this case functioning as a bridge between a victim and the organizations providing assistance, can turn actors into key actors if this function is perceived as particularly relevant within a specific field. This appears to have been the case with the Support Centres for Domestic Violence and the Youth Care Agencies.

Nevertheless, being credited with a key role does not mean that actors also fulfil this role in practice, as was the case with the Youth Care Agencies. Bourdieu's work explains this through the concept of *illusio*: actors will only become part of a field if their interest is aroused by the substance of that particular field and they are therefore willing to "play the game" of that particular field. Apparently the Youth Care Agencies' illusio was not (or not yet) triggered by the issue of honour-related violence. However, it remains unclear why.

9.5 The financiers

The 2007-2008 study revealed that many of the activities observed were made possible through government funding[101]. The sources of that funding varied from regular state funding to provincial funding and municipal funding. Many of the key actors within the HRV field were funded by these government institutions: the police, women's shelters, the educational sector, the Support Centres for Domestic Violence and the Youth Care Agencies. In addition, some projects were funded by the interministerial programme to combat honour-related violence, such as the school pilot. Other activities were made possible through supplementary state subsidies, such as the citizens' initiatives *Verwaalde gezichten* and *Kezban Foundation*[102].

---

101. I deliberately use the label "government funding" rather than "state funding". State funding refers to funding by the national government. Government funding, in contrast, refers to funding by any government institution, such as the national government and the provincial and municipal authorities.

102. This variety of different funding flows rendered it impossible to calculate the total amount of funding allocated to the HRV field.

This does not imply that the state was able to directly exert its power over the HRV field. In the Netherlands, many government-funded functions have been transferred to other government institutions such as municipal or provincial authorities. This process is generally referred to as "decentralization"[103]. In 2007-2008 this was the case with the police, for instance. As a consequence, the national government was obliged to make separate arrangements with each police region. Chapter 11 provides a further exploration of the state's options to steer the emerging HRV field in a particular direction.

This section illustrates how various government institutions used their role as financers to facilitate the emergence of the HRV field. At the same time, their power was limited by the general trend towards decentralization in the Netherlands. As such, while the government's economic capital was crucial for the field's emergence, it did not offer the government a position of complete domination.

9.6 The regular function

Within the emerging HRV field the following actors performed relevant "regular-function" roles: the police, women's shelters, municipal authorities, Support Centres for Domestic Violence, Youth Care Agencies, the state, the media and subject-matter experts. What set these actors apart was that their regular work involved responsibilities that were deemed to be particularly relevant within the emerging HRV field.

For instance, this included the media's role to expose matters. One journalist, for example, explained her involvement with honour-related violence as follows: "I just get stuck in. I think it's very important to be clear about what you're dealing with, to be able to see clearly what the problem is and not work through a veil." The media therefore fulfils an agenda-setter role as part of its regular function. Likewise, the Support Centres for Domestic Violence fulfil a bridge-builder role as part of their regular role. This illustrates that an actor's regular role may coincide with one of the other key roles within the emerging field.

While some actors perform key regular functions within the emerging field, others take on new roles. As a case in point, the migrant organizations took on the role of *mentality changer*. Other actors such as the state had high hopes of the mentality-changing role of the migrant organizations. Bringing about a mentality change, however, is not an easy task. According to two representatives from an umbrella organization, a new balance needed to be found between the individual and the community, one in which violence was no longer regarded as a solution:

---

103. See Chapter 11 for more information on these decentralization processes in the Netherlands.

> Interviewee 1: "A new balance must be found between the individual and the group. (...) [S]o when people from eastern Turkey receive a message that says, 'You have to commit a murder', they don't just go out and do it and think that it's all about honour."
> Interviewer: "But what sort of new relationship between individuals and the group are you aiming for?"
> Interviewee 1: "That people are responsible for their own behaviour; that there are more aspects to it than just authority over the women in your immediate surroundings."
> Interviewee 2: "(...) But that's a process. It's all about making it clear that using violence is never legitimate for any purpose. That it doesn't solve anything; people need to become aware of this, that they won't solve any problems and will only make other people angry. This is a specific development process that each individual has to undergo. It's only effective if people can be critical of themselves. We're trying to set off a particular process, so that people become less vulnerable to influences from outside, and you can then deal with this in a very different way."

Another representative of an umbrella organization for migrant organizations indicated that such a process takes time and that an alternative must be presented:

> Interviewee: "You can't say to people, 'You have to change your system' without offering…"
> Interviewer: "An alternative."
> Interviewee: "Yes. Because otherwise they'll move into a kind of existential hole and you can't subject anyone to that and they won't buy into it either. Because they need to continue to understand their world. (...) One factor is extremely important and that's 'time'. You can't avoid the aspect of time. Because people simply need time to develop in a particular way."

These quotes clearly show that bringing about a change in mentality in relation to honour-related violence is not easy. It requires time, behavioural alternatives and efforts by all parties involved.

The foregoing also illustrates how a specific function can draw actors into an emerging issue-based field if the issue at hand has particular bearing on their work. However, performing a relevant regular-function role in and of itself is not enough to turn an actor into a key actor. In order to become a key actor, the actor must combine a regular function role with another role, such as like agenda setter, expert or financer.

In terms of capital, all these actors have access to an embodied form of informational capital that is of particular relevance within the emerging HRV field: the police's experience with investigating murders, for example, and women shelters' experience with assisting threatened women. Moreover, these key actors will have built up this embodied informational capital within other fields in which they hold similar positions, for instance the domestic violence field. Bourdieu describes this process as *homology across fields,* referring to the concept that actors hold the same types of position within different fields (Bourdieu and Wacquant 1992:106).

Migrant organizations, in contrast, assumed an entirely new role within the HRV field: the role of mentality changer. As a consequence, other actors were apparently reluctant to accept them as full and equal partners, accepting them neither as experts nor as agenda-setters. Chapter 11 takes a closer look at the position of migrant organizations in relation to other organizations

9.7 Concluding remarks

Based on the descriptions of the key actor and the key roles within the emerging HRV field, it can be concluded that the following types of capital were deemed to be of particular importance within the emerging HRV field in 2007-2008: *informational capital, social capital* and *economic capital*. Moreover, these descriptions can be used to present a distribution of these types of capital over the separate actors: *experts* have access to informational capital, as do actors who fulfil a *regular-function role* within the emerging field, *financers* have access to economic capital and *bridge builders* have access to social capital.

The foregoing illustrates that the three "fundamental species" of capital that Bourdieu distinguishes – economic, cultural and social capital (Bourdieu & Wacquant 1992:119) – are all present within the emerging HRV field. Within the HRV field, governmental institutions such as the state and municipalities have access to economic capital, giving them a position of power. Migrant organizations, in contrast, claim a key position within the HRV field based on their social capital.

Still, the capital that is pursued most within the HRV field is informational capital, also termed cultural capital by Bourdieu. This type of capital seems to function as *symbolic capital*, as it is the most valued type of capital within this field. As a consequence this type of capital also generated the greatest struggles within the emerging field.

From this table it can be deduced that all key actors within the emerging HRV field had access to some type of *informational capital*. Actors who fulfilled a regular function had access to the embodied type of informational capital. This pertains to the actor's *practical knowledge* which has become engraved on his habitus through processes of socialization within his working environment and/or through taking part in a pilot project. Migrant organizations also had access to this embodied type of informational capital, though in their case it pertained to their *member knowledge*: knowledge built up through socialization processes within their community. Both the media and the state had access to the institutional type of information, being perceived as legitimate sources of information. Lastly, subject-matter experts were the only actors who had access to embodied, institutional and objectified informational capital, previously described as expert knowledge. Having access to informational capital therefore appears to contribute to becoming a key actor within the HRV field.

Table 5. Distribution of capital over the key actors within the emerging HRV field.

Actors	Roles	Species of capital
Police	• Agenda setter • Expert • Regular function	• Informational capital (institutional and embodied)
Municipal authorities	• Expert • Financier • Regular function	• Economic capital • Informational capital (embodied)
Women's support services	• Agenda setter • Expert • Regular function	• Informational capital (embodied)
Support Centres for Domestic Violence	• Bridge builder • Regular function	• Social capital • Informational capital (embodied)
Youth Care Agencies	• Bridge builder • Regular function	• Social capital • Informational capital (embodied)
The state	• Agenda setter • Financier • Regular function	• Economic capital • Informational capital (institutional)
Educational sector	• Expert • Bridge builder • Regular function	• Social capital • Informational capital (embodied)
Migrant organizations	• Agenda setter • Expert • Bridge builder	• Social capital • Informational capital (embodied)
Media	• Agenda setter • Expert • Regular function	• Informational capital (institutional)
Subject-matter experts	• Agenda setter • Expert • Regular function	• Informational capital (embodied, institutional and objectified)
Citizens' initiatives	• Agenda setter • Expert	• Informational capital (embodied)

State power

This chapter describes the actors that can be denoted as "*key actors*" within the emerging HRV field: the police, women's shelters, municipal authorities, Support Centres for Domestic Violence, the Youth Care Agencies, the state, educational institutions, migrant organizations, citizens' initiatives, the media and "subject-matter experts". These actors are denoted as key actors based on the number of mentions that they received from interviewees and in policy documents. Moreover, these are the actors that organized and/or were present at meetings on the issue of honour-related violence.

How these actors are positioned relative to one another, and therefore which type of capital is deemed most valuable within the emerging field, is examined more closely in Chapters 10 and 11. Here I focus primarily on what the foregoing tells us about the state's power.

In Chapter 8 I argued that the configuring function of the parliamentary debates described went beyond the political field. The discussion presented above of the key actors, their roles and their capital highlights that one of the state's key values – developing a solid knowledge base – did indeed transfer to the emerging HRV field. Not only did all key actors have access to some type of informational capital, one of the key struggles within the emerging field also pertained to the question of which type of informational capital was the most valuable.

Moreover, contrasting the key actors within the emerging HRV field with the actors that were perceived to be fundamental by actors within the political field makes it possible to further assess the state's power: was the state indeed able to define the key positions within the HRV field? Within the political field, the following actors where deemed to be fundamental in the battle against honour-related violence: the police (the Multi-Ethnic Policing Unit in particular), women's shelters (FO in particular), the Public Prosecution Service, schools, municipal authorities, subject-matter experts and migrant organizations. A comparison with the key actors described in this chapter reveals that only one political key actor is missing: the Public Prosecution Service[104]. Moreover, other key actors within the HRV field, for example the Support Centres for Domestic Violence, the Youth Care Agencies and citizens' initiatives, were also mentioned in the political field, albeit not as frequently as the others.

Actors that functioned as key actors within both fields had in common that they either functioned as key instigators for the media's attention for honour killings – women's shelters (FO), schools (Zarife's school) and subject-matter experts (Clementine van Eck) – and/or took part in one of the pilots set up by the state: the police pilot, the school pilot, the municipality pilot and the migrants organizations project. By initiating large-scale pilots the state contributed to the visibility of certain actors within emerging issue-based fields. As a consequence those actors stood out, both in the political field and within the emerging HRV field.

---

104. As explained above, while the Public Prosecution Service is part of the HRV field, it nevertheless does not hold a key position within this field.

10. Discussions about the label of honour-related violence

> One of the major powers of the state is to produce and impose (especially through school systems) categories of thought that we spontaneously apply to all things in the social world – including the state itself. (Bourdieu et al. 1994:1)

Bourdieu's work directs attention to the dominant role of states in developing categories and advancing theoretical unification. He argues that as time passes these categories become so common that societies perceive them as normal, as absolute. He therefore urges scholars not to blindly ratify these categories but to question them by going back to their genesis (Bourdieu et al. 1994:1).

The preceding chapters traced the genesis of the label of honour-related violence back to its development by Ferwerda and Van Leiden in 2005. Moreover, a reconstruction of the emergence of the issue of honour-related violence within the media field[105] and the political field[106] led to a description of the context in which this category emerged. Charts have been drawn to illustrate the rise of this category within both fields[107]. However, those charts do not provide any information about how this label was applied: *how do people define honour-related violence in practice?*

This question is relevant for three reasons. Firstly, for an issue-based organizational field to emerge field members need to be committed to the field's central issue (Hoffman 1999). Moreover, according to Hoffman (1999:352), one way to determine that a new organizational field has indeed emerged is by establishing that a large group of actors have developed a shared information load[108]. By answering the preceding question it therefore becomes possible to assess whether a Dutch HRV field was indeed emerging.

Yet developing a shared information load does not necessarily mean that all actors are using exactly the same definition. Grodal (2007) finds that while it is important to have a common label, it is also important to leave actors enough freedom to *translate* the label to their respective working environments. She summarizes this process of *meaning making* within the nanotechnology field as follows:

---

105. See Chapter 5.
106. See Chapter 8.
107. See Chapter 4.
108. See the general introduction.

> Involvement of new communities is central to the emergence of a new organizational field. In the beginning of a field, a label is created within a community and infused with meaning. Multiple mechanisms like excitement, translation, legitimation, decoupling, naming, and labeling drove changes in meaning, which again facilitated the adoption of the label by new communities. If other communities do not adopt the label a field does not evolve, but continues to be a social world. A necessary condition for a field to evolve is, thus, new communities' adoption of the label. It is, however, not possible for new communities to adopt a label without changing the meaning of the label. By definition, communities possess different webs of meaning and they use symbols in different ways (Becker 1982, Strauss 1978). When the label is integrated into a new symbolic system its references change. (Grodal 2007: 172-175, 178)

A given level of ambiguity therefore creates the freedom that actors need to "translate" the definition to their own working environments, which in turn facilitates their commitment to the emerging field.

Secondly, studying the definition-in-use also renders it possible to assess the state's power: this will help to assess whether actors have indeed integrated this definition into their habitus – a process that Bourdieu describes as *doxic submission*. Doxic submission consequently means endorsing a field's doxa, which refers to the dominant classifications within a field.

Lastly, answering the question about the definition-in-use also highlights what types of knowledge informed the key actors' definitions of honour-related violence. As explained in Chapter 9, three types of knowledge could be observed within the emerging HRV field: *expert knowledge, practical knowledge* and *member knowledge*.

The following quote illustrates how some actors actively worked to develop their knowledge of the issue of honour-related violence;

> Interviewer: "And how did you gain your experience in relation to honour-related violence?"
> Interviewee: "Well, it's actually a combination of working on it myself, so speaking to a lot of people. Listening to stories, contacts, visiting conferences, reading books on the subject. (…) Many films have been made but many books have also been written, there are women all over the world who have a personal history of honour violence, who have survived it, or who know someone who hasn't and who then write a story about it. So this involves books, articles, scholarly journals; we've also read a great deal about the approach to honour-related violence abroad. A great deal of research is being conducted in Turkey and in countries such as Germany and Britain, and in Scandinavia there's now masses of information about '*honour-related killings*'. (…) The UN is now also getting involved; it's even drawn up a charter, not so well known (…). (Project leader at a women's shelter)

Clearly, this interviewee combined a variety of learning methods. Besides actively acquiring knowledge about the issue by reading about it, he also developed his knowledge through his day-to-day work. Many of the interviewees came into contact with confirmed and potential victims and/or perpetrators of honour-related violence in their work. Their experiences helped them to build their own database of what honour-related violence comprises, described above as practical knowledge.

Lastly, some interviewees were able to grow their understanding of honour-related violence based on their own experiences, as was the case with this social worker:

> I'm a Hindu and grew up with a respect for honour. I know how important it is. You don't do anything that would impact your family's honour, so you do nothing outside the set rules. You behave as you were brought up. And don't do anything that will cause people to gossip and that would shame your parents. (Social worker at a women's shelter)

Above, this type of knowledge is termed member knowledge. It is important to distinguish between these types of knowledge in order to understand the differences between the definitions-in-use.

In this chapter I therefore show how honour-related violence was described by 75 prominent members of the emerging HRV field. Those interviewees represent organizations that actively worked against honour-related violence, for example the interministerial programme to combat honour-related violence, Rotterdam's and Amsterdam's partnership networks, the umbrella organization for women's shelters, the National Expertise Centre on honour-related violence (police) and migrant organizations. The interviewees should therefore be considered to be informed representatives of the emerging HRV field.

10.1 The Working Definition versus the Definition-in-use

> (…) [Y]ou have to have a shared working definition. This is often lacking among partners in a network. You need to see the whole group as a problem and not reduce it to the individual roles of people. That still happens.

The above quote was spoken by a representative of the police. In his interview he highlighted the importance of a shared definition. A shared definition, in his opinion, formed the basis for an effective collaborative effort. Nevertheless, at the same time he acknowledged that not everybody applied the same basic principles, for example holding the whole family accountable.

In a similar vein, a representative of the Amsterdam network for honour-related violence reflected on the formal definition as follows:

> (…) [I]t struck me as a bit odd, when you asked, "What is honour-related violence?" I thought that it's a bit strange that even though I've read the definition many times, I actually don't find it so expressive or so arresting that I wish to use it. So it's a bit strange but that might have more to do with me than the definition, it could well be.

Evidently, both interviewees felt that the formal definition had not yet been fully assimilated into the emerging HRV field's logic by 2007-2008. In this section I therefore highlight the similarities and differences between the formal state-approved definition and the *definitions-in-use*. Moreover, I argue that differences between the interviewees' definitions-in-use stem from differences in their positions within the emerging field, which influence the types of knowledge that the interviewees developed.

Each of the following subsections starts with Ferwerda and Van Leiden's working definition (2005). The bolded text is the part of the definition that is subsequently compared with the interviewee's definition-in-use.

> **Honour-related violence means any form of physical or mental violence** perpetrated from within a collective mentality, in response to a breach of honour (or the threat of such a breach) concerning a man or woman and therefore his or her family, where the outside world is or might become aware of the breach. (Ferwerda & Van Leiden 2005:25)

According to the working definition, honour-related violence encompasses both physical and/or mental violence. Nevertheless, all interviewees initially focused on the more typical forms of honour-related violence such as honour killings, repudiation, abandonment and suicide. However, in the course of the interview they would also mention other forms of violence such as buying-off, forced relocation and psychological violence used to make people conform to the prevailing standards and values[109].

Interestingly, what was regarded as violence by some was not perceived as such by others. For example, one interviewee did not regard abandonment in the country of origin as a form of violence, stating, "The girl was taken on holiday and then left behind. Alright, not a major problem so far" (Representative of a Municipal Health Service). In contrast, schools regard this as one of the most significant threats to their student populations. In other words, whether or not an act was considered to constitute honour-related violence seemingly depended on the interviewee's day-to-day experiences with victims and/or perpetrators of honour-related violence.

As a consequence, two definitions came to the fore within the emerging a HRV field: a narrow definition and a broad definition of violence. The *narrow definition of violence* focused on the more visible and criminal forms of violence, while the *broader definition of violence* also took less visible and more subtle forms of violence into account. The definition that was then applied depended on the individual's own role within the HRV field.

---

109. The types of violence that were mentioned partially correspond to the types of violence recognized by Ferwerda and Van Leiden (2005: 31-3). Still, a number of other types of violence were not specifically mentioned by the interviewees, such as "pride killing" and "counter-tarnishing". Pride killing is deliberately killing an honour-violator and counter-tarnishing is "damaging the family honour of the honour violator, for example by raping or abducting a member of their family" (Ferwerda & Van Leiden 2005: 32).

The police, for instance, being responsible for criminal cases of honour-related violence, are usually confronted with serious and physical forms of violence. They therefore focused on the types of violence that, as one interviewee put it, were "worthwhile for the police". As a consequence forms of honour-related violence that were not criminal offences, such as abandonment, psychological pressure or repudiation, fell outside their remit. Moreover, the police's focus on criminal offences also led to a focus on the perpetrators of honour-related violence and so on the possibility of multiple perpetrators. This explains why the police also strongly emphasized the importance of the collective element of honour-related violence.

In contrast, schools fulfilled a preventative role within the HRV field: they aimed to pick up on honour-related violence as early as they possibly could. As a consequence they employed a much broader definition of violence. The two pilot schools for instance in fact labelled the issue as "honour questions" and "honour issues" rather than "honour-related violence". *Honour issues* then encompassed tense situations in which honour played a role but that had not yet escalated into actual violence. Schools therefore focused on early signals of honour issues, e.g. where pupils stopped attending school, stopped participating in extra-curricular activities, were unable to take part in work placements or began to avoid other pupils/teachers (Philips 2008).

Lastly, migrant organizations also chose to operationalize honour-related violence in a broader sense, for instance male/female relationships. These themes were perceived as more accessible to their grassroots. Moreover, effecting a change in mentality demanded an open debated of the standards and values forming the basis for that mentality, such as the assumptions about male/female and parent/child relationships.

Based on conversations within the Moroccan community, the *Samenwerkingsverband Marokkaanse Nederlanders* (SMN), a partnership organization for Moroccans in the Netherlands, developed the following definition of honour-related violence:

> [V]iolence that is used as a result of an incident in which the honour of an individual or a particular family is damaged or breached. A sense of justification exists in terms of restoring the damaged honour (…). (SMN 2008: 9)

In contrast, *Vluchtelingen-Organisaties Nederland* (Refugees Organizations in the Netherlands), gave the working definition as follows:

> Honour-related violence arises as a result of the assumption that the woman is the "property" of the man and her family, to which an honour status can be ascribed. Social pressure, gossip and shame determine the manifestation and severity of the violence. Honour-related violence therefore arises out of a mentality in which the individual's right to self-determination is systematically oppressed. It hampers the personal development of girls and women on all possible levels (mental, physical and economic). (Dekker and Özgümüs 2008: 16)

A similar operationalization can be found in relation to the *Inspraak Orgaan Turken in Nederland* (IOT), the participation organization for Turks in the Netherlands, which approached honour-related violence by proposing that "a change in the traditional position of women and the relationship between men and women" (IOT 2008: website) is required.

The foregoing examples again illustrate how each actor held a separate position within the field and as a result utilized its own specific definition. Moreover, various organizations that together formed the HRV field actor 'migrant organizations' sometimes used slightly different definitions. VON had for years dedicated its efforts to stopping violence against women; as a consequence they opted for a gender-specific definition. SMN, in contrast, chose to operationalize the definition in a manner that connected to the forms of violence that occurred within the Moroccan community.

> *Honour-related violence means any form of physical or mental violence **perpetrated from within a collective mentality, in response to a breach of honour (or the threat of such a breach)** concerning a man or woman and therefore his or her family, where the outside world is or might become aware of the breach.* (Ferwerda & Van Leiden 2005:25)

While honour is a key concept within this definition, the definition does not in fact state what honour actually encompasses. According to the formal definition, honour-related violence is a response to a breach of honour, conducted by a perpetrator who is stirred up by a collective mentality.

Some of the interviewees nevertheless sought to define what honour encompasses. For instance, according to one interviewee, "Honour is all a matter of status, your standing in the community. Living up to the prevailing standards and values is part of it, as is breaching them" (representative of a municipal health service). Most interviewees, however, did not specify what they understood honour to be. According to this group of interviewees, honour-related violence was violence arising as a result of a breach of unwritten rules, traditional standards and values. One interviewee expressed this as follows: "It's deeply rooted, it's all a matter of standards and values, mentality and economic circumstances" (representative of a municipal welfare organization). Only a small number of interviewees actually specified the issues to which these standards and values related, however. One interviewee, for instance, explicitly linked honour-related violence to oppression of women:

> Precisely because of the fact that it comes from another – not like domestic violence – from another school of thought, another mentality, the oppression of the … We primarily see it as oppression of the woman, because this is how it occurred, we say, this is completely different, we're not just talking about murders, we're also talking about systematic isolation and oppression of women and that's different to domestic violence, that's a completely different form of violence. (…) And honour, I don't want to say that it doesn't exist for the Dutch, of course we have honour, but the mentality that

you need to oppress a woman, ehm, people wouldn't consciously say that but the fact that a woman is required to behave according to particular a code, that's the basis for us and you also have that in certain subgroups and that doesn't mean that all Turks or Kurds have this but certain subgroups among the Turkish and the Kurdish communities do (…). (Representative of a migrant organization)

The interviewee therefore not only associated honour-related violence with a culture of "systematic isolation and oppression of women", he also contrasted this with Dutch culture and with domestic violence.

By and large, however, honour-related violence was not explicitly defined as a cultural object. Only a small number of interviewees spoke of cultural violence or an honour culture and a "we" culture in connection with honour-related violence. Still, it can be inferred from the emphasis that the interviewees placed on standards and values and/or mentality that all interviewees shared the common assumption that honour-related violence is indeed a form of violence that can be associated with certain cultures. They subsequently connected honour-related violence to specific migrant communities. This point is addressed at greater length in the following section.

The fact that honour-related violence involves a collective form of violence was also handled more indirectly, for example when people provided examples of honour-related violence that they had faced in their day-to-day work. In addition, the role of the collective in honour-related violence was made explicit when interviewees explained the difference between honour-related violence and domestic violence. The following quote illustrates this demarcation:

There's a difference between honour revenge and domestic violence. To me, it's certainly important whether the family and the environment are involved. If they are, then it's not domestic violence. Domestic violence is perpetrated purely by an individual, unconsciously or as a result of frustrations. (Representative of a Municipal welfare organisation)

According to this interviewee domestic violence is always an individual act. Moreover, unlike honour-related violence, domestic violence is not premeditated.

The fact that interviewees particularly focused on the collective element when discussing the distinction between honour-related violence and domestic violence is linked to the idea that this collective element also means that these types of violence need to be handled in different ways:

I think that honour-related violence is a form of domestic violence but, in terms of how it takes shape, it's different to domestic violence because it doesn't generally involve multiple perpetrators. So you need a different approach; you need to use different instruments. A domestic exclusion order[110] doesn't make much sense when applied to

---

110. Called *huisverbod* in Dutch.

honour-related violence, because if you remove the father, the brother or uncle will do it. You need a completely different approach. (Representative of the Ministry of Justice)

This shows that interviewees worked on clearly marking the boundaries between honour-related violence and domestic violence.

This element of the definition was stressed in particular by the women's shelters. Past experiences, and particularly Gül's murder, had led to a focus on women's safety and the development of a risk assessment instrument. That instrument firstly sought to make a distinction between domestic violence and honour-related violence. For this purpose it distinguished between the individual perpetrators of domestic violence and the collective perpetration of honour-related violence. Secondly, the instrument also tried to assess whether the breach of honour was common knowledge among the wider family, as awareness of such a breach often put pressure on the immediate family to take action or caused other relatives to become involved. The women's shelters then used the results of this risk assessment instrument to determine whether mediation was possible. The level of the threat also determined whether the woman or man needed to be provided with shelter or housed at a secret location, a refuge. This instrument again illustrates how each actor operationalized the definition in a way best suited to its own role within the emerging field.

> *Honour-related violence means any form of physical or mental violence perpetrated from within a collective mentality, in response to a breach of honour (or the threat of such a breach)* ***concerning a man or woman and therefore his or her family****, where the outside world is or might become aware of the breach.* (Ferwerda & Van Leiden 2005:25)

The fact that both men and women could become victims and/or perpetrators of honour-related violence is the third element of the working definition. At this level, the meanings assigned to honour-related violence by interviewees differed slightly from the working definition. The examples provided by the interviewees show that they all assumed victims to be women initially. These examples often involved young girls who had behaved improperly, who had behaved in an overly "Western" manner, or had entered into a relationship with an "inappropriate" boy and so incited their family's anger. In addition, the examples regularly concerned women who had separated from their partners as victims of honour-related violence.

During the course of the conversations, however, many of the interviewees explicitly indicated that men could also become victims of honour-related violence – for example being required to enter into a forced marriage or being homosexual. Being forced to commit honour-related violence was also mentioned by several interviewees.

Fewer interviewees imagined that women could play the role of perpetrator. Particularly interviewees with member knowledge seemed to be aware of this possibility. For example, a Turkish interviewee said, "(…) [W]e mustn't set women apart from the men. Women do the same things. Those bloody aunts, I always call them. The first bit of gossip is usually sent on its way by an aunt" (representative of a migrant organization). The role of women is also considered by police representatives; one interviewee gave the following example:

> Interviewee: "What you see in every case is that both men and women can be perpetrators and both men and women can be victims."
> Interviewer: "In what way are women perpetrators? People are not yet convinced of this."
> Interviewee: "If we're talking in legal terms, you have intellectual perpetrators. This is a system where women also monitor women. Some women also take on the role of maintaining honour within the family."
> (…)
> Interviewer: "But do you also know of women who perpetrate violence? Does that also happen? That they use physical force?"
> Interviewee: "No, that's not their role. But I was involved in one case. It involved an eighteen-year-old Moroccan boy who was engaged to a Dutch girl of the same age from a lower social family from the neighbourhood. The girl became pregnant by the boy. The family was against this. The mother and the sister [of the boy] offered to let the birth take place at their house. And that's what happened. They brought clean sheets for the birth. And then the mother and sister tried to flush the child down the toilet but its will to live was too great. The son then tried to cut the child into pieces but he couldn't go through with it and so the child was stuffed in a plastic bag and thrown in the water. The child died. (Police officer)

The foregoing examples illustrate how women can act as perpetrators. Moreover, they also illustrate that who is regarded as a potential victim and/or a potential perpetrator depends on the position within the emerging field. By referring to the women's involvement as intellectual perpetration, for instance, the latter interviewee clearly alludes to his position within field, namely as a police officer with a crime-related task.

> *Honour-related violence means any form of physical or mental violence perpetrated from within a collective mentality, in response to a breach of honour (or the threat of such a breach) concerning a man or woman and therefore his or her family,* **where the outside world is or might become aware of the breach**. (Ferwerda & Van Leiden 2005:25)

The final part of the definition refers to outsiders knowing of the actual or potential shame on the family's honour. This component of the definition regularly came up in the interviewees' accounts. According to the interviewees, knowing (or not knowing) about the breach of honour affects how much room an individual has to manoeuvre; mediation is still possible if the breach of honour has not yet been exposed outside the family.

In addition, interviewees emphasized that the extent to which the breach of honour is known to others has consequences for the victim's safety. If the breach of honour is public knowledge, his or her family will perhaps face pressure within their community to take action. The following case illustrates this:

> You see, as long as you can keep the breach of honour a secret, it's not a big problem. (…) It's only once it gets out that the problems begin. And then you notice that people start getting involved, particularly those from your own community, and it starts to get tricky. I had a case that was very … well, a bit funny; it was a girl who was suspected of having a relationship with an older Dutch man. This was not appreciated [by her family, NVB]. The girl was taken on holiday and then left behind. OK, not a major problem so far. We were working on it. And this older man, he contacted the Moroccan embassy and said something along the lines of, "She's being held against her will." And in no time at all, the family in Germany also started to receive phone calls from people saying, "Hey, why's that guy looking for your daughter?" So then we really had a problem. Yes, it was well intended but it didn't really work out. Because then we really had a problem. Because they then had responses along the lines of, "Why's that guy looking for your daughter?" What sort of nonsense is that? And why is this man involved… who is he? Yes, that was the problem, so you have to be careful. (Representative of a municipal health service).

In this quote, the interviewee also referred to a component of honour-related violence that is perceived to be very relevant: gossip. Without gossip, the family in Germany would never have heard about the relationship between the girl and the older man.

Various interviewees indicated that gossip is one of the most significant risks in terms of escalating issues of honour-related violence. The examples provided by the interviewees show that they therefore often corroborated the stories that the families wished to present to the outside world in order to gain time for mediation. For example, a family may announce that their daughter is at boarding school, even though she is actually staying in a women's shelter.

In general, it can be concluded that the majority of the specifics given by the interviewees correlate with the main elements of the formal definition of honour-related violence. Still, while all the interviewees were aware of the working definition, they mostly based their descriptions of honour-related violence on their own practical knowledge, which they had developed through their day-tot-day working practices. The differences in the interviewees' day-to-day jobs also led to differences in their definitions of violence, some utilizing a broad definition of violence and others utilizing a narrower definition.

Field members particularly highlighted those elements of the definition that impacted their own working practice, for instance the collective element of honour-related violence and the degree to which the breach of honour has become public knowledge. The interviewees' stories about honour-related violence also show that they specified what honour-related violence actually was in much greater detail than the formal definition provided. This includes the notion that honour-related violence particularly occurs when a relationship between partners or between parents and children comes under pressure. Additionally, interviewees were far more specific than the definition on the subject of what communities were involved, what forms of violence they saw and in what situations honour-related violence occurs. The next section therefore deals with these specifics that go beyond the formal definition.

10.2 Moving beyond the definition

> I don't see much difference between the Kurds, the Turks and the Moroccans. The mentality's the same. One group does it in one way; the other goes slightly over the top. (Representative of a municipal welfare organization).

This quote effectively summarizes the principal image of the communities in which honour-related violence occurs: different types of violence but one mentality. Each of the interviewees, whether at their own initiative or when prompted, talked about the communities in which honour-related violence plays a part. They also often made a distinction between the types of violence that occur in the separate communities.

For instance, the idea regularly surfaced during the interviews that honour killings primarily occur within the Turkish and Kurdish communities, whereas abandonment and repudiation are more likely within the Moroccan community. One interviewee, for instance, described "Moroccan violence" as follows: "We know that the Moroccans often take family members to Morocco and then leave them there; then they're simply repudiated and mutilated" (representative of a municipal welfare organization). A journalist described the differences between Turks, Moroccans and Hindustanis in the following manner:

> Yes, there are many [honour killings] in Turkey. That's my impression, having been involved in many conversations. But I can't substantiate this at all. The only thing that's certain is that the "repudiation" option is used more frequently by Moroccans. And that things often calm down for Moroccans after a few years and then the issues can be sorted out. This doesn't happen with Turks or Kurds. I'd give a Moroccan a much better chance of survival. (…) I've never seen a Moroccan father murder his daughter because of an honour-related problem. Exclusion happens a great deal, though. And with Hindustanis, you see a high rate of suicide but you never know if it was forced suicide or voluntary suicide. So there are huge differences between the various groups.

These quotes illustrate that field members principally differentiated between the more visible forms of violence such as honour killings, repudiation, suicide and abandonment. Limiting boys' and girls' freedom to make their own choices, for example, was not explicitly linked to a particular community.

The interviewees referred not only to Turkish, Kurdish, Moroccan and Hindustani communities. Afghan, Iranian, Iraqi, Pakistani, Egyptian, Surinam, Somali, Ghanaian and Sudanese communities were also mentioned as being relevant. A number of interviewees also indicated that honour-related violence sometimes involves Dutch "natives". According to one interviewee, for instance, the pressure to adapt to the prevailing standards and values within orthodox Christian communities is almost as high as it is for migrants. Nevertheless, the majority of the interviewees saw honour-related violence as an alien problem.

Some interviewees also indicated that differences sometimes exist within a single community. This point was mainly raised by interviewees with member knowledge. They reflected on regional differences in the country of origin, but also on the various ethnic and religious streams within a single community and on the distinction between growing up in the countryside or in the city.

The examples given by the interviewees also illustrate that a single honour-related violence case often involves more than one community. As a result, some cases encompass relationships between migrants and natives but also between two individuals from different communities. This is also the case in the following example:

> The Hindustani girl had a relationship with a Moroccan boy. She became pregnant. She didn't dare tell her parents. She decided to run away or ... [to commit suicide, NVB]. But the boy wanted to marry her. But the Moroccan parents were also opposed to this at first. They said. "If you marry a Buddhist, you'll soon have problems." He said, "I choose my life, and she chose me." The girl's parents were also against it: "There are plenty of Hindustanis here, you can choose someone else. You can't go and live in Morocco later." With our help and influence, the Hindustani girl's family was invited to the temple. We drank tea and talked. Finally, they consented to the marriage, and the girl's parents said, "Child, you do what you need to do." (Representative of a municipal welfare organization)

This quote also illustrates the types of situations that might lead to honour-related violence: in this case an unwelcome relationship between two young people from different communities. The following section offers a closer examination of the types of situations that were perceived as particularly critical.

Dangerous situations

The quotes presented so far clearly show that interviewees quickly operationalize honour-related violence into concrete situations. Further analysis of those examples demonstrates that a number of specific situations exist in which they recognized honour-related violence, such as forced marriage, loss of virginity, pregnancy out of marriage, a forbidden boyfriend/girlfriend, promiscuous behaviour[111], gossip, leaving the partner/separating, cheating, running away, confrontations between parents and children and, lastly, having a partner from a different religious or ethnic background[112].

This list shows that the interviewees specifically recognized honour-related violence in situations where the relationships between men and women or between parents and children come under pressure or where the issue concerns chaste conduct by women and girls. In other words, the standards and values that form the foundation for honour-related violence are implicitly operationalized to standards and values that relate to male-female relationships and the chaste ideal (of women). A possible explanation for this "implied" explanation lies in the fact that these underpinnings are so self-evident that interviewees do not feel any need to expound on them explicitly.

Some interviewees also explicitly mentioned the role of religion in connection with honour-related violence. Yet religion was not seen as a source of honour-related violence: many of the interviewees expressly denied any link between religion – and more specifically Islam – and honour-related violence. Religious differences, however, are regarded as a reason for honour-related violence, specifically where young people choose a partner from a different religious background.

Additionally, a small number of interviewees related honour-related violence to emancipation processes within migrant communities. Those interviewees also suggested that in the short term emancipation might lead to more honour-related violence. For instance, some interviewees indicated that they were often confronted with problems between parents and their children that arose when children refused to agree to an arranged marriage. Some interviewees also felt that growing up in a Dutch context amplified these problems.

The following interviewee, from a Moroccan background, provided a particularly appropriate explanation:

> Immigration has brought about a gap between the first and second generations. I have yet to meet a Moroccan who can really talk comfortably to his parents about any subject. And that has to do with the honour culture of recent years. (…) We're brought up with the idea that "you can't have sex before marriage; if you're a girl, you're not allowed to have a boyfriend." Boys are. Have girlfriends that is, because boys can't have boyfriends either. There's a difference in how boys and girls are raised, and there are expectations in terms of marriage and having children. And the single life is not an issue. It's not an option or choice you can make. And a decent woman will also stay married, separation is not good. There are all sorts of ideas but that's the ideal image;

---

111. Promiscuous behaviour, according to the interviewees, includes all types of behaviour such as short skirts, contact with boys and so on.

112. The reasons provided by the interviewees largely correspond to those set out by Ferwerda and Van Leiden (2005: 35-6). Ferwerda and Van Leiden additionally list rape, arguments about possessions, the removal of children and elopement as possible reasons for honour-related violence.

but reality has well and truly taken over. Because we get pregnant, we have abortions, we give birth to illegitimate children. (…) And if boys can have girlfriends, girls can have boyfriends too. Because those girls are the girlfriends. (Representative of a migrant organization)

This quote reveals that the processes of immigration and emancipation are challenging the gender stereotypes within the Moroccan community. The fact that a number of interviewees noted how emancipation and immigration have influenced the existence of honour-related violence also indicates that the interviewees did not interpret the cultural component of honour-related violence as a static phenomenon. On the contrary: their stories illustrate that they saw it as being influenced by processes of immigration and emancipation.

10.3 Concluding remarks

The foregoing explanations lead to the following answers to the questions posed at the start of this chapter. Firstly, the interviewees did in fact develop a shared understanding of the issue of honour-related violence. As such, one of the factors signalling the emergence of a new organizational field can be said to exist. Secondly, the interviews confirm that theoretical unification was taking place. While interviewees were unable to quote the formal definition, their descriptions generally corresponded to its key elements. Lastly, it can be concluded that the interviewees primarily based their knowledge of the issue on their day-to-day experiences with either victims or perpetrators of honour-related violence. In the following sections I explain these conclusions further.

Developing a shared understanding of honour-related violence

Although the interviewees emphasized slightly different aspects of the phenomenon of honour-related violence, in general they agreed on its key dimensions. In terms employed by Hoffman (1999), the interviewees had developed a shared information load, a shared understanding, of the issue. For instance, all the interviewees acknowledged that honour-related violence encompasses a wide variety of types of violence, both physical and mental. Moreover, they recognized that both women and men could become victims of honour-related violence. The interviewees also agreed that this type of violence is connected to certain cultures but not to a particular religion, for example Islam. The examples they presented also illustrate how they identified this type of violence in situations where a relationship between husband and wife and/or between parents and children was under pressure. Moreover, they collectively indicated that it matters whether the outside world knows about the breach of honour. Lastly, almost all the interviewees used the collective dimension of honour-related violence as a means to distinguish this type of violence from domestic violence.

Yet the preceding sections also highlight differences in emphasis. The police, for instance, use a *narrow definition of violence*: they focus on criminal offences and therefore on the more physical forms of violence such as honour killings. Schools, conversely, use a *broad definition of violence*: they try to identify honour issues before they escalate into honour-related violence and therefore also focus on less tangible signals such as if a pupil starts missing classes. These differences offer a strong suggestion as to why some interviewees believed that multiple definitions were applied within the field of honour-related violence: different actors operationalize honour-related violence from the perspective of their own positions, their own roles within the HRV field.

This type of ambiguity regarding the definition does not necessarily pose a problem for field emergence. Grodal (2007) finds that while it is important to have a common label it is also important to leave actors enough freedom to *translate* the label to their own working environment: a degree of ambiguity creates the space that actors need to "translate" the definition to their own working environment, which in turn facilitates their commitment to an emerging field.

Theoretical unification and doxic submission

According to Bourdieu et al. (1994:7) states are powerful because of their ability, among other things, to develop categories of thought that gain a universal character, thus creating *theoretical unification*. A superficial inspection might lead to the conclusion that theoretical unification had not taken place within the emerging HRV field in 2007-2008 (or at least not yet), given that none of the interviewees were able to quote the formal working definition commissioned by the Dutch state. Moreover, the interviewees all highlighted slightly different elements of the phenomenon of honour-related violence.

However, a closer analysis of the descriptions provided reveals that the interviewees' account in fact include each element of the formal definition. Moreover, the key contributions made by the state were also present within the emerging field. Firstly, as in the formal working definition, all the interviewees acknowledged that honour-related violence refers to more types of violence besides honour killings alone, that it includes both female and male victims and that it is not explicitly connected to Islam. Secondly, like the political field, all the interviewees saw honour-related violence as a distinct social problem and so as separate from domestic violence. I therefore posit that theoretical unification was indeed taking place within the emerging field. Moreover, as explained above, the various actors were already translating the issue to their own working environments and so integrating it into their own habitus – a key element of doxic submission.

Practical knowledge versus expert knowledge

The foregoing analysis of the interviewees' definitions-in-use also illustrates how they drew primarily on their practical knowledge when describing the issue of honour-related violence. Some were also able to complement their descriptions using facts derived from their member knowledge. This seeming prioritization of practical knowledge over expert knowledge is interesting here: the interviewees also referred to subject-matter experts as the *real* experts on honour-related violence. Moreover, their descriptions did in fact contain the key elements of the formal working definition developed by an independent research organization.

This paradox can be explained as follows. Actors evidently initially base their knowledge of the issue on the available expert knowledge. However, once they have committed themselves to a field, they start to build their own practical knowledge, which is based on their day-to-day experiences with victims and/or perpetrators of honour-related violence. They then start to "translate" the definition to their own working environment and so integrate it into their own habitus.

The shift from expert knowledge to practical knowledge observed here therefore potentially indicates a next step in the emergence of an issue-based field: first the issue is raised within the media field, next it is legitimized by the state, after which it is adopted and translated to the individual's working environment.

Methodological reflection

The interviews that I conducted as part of the 2007-2008 study were with *front runners*, as they are known: members of organizations which, at the time, were actively working to combat honour-related violence. As a consequence they were able to describe how their organizations dealt with this particular issue. Moreover, the preceding analysis highlights that those interviewees, while representing a very diverse group of organizations, shared a number of basic assumptions about the issue of honour-related violence.

Nonetheless, the findings potentially also give the impression that the members of the organizations represented here were all properly informed about this specific type of violence. That was not the case. In fact, the interviewees often complained that their own organization and/or their partner organizations lacked the necessary knowledge. Moreover, as discussed in Chapter 9, two studies conducted in the educational sector revealed that representatives of these organizations based their knowledge of honour-related violence principally on the media's representation of the problem. While some field members were already translating the issue to their own working environments and integrating it into their habitus, therefore, others were still familiarizing themselves with the issue.

11. Collaborative practices within the HRV field

> As a result of the problem's complexity, combatting honour-related violence demands an intensive collaborative effort from all the parties concerned: the government, regulatory authorities and migrant groups. This collaborative effort is not a question of choice but is the only way to successfully bring honour-related violence to a halt.

These words were spoken by Albrecht (2006: 5-6), a "network manager" in Rotterdam's *honour-related violence network* (HRV network). As explained elsewhere, the municipality of Rotterdam functioned as the *pilot* for the Dutch municipal measures to tackle honour-related violence. A key element of this pilot was the concept that tackling honour-related violence required the organizations involved to work according to the principles of "*ketensamenwerking*", literarily translated into "chain collaboration", but denoted here as *network collaboration*. In fact, *ketensamenwerking* was a buzzword in 2007-2008: many organizations were seemingly part of one network or another within the HRV field. For instance, the police, women's shelters, public prosecutors, the youth care agencies, etc. all took part in the Rotterdam and Amsterdam HRV networks.

At the same time, the 2007-2008 study revealed that not all municipal authorities were in the process yet of developing these types of HRV networks. Moreover, the general decentralization trend within the Netherlands led to local differences between collaborative practices. As a consequence, Amsterdam's HRV network was different from Rotterdam's. Not only this, but network collaboration was not the only type of collaborative practice that could be observed within the emerging HRV field. For instance, at the national level the state worked with the umbrella organizations for migrant organizations to bring about a change in mentality within the involved communities.

In this chapter I further substantiate my proposition that a Dutch HRV field was indeed emerging, since field emergence is also marked by increased interaction between specific actors (Hoffman 1999). By describing these collaborative practices I illustrate how the emergence of the issue of honour-related violence indeed led to new and/or intensified collaborative practices between actors.

By analysing these collaborative practices I also seek to examine the extent to which elements of the interministerial programme to combat honour-related violence can be identified within the emerging HRV field. As explained in Chapter 8, that programme consisted of several distinct elements: 1.) an integrated approach to the problem, 2.) a focus on developing a reliable knowledge base, 3.) a focus on collaborative effort and 4.) a focus on three particular domains, namely prevention, protection and prosecution.

Lastly, a study of these collaborative practices provides information about the emerging configurations of the Dutch HRV field, as these practices provide information on how various actors were positioned in respect of each other and so about the value of their capital. Moreover, it reveals the key struggles and therefore the power dynamics within the emerging field.

Nevertheless, the scope of this research does not allow for a detailed analysis of all these practices. I therefore focus on those collaborative practices that generated the largest amounts of activity – e.g. drafting documents, organizing conferences, meeting on a regular basis – and/or brought together many of the key actors. Another complicating factor in describing these collaborative practices is that they took place within an emerging field. As a result, many of them were still evolving. Therefore, I sometimes also describe collaborative practices that were still under development, or that only occurred within specific municipalities. As such, I present general descriptions of the main collaborative practices within the emerging HRV field.

The following section first sketches the emerging configurations within the Dutch HRV field, i.e. the positions of the various actors and the types of collaborative effort that they formed. In the subsequent sections I then further address the key collaborative practices that could be observed in 2007-2008: 1.) partnerships between the state and the umbrella organizations for migrant organizations, 2.) partnerships between national actors and local actors, 3.) partnerships between network partners and 4.) partnerships between network partners and migrant organizations.

11.1 Emerging field configurations: a schematic representation

The 2007-2008 study showed that the key actors within the emerging field supported a *two-track policy* for tackling honour-related violence. On the one hand, they argued that honour-related violence should not be tolerated in the Netherlands and that therefore action needed to be taken against this type of violence. On the other, they argued that efforts should be made to change the mentality within the communities concerned. This two-track policy was subsequently translated into a role distribution across actors: actors working in law enforcement and providing assistance on the one hand, and actors working to bring about a change in mentality on the other.

In the first track, key actors such as women's shelters, the Support Centres for Domestic Violence, the Youth Care Agencies and the police developed reliable network collaboration at the local level. The second track involved efforts to realize a change in mentality within the communities concerned. This role was primarily assigned to and claimed by migrant organizations. In this context, actors also defined two types of mentality change: on the one hand, migrant organizations were expected to bring about a new mentality in relation to honour-related violence, while on the other they were asked to change the attitudes towards the available support services.

This two-track policy was also visible from the actors' respective positions on the issue of honour-related violence: the emerging HRV field appeared to consist of two subfields, each characterized by a different focus: protection/prosecution or prevention. Moreover, while actors representing different subfields sought to combine their efforts, clear demarcation processes between both fields were also visible. The following diagram shows how key actors within the HRV field were positioned in respect of each other. The arrows also indicate the various collaborative practices observed between these actors.

Figure 7: Collaborative practices within the Dutch HRV field

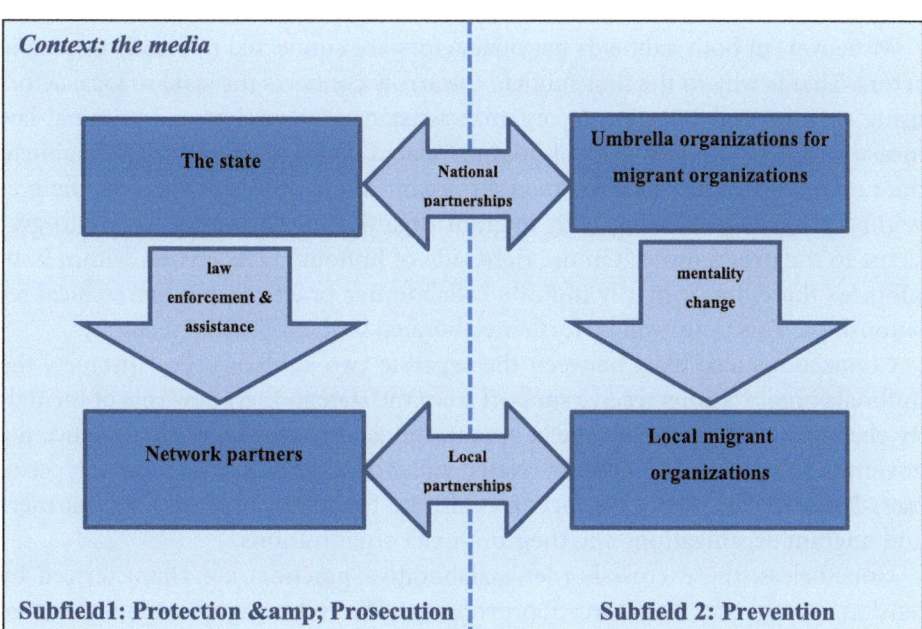

Naturally this diagram is a simplified representation of reality, which inevitably leads to a loss of information. For instance, it only shows the principal collaborative practices observed within the emerging HRV field in 2007-2008. Some actors moreover operate in the area where assistance and mentality change overlap, for example schools and some citizens' initiatives. As noted in Chapter 9, schools are expected to identify possible honour issues at an early stage and, if necessary, make referrals to other actors while simultaneously being expected to endeavour to change the mentality of their student populations. Moreover, to add clarity, the various sectoral umbrella organizations such as *Federatie Opvang* (FO) have been omitted from the diagram. Nevertheless, they played an important role in the collaborative efforts between the state and local network partners.

Yet accentuating certain characteristics of reality makes it possible to represent that reality more effectively. In this case the diagram is a useful tool for learning about how the key actors were positioned within the emerging issue-based field in 2007-2008. Moreover, it illustrates that *the HRV field was apparently made up of two subfields.*

In the *first subfield* the actors focused on law enforcement and assistance. This first subfield can therefore be linked to the *protection* and *prosecution* projects of the interministerial programme against honour-related violence. The *second subfield* consists of actors focusing on bringing about a change in mentality. As such, this field can be linked to prevention, being the third pillar of the interministerial programme.

Moreover, in both subfields national actors are connected to locally operating actors. That is why in the first subfield the arrow connects the state to local actors using network collaboration to organize assistance for victims and criminal-law measures against perpetrators of honour-related violence. In the second subfield the umbrella organizations for migrant organizations give substance to the *prevention project* by working with migrant organizations working locally to give shape to the programme "On the right side of honour". The arrows within both subfields therefore primarily indicate collaborative practices, *not* hierarchical relationships. This point will be further elaborated in the following sections.

Connections also exist between the separate two subfields. For instance, the umbrella organizations receive support from the state in their new role of mentality changers. In turn, the umbrella organizations also endeavour to influence the government's policies on honour-related violence. At the local level these types of *cross-border collaborative practices* can also be found between network partners and migrant organizations and their umbrella organizations.

Nonetheless, these cross-border collaborative practices are characterized by tension, struggles and demarcation processes. The following quote is illustrative of the tensions:

> Safety is not the core duty [of migrant organizations]; we don't have the authority to take this responsibility upon ourselves. If we see an indication that "things aren't going well here", we must not pretend to be able to provide assistance, but must immediately ask the law enforcement agencies whether they see the same things as we do.

This quote by a representative of a migrant organization stresses why network partners and migrant organizations need to work together, while simultaneously marking out the difference in their roles. Besides clearly demarking each other's responsibilities, other interviewees also showed a lack of confidence, a lack of trust, in each other, which again indicated the existence of two separate subfields. The following sections offer a closer examination of these tensions and struggles.

11.2 Collaborative practices between the state and umbrella organizations

In 2007-2008 collaborative practices could be observed at various levels, including at the national level, where collaborative efforts were pursued between the state and the umbrella organizations for migrant organizations. More specifically, these efforts were given substance by the Ministry of Housing, Communities and Integration and the four umbrella organizations that participated in the programme "On the right side of honour": refugee organization VON[113], Turkish participation organization IOT[114], Moroccan partnership organization SMN[115] and Overijssel-based Turkish group STO[116].

In part, the partnerships between the state and these umbrella organizations were highly formalized. The Minorities Policy (Consultation) Act[117] had been introduced in 1997, giving shape to the formal implementation of national minorities consultation platform *Landelijk Overleg Minderheden*, or "LOM"[118]. The goal of this platform was to facilitate exchanges of information between the government and migrant organizations. LOM comprised seven umbrella organizations, including those participating in the programme "On the right side of honour" (LOM Samenwerkingsverband 2008: website).

However, the emergence of the issue of honour-related violence caused the collaborative efforts to intensify. For instance, following the school shooting in Veghel in 1999, the state called on IOT to specifically work on the issue of honour-related violence. One interviewee recalled this period as follows:

> Interviewee: "It started in 2000, when Van Boxtel summoned IOT and said that he'd rather not see the kind of thing that had happened in Veghel. He said it was *eerwraak* that had started it [and that this] had to be debated at some depth among the rank and file. So that's what we did."

---

113. VON (*Vluchtelingen-Organisaties Nederland*) represents four hundred local refugee organizations, including Kurdish, Afghani, Palestinian, Somali, Iranian and Iraqi refugees. These local migrant organizations are affiliated with or departments of federations and platforms that are united within VON (Dekker & Özgümüş 2008:7).

114. IOT (*Inspraak Orgaan Turken*) champions the interests of Turks in the Netherlands and is made up of nine federations that are affiliated with IOT. The federations represent the various religious and cultural aspects that are present within the Turkish community and form an umbrella for 250 local migrant organizations (IOT 2016: website).

115. SMN (*Samenwerkingsverband van Marokkanen in Nederland*) represents the interests of Moroccans in the Netherlands. Unlike VON and IOT, however, SMN has a network structure. Its work revolves around improving the formation of networks and the degree of organization among Moroccans in the Netherlands (SMN 2008: website).

116. STO (*Samenwerkende Turkse Organisaties in Overijssel*) also works on behalf of Turks in the Netherlands, but operates within a specific region, i.e. Overijssel province.

117. In Dutch: *Wet Overleg Minderheden* (or "WOM").

118. The Minorities Policy (Consultation) Act was repealed in 2013. The subsidies for the umbrella organizations represented in the LOM ended in 2015.

Interviewer: "And did you agree?"
Interviewee: "There was a great deal of resistance to begin with. The board members were of the opinion that it wasn't our task because our role is to represent [our members'] interests. Another argument was that there was enough negative attention already and we shouldn't air our dirty laundry in public. Then there were responses along the lines of, 'If it had been my daughter, I'd have done the same thing.'"
(...)
Interviewer: "And how (...) did you tackle this resistance?"
Interviewee: "Van Boxtel really had to work hard. He said, 'Listen, I have participation organizations to provide explanations and to find out how particular issues are perceived within particular communities, and if I want to know these things, you're going to find out for me.' A project was then set up (...)."

This quote illustrates how the state used the LOM platform as a means to reach the demographic at which its policy was aimed. It also reveals one of the key tensions in this partnership: umbrella organizations are part of the civil society, and their principal role is to represent their supporters' interests. This is in fact a mandatory condition, one which was stipulated in the Minorities Policy (Consultation) Act: in order to take part in the LOM, umbrella organizations needed to have a broad support. As a consequence, the umbrella organizations could not move too far ahead of the people they represented. At the same time, by attaching conditions to its funding, the state pushed them to do exactly that.

This tension became even more apparent when four LOM partners initiated the programme "On the right side of honour" as part of the social prevention project set up under the interministerial programme to combat honour-related violence. As shown in Chapter 8, parliament scrutinized the government's approach to tackling honour-related violence. The MPs even temporarily assigned priority project status to honour-related violence to ensure that they were properly informed about the state's progress. As a consequence, the umbrella organizations were also held accountable by the state, which needed the umbrellas' progress reports to keep the MPs satisfied. In this manner, the umbrella organizations seemingly became *policy implementers*.

The following quote by Van der Laan, then Minister of Housing, Communities and Integration, also clearly illustrates this:

As representatives of the federation of Turkish participation organizations in the Netherlands, you have just signed a protocol for how you will deal with honour-related violence in our country. (....) By doing so, you have undertaken to assume responsibility for bringing the issues into the open and preventing and tackling honour-related violence." (Van der Laan, 25 November 2008, website)

This demonstrates how Van de Laan held the umbrella organization accountable for realizing a change in mentality within its rank and file.

The next quote from a policy advisor further illustrates the tension in the state's approach towards umbrella organizations:

Migrant organizations are organized citizens and are part of the civil society. They are not the implementing authorities of a ministry. Cooperation is entered into on the basis of the shared responsibility of the migrant umbrella organizations. (…) This is given shape within the programme: the initiative for change must also come from below. This will then be supported and organizations have the necessary freedom in terms of how they put the issue on the agenda within the communities. As a result, effective substantiation and efficacy will be investigated, as will justification in terms of effort and resources. This takes place through discussions and information exchanges and through reports and assessments.

This means that, while this representative of the Ministry of Housing, Communities and Integration acknowledged that umbrella organizations were part of the civil society and therefore free to determine for themselves how to bring about the change, the representative simultaneously acknowledged that the state would hold them accountable by demanding reports and assessments of their efficacy.

Various documents from the umbrella organisations illustrate how they adapted to this "output control" by the state. For instance, they explicitly consider the "return" on projects that were carried out as part of the programme "On the right side of honour". For example, in its manifesto *Vluchtelingen als change-makers* ("refugees as change-makers") refugee organization VON specifically examines the question "What may you expect from us?" (Dekker & Özgümüs 2008: 13-14). IOT, the participation organization for Turks in the Netherlands, went so far as to supply precise figures for their output. Its *Deelplan eergerelateerd geweld 2007-2010* ("honour-related violence subplan 2007-2010") promised the following output:

> In reality, this means that IOT and its affiliated federations will realize the following during the plan period:
>
> – Thirty Turkish organizations in 10 municipalities will enter into collaborative partnerships with the police, women's support services and other relevant organizations in order to realize an approach to honour-related violence.
> – The managers of 200 local Turkish organizations will be familiar with the operational protocol and will have been approached by their own federations in order to endorse the protocol.
> – All federations affiliated with IOT must organize activities connected to the topic of honour-related violence.
> – Within the Turkish community, 20,000 people will be contacted to share information with them about the roles and methods of the police and women's support services and others in connection with actual and threatened honour-related violence.
> – Five hundred people will be familiar with behavioural alternatives with respect to honour-related violence, particularly the course and discussion groups for young parents about upbringing, as set out below.

> It will require a tremendous effort from IOT's associated federations and their local organizations to implement the activities described in this plan. An estimated 150 volunteers will be required to carry out these activities. (IOT 2008: website)

However, the umbrella organizations did not simply carry out their allocated tasks passively. As bridge builders, the umbrella organizations were also very much aware of their position of power, and they used that position to claim a position as policymakers. This is illustrated effectively by the following quote:

> But also because we said: if you [the programme to combat honour-related violence] wish to achieve something, if we want to achieve something, then it must be regarded as a societal problem, we must be seen as a valuable partner; the migrant organizations, they're the problem owners. The police and women's support services are very important in the network but without the migrant organizations you'll not get anywhere, you'll have no points of entry, nothing. That came across quite well at the time. We made it clear to the Minister of Justice. (...)

However, as the debate evolved, it also became clear that migrant organizations did not always feel acknowledged as full and equal partners. Moreover, they felt misrepresented in the protection and prosecution programme: while they worked to bring about a new mentality towards service providers, the service providers did not reciprocate:

> You have these three pillars, don't you? Safety and protection and the criminal-law measures. (...) But [within these pillars] no specific reference is made to the fact that opportunities have to be made for partnership and networking [with the migrant organizations]. Whereas this point is made very explicitly in our programme ["On the right side of honour"] (...). That's fine, but opportunities need to be found for this in all of the programmes. Collaborative efforts without reciprocity do not exist. That's what we're struggling against, with the programme coordinator among other people.

The struggle described here is one of the key struggles within the emerging HRV field: migrant organizations seek acknowledgement as network partners while network partners such as the police and municipal authorities see a different role for them. This point was already mentioned in Chapter 9 and is considered at greater length in section 11.5, where I describe the local cross-border collaborative practices.

At the national level, the umbrella organizations utilized various strategies to gain a position as *policymakers*. For instance, they wrote letters to the ministers in charge of the various efforts. During the research period, this strategy was seen with particular frequency after Zeynep Boral's murder in 2007. The umbrella organizations "used" that honour killing to bring various shortcomings to the attention of the Minister of Justice, who was responsible for coordinating the interministerial programme. One interviewee explicitly reflected on this strategy as follows:

> Right after the double murder occurred in Alkmaar, we sent a letter to [Minister of Justice] Hirsch Ballin. In our letter to the minister, we said that he wasn't providing proper administrative control of the police's approach. There was no administrative control. We were afraid that things could go wrong as a result. (...) This administrative control is still not in place. They know this already. This is one of our disagreements.

Besides their direct attempts to influence the state through letters, the umbrella organizations also used an indirect steering mechanism. They actively used their position as agenda setters to sound the alarm about the HRV field's shortcomings within the media field and/or the political field. For instance, they co-organized the commemoration of Zeynep's murder in 2008. This commemoration was attended by her family, as well as by many members of the HRV field, including Arib, MP for PvdA (the Dutch labour party). The commemoration subsequently also generated a great deal of media attention.

The foregoing also demonstrates how, like the previously discussed shootings of Kezban, Hassan, Zarife and Gül, Zeynep's murder functioned as a *key field-configuring event*. Various actors used it to illustrate the state's shortcomings in its handling of honour-related violence. Moreover, again like the previous shootings it generated a great deal of discussion about the applicability of the label of honour killing. Yet its function was not entirely identical. While the previous incidents had contributed to the emergence of the issue, Zeynep's murder occurred at a time when the interministerial programme was already in place, and it generated a great deal of discussion about both the adequacy of the measures developed and the speed of their implementation.

All this illustrates how the emergence of the issue of honour-related violence altered and intensified the existing collaborative practices between the state and the umbrella organizations for migrant organizations. Firstly, the umbrella organizations' social capital within the honour-related violence field became more valuable as the state began to depend on them to bring about a change in mentality among their grassroots. Secondly, the attention for this particular issue in the media and among MPs meant that migrant organizations could capitalize more on their role as agenda setters. As the state's actions were already under scrutiny from both sets of actors, the umbrella organizations found a willing public for their critical comments and so could also challenge the state's position indirectly.

In terms of Bourdieu's writings, it can therefore be concluded that in this particular field the state's power was limited. The state was able to use its funding to impose "output control" on the umbrella organizations. However, due to the specific nature of this issue-based field, the umbrella organizations were able to push back and make demands of their own: recognition as a full and equal partner.

11.3 Collaborative practices between the state and local network partners

Besides working with each other, the state and the umbrella organizations for migrant organizations also worked with other actors within the HRV field. The state worked with actors that took part in local HRV networks such as the police, women's shelters, municipal authorities and the Support Centres for Domestic Violence. Similarly, the umbrella organizations needed to work with local migrant organizations in order to give shape to the programme "On the right side of honour". Nonetheless, as the programme "On the right side of honour" was not yet being implemented at the time of this study, this section focuses on the state's collaborative practices with local actors.

Decentralization processes

The collaborative practices observed between the state and local actors such as municipal authorities were nothing new. In fact, the state worked with those same local actors on a wide range of issues. Yet the emergence of the issue, and the subsequent interministerial programme altered the content of those collaborative practices. Below, I therefore present a few examples of those practices. However, as they were influenced by the general *decentralization trend* that crept into the Netherlands at the beginning of the 1980s (Boogers et al. 2008) I begin with some brief information about that development.

Since the 1980s and 1990s, the Dutch state has shifted many of its duties and responsibilities to administrative authorities situated lower down in the hierarchy, such as provinces and municipalities. An inescapable aspect of these decentralization processes is the privatization of former government institutes. Those organizations have become independent administrative authorities (*zelfstandige bestuursorgaan, zbo*) that, when formed, are assigned a specific list of tasks and objectives. As a consequence, when new tasks are given to an independent administrative authority, this triggers negotiations about the financial implications of the new task (Van Thiel 2003: 2-5).

The idea behind these *decentralization processes* was that they would lead to custom-designed and more integrated policies. Moreover, it was expected that the actors would be able to respond more adequately to evolving circumstances. Lastly, these processes were expected to enhance the state's democratic legitimacy, as civilians could voice their concerns more easily at the municipal level. The downside of these processes was that municipal autonomy meant that the local implementation of policies was not necessarily identical (Boogers et al. 2008:9-10).

According to Van Thiel (2003: 23) this "horizontalized" the relationship between the state and other actors, as the state's top-down administrative control diminished. This *horizontalization* subsequently led to the creation of what are sometimes termed "second generation instruments", which are characterized by a more discretionary approach between the actors concerned. An example of this type of second generation instrument is the establishment of covenants between actors.

The question that subsequently arises is whether these decentralization processes made the state any less powerful, thus debunking the theory devised by Bourdieu et al. (1994) on state power. In the following I therefore focus chiefly on how the state sought to retain its previous level of power and influence over other key actors within the emerging HRV field.

Collaborative practices between the state and network organizations

The described decentralization processes impacted the collaborative practices observed within the emerging HRV field. They particularly shaped the partnerships between on the one hand the ministries that determined the interministerial programme to combat honour-related violence and on the other the executive organizations represented in the HRV networks.

For instance, at the time of the 2007-2008 research, negotiations were ongoing between the Ministry of Health, Welfare and Sport and municipal authorities about setting up forty shelters for male victims of honour-related violence. In the end, a covenant was established between the four largest municipalities[119] and the ministry, stipulating that the ministry would provide half the funding to develop the shelters. Precisely how the shelters were to be organized was left to the municipalities to decide.

One interviewee working for the Ministry of Health, Welfare and Sport described the relationship between the ministry and the municipal authorities as follows:

> Interviewee: "(...) but municipal authorities give direction to the domestic violence approach at a local level. We of course can't do that from here [the ministries]. We can set conditions, provide instruments, but the 'doing' has to take place at a local level and we try to facilitate this. (...)"
> Interviewer: "This directing role of municipal authorities, you believe that this can't be done in any other way?"
> Interviewee: "No, I can't tackle domestic violence from here."
> Interviewer: "It's remarkable that every municipality does it in a different way. (...)"
> Interviewee: "Yes, we're trying to streamline this. One of the most important points in our new approach [to tackling domestic violence] is the creation of a national model. We're doing this together with the four largest cities; they're already working on it. We think this is an exciting initiative and we'd like to work with them to develop it further, so we have a model that we can offer to municipal authorities. We can't impose it; that

---

119. The cities of Amsterdam, Rotterdam, The Hague and Utrecht.

would require a legal obligation. If you wanted to do that it would take another three years, but we don't really see the point. It's more a matter of facilitating: you offer it to them and hope that they use it, that they adopt whatever elements are useful to them."

This interviewee felt that it made sense to organize the efforts to tackle domestic violence at the municipal level, since municipal authorities are closer to the individuals concerned. At the same time the ministry tried to facilitate these efforts, for instance by developing instruments and models, and so sought to contribute to uniformity in the implementation of the domestic-violence policy at the local level.

This illustrates how the Ministry of Health, Welfare and Sport tried to control the honour-related violence: through financial incentives and by providing models and instruments. The Ministry of Justice organized its criminal-law measures for tackling honour-related violence in a similar manner. The focus here is primarily on the ministry's partnership with the police, which was also ministry's main focus during the research period.

The ministry's partnership with the police was complicated by a number of factors. First, at the time the police fell under the responsibility of another ministry: the Ministry of the Interior and Kingdom Relations. Additionally, each of the twenty-five police regions were independent administrative authorities (*zelfstandig bestuursorganen*)[120]. As a consequence, negotiations needed to be conducted with each region separately to convince them to adopt the honour-related violence measures developed by the Multi-Ethnic Policing ("MEP") Unit. The following quotes from a representative of the Ministry of Justice illustrate this complexity:

> What I do is relatively simple, it's concrete, the criminal-law chain is clear. But at the same time it's also quite complex. You can't organize all the police organizations at once. (...) They're unwieldy organizations that are very busy. And then you come along with your [interministerial] programme and they have to just [pick it up]…
> And then there are forces that stand in your way and say, "We don't have any capacity." And I think that's a legitimate concern. Because the state, of course, imposes all kind of tasks and if you don't provide any funds… There's money for the programme but that will stop in 2010. (...) And it's all very well for the House of Representatives and the Cabinet to say, "They have to work more efficiently and more effectively", but you can't keep that up indefinitely.

Clearly, this interviewee sympathized with the struggle that the police face in taking on new tasks. At the same time, his quote illustrates how the state's partnerships with other actors are shaped by the political dimension.

The fact that the state needed to conduct individual negotiations with each police force may well have contributed to the concerns among umbrella organiza-

---

120. In 2013 the police was centralized into a single national police force.

tions for migrant organizations about the "administrative control of the police's approach". These individual negotiations caused differences in the speed at which the various police forces adopted the MEP method. Moreover, as with the municipal authorities, it was left to the individual police forces to decide for themselves how to implement the MEP method. The same interviewee explained this as follows:

> Interviewee: "And in answer to the question, 'Where should [the approach to tackling honour-related violence] be accommodated?' one force places it within the 'enforcement' unit while another places it in the 'detection' unit. Many forces accommodate it within their 'research and management information' units. So there's a huge variety."
> Interviewer: "They're allowed to decide this for themselves?"
> Interviewee: "Yes. I try not to get involved. Our only goal is to ensure that the MEP method is applied everywhere."

This explains the differences in local measures against honour-related violence.

However, like the Ministry of Health, Welfare and Sport, the Ministry of Justice sought to unify the police force's approach. For instance, it supported the efforts to organize "national contact days": conferences that afforded the local points of contact for HRV the opportunity to exchange experiences with one another and to learn how other police forces gave shape to their efforts against honour-related violence. In addition, the Ministry of Justice also worked to improve the levels of expertise among all police officers. Part of this involved developing courses with input from the Police Academy. Furthermore, in partnership with the Ministry of Health, Welfare and Sport, the Ministry of Justice supported the development of a model covenant setting out how the Public Prosecution Service, the police and women's support services could work together in their fight against honour-related violence[121]. The ministry also worked with the Ministry of the Interior and Kingdom Relations to develop a brochure explaining what forms of information actors could exchange with one another without violating privacy laws. This was an important instrument, as information sharing between actors such as women's shelters and the police was perceived as crucial for effective cooperation in the fight against honour-related violence.

Clearly, the general decentralization trend limited the state's administrative control within the emerging HRV field. However, by applying its informational and economic capital the state was nevertheless able to motivate other actors to take action. At the same time, the state was not in a position to stipulate the details of those actions. Consequently, local differences occurred within the emerging HRV field. As is shown in section 11.5, those local differences amazed and

---

121. This model covenant is called *Samenwerken voor de veiligheid van (potentiële) slachtoffers van eergerelateerd geweld* ("working together for the safety of existing and potential victims of honour-related violence") (De Boer 2008).

frustrated migrant organizations, as they expected working practices and development speed to be similar throughout the Netherlands.

11.4 Network collaboration within the HRV field

At the local level, the emergence of the issue of honour-related violence gave rise to the development of a very specific type of collaborative practice: network collaboration (*ketensamenwerking*). The aims of these HRV networks were 1.) to provide the necessary assistance to victims of honour-related violence and 2.) to co-ordinate criminal investigation into honour-related violence cases. At the time of the 2007-2008 study, Amsterdam and Rotterdam in particular were developing these HRV networks, which were still under construction. The following quote from a police representative provides a vivid description of the status quo:

> I came to work here on 1 April and felt as if I had to jump straight onto a moving train, if you'll excuse my use of that metaphor. In terms of speed, it really is a high-speed train. From time to time, I also think that it's going too fast. Looking at my own organization, as well as other organizations that are connected to the network approach, it's clear that not everyone has been able to "sell" themselves, and the network and the approach and the theme, within their own organizations. Looking at the police alone, the major shortfalls at the moment lie in the knowledge about the issue among my peers – among the people who actually have to deal with it, whether sitting at their desk taking reports, or taking reports out on the streets, or as neighbourhood officers hearing stories while walking, cycling or driving around, or officers who have to handle a particular statement.

According to this interviewee, therefore, network collaboration was evolving very rapidly, perhaps too rapidly, as the partners in the networks struggled to bring their own organizations up to speed. The quote also demonstrates how the complexity of the fight against honour-related violence lay not only in the complexity of the issue, but also in the complexity of network collaboration: working in networks demanded not only clear-cut arrangements between the partners, but also the necessary setup at each organization for working according to this method. In the following I therefore examine both the internal and the external challenges of network collaboration. First, however, I provide a brief explanation of the concept of network collaboration.

Network collaboration: a theoretical explanation

Networks can be regarded as a particular form of inter-organizational partnership. Van der Aa and Konijn (2004: 17) describe this type of partnership as follows:

> Networks bind organizational processes that together might be significant for a client. (…) The purpose of networks is to combine the responsibilities that might be fragmen-

ted across autonomous organizations, to form a comprehensive and functional entity. (…) The underlying idea is that the working processes of many organizations are, in fact, partial processes, steps in a client's trajectory (…).

A network has a specific aim to which the various partners are committed. In addition, networks ideally have a repetitive nature, are non-hierarchical in terms of their setup and have an operational focus (Van der Aa & Konijn 2004; Goedee & Entken 2006). Lastly, according to Beemer at al. (2003) the core values that guide network collaboration are flexibility, customization, demand orientation and trust. Network collaboration can therefore also be interpreted as giving shape to the decentralization processes described above, which focused on custom-designed and integrated policy implementation.

Working in networks requires a new way of forming partnerships. Working as part of a network demands a change in the organizational culture: the focus should no longer be on the organization's interests but on the interests of the network as a whole. However, research into organizational culture changes demonstrates that thought processes and operational methods take a long time to change (Bate 1994; Boonstra et al. 2003; Koot and Dobbinga 2004; Martin 1992; Tennekes 1995; Veenswijk 1995). Moreover, Van der Aa and Konijn (2004: 20) explicitly state that these changes are not easy to realize in the public sector, where notions of hierarchy and bureaucracy often dominate and numerous interests jostle for position.

Consequently, as one interviewee noted, "A network approach might look very attractive on paper, but it has to be substantiated." In other words, the organizational process must be set up in a way that ensures that in practice people actually think and work in accordance with the network approach. The question that subsequently arises is whether actors within the emerging HRV field had already adapted to this new way of working.

External partnerships with network partners

The vast amount of documentation about network collaboration and the countless meetings that took place between network partners initially created the impression that by 2007-2008 network collaboration was a firmly established practice within the emerging HRV field. However, closer inspection reveals that these practices were still a work in progress. The discussions between network partners demonstrate that it takes time to organize external partnerships (and to adjust the internal processes).

For instance, a Rotterdam-based partner mentioned how partners still needed to adjust to network collaboration:

> Of course, along the way (…) you get *to the point* more quickly, but it remains a case of carefully addressing things. Whenever something appears to not work in practice, you have to adjust. You shouldn't continue with it.

> (…)
> Practical experience is gained together, so whenever you give off signals such as "my organization can't connect to this" or "I get the impression that we're wide of the mark with this point or that", then you need to work on it together.

This also illustrates how the results of the network as a whole depend on the ability of the individual organizations to adjust to the demands placed on them by the network. Therefore, according to this respondent, the partners needed to respect each other's positions and try to resolve their individual problems together.

An Amsterdam-based network partner also described the development within his own municipality, focusing primarily on the internal organizational issues still facing the organizations concerned:

> So, these types of growing pains, as I call them, are still part of the reporting procedure, and naturally they need to be eliminated. Still, this will take some time because we have I think around 25 neighbourhood teams in Amsterdam and numerous employees with the police who have to deal with this and who won't all know what to do (…). This also applies to support centres [for domestic violence]: not every employee will immediately realize that he's dealing with honour violence. (…) Right, so we're also working on this within the network, to ensure within the network consultation process that the "discovery points", shall we say, perhaps doctors, other professionals, housing corporations, in-home caregivers… That they develop the necessary awareness, knowledge, that they know where to go to report things. (…)
> So if you ask me what a good approach is, that would be the approach that we just outlined, but properly implemented. Properly implemented, so that all the organizations know, "That's how to do it. And this I where I can go. And I'm confident that if I go there with a report, that something will happen with this information. That the report will be investigated carefully and effectively. That safety issues will be taken into account, not just the assistance." So that the various partners trust one another… That's really important. And it's something you have to earn, you have to win it. You can't enforce it with a covenant or pretty words. No, you just have to earn it. By demonstrating that it works.

Both these quotes clearly illustrate that the working arrangements between the network partners were still being refined on the basis of practical experience: only practice reveals whether the various roles allocated on paper can be properly fulfilled by the actors in question. The second interviewee also indicated that actually tackling the problem of honour-related violence meant that all the employees involved needed to understand both the issue and the collaborative practices.

At the same time, being primarily a matter of customization, network collaboration demands flexibility. As a consequence, the tasks that a particular actor fulfils may vary for each case of honour-related violence. The quote below, been taken from a conversation with a police officer, illustrates this idea:

> That also depends on the specific case. Sometimes an employee from the Support Centres for Domestic Violence has such a good relationship with the victim or the victim's boyfriend that, if we have any questions for the boyfriend, I'd rather use the existing relationship than become involved as a stranger.
> Sometimes you might have picked up a signal from a girl and you know that her family are going to Morocco or Iraq for an extended visit. The people in her immediate circle, social workers or a friend, might be extremely worried about this because they've heard chatter about forced marriage or other issues. Then you can ask a colleague on the neighbourhood team to pay a visit in plain clothes in order to gauge the situation, or at least show that the police or those providing assistance have concerns about certain issues; however, they'll need an excuse to charm their way inside.
> Sometimes it's much more concrete: if a father hits his daughter at school or something like that, then you can assume that the school, the girl's friends and the police are aware of it. Then it's more logical for a neighbourhood officer to gauge the situation with an approach along the lines of "Sir, we have some concerns". You might also tell these kinds of people that we're concerned and this might be interpreted as concerning the daughter, health, finances, lack of a job and so on. (...) At the same time, you also need to be clear that it's a matter of Dutch criminal law and legislation. His actions aren't permitted.

In other words, the network approach adopts a situation-specific approach to honour-related issues; actors may fulfil various tasks depending on the case confronting them. At the same time, the quote shows that some regular-function roles always belong to one and the same partner. The trick is to find the right balance between ensuring that the roles and tasks of the network partners remain sufficiently clear, while also allowing for sufficient flexibility in handling honour-related violence issues, which all have their own characteristics.

Network collaboration: the internal challenges

The explanation of network collaboration presented above shows that an actor's ability to adjust its organization to network collaboration is just as important as, and perhaps even more important than, developing arrangements with external partners. However, various interviews and documents illustrate that this internal adjustment to network collaboration was still lacking in 2007-2008. According to Janssen (2008), a researcher at the police's National Expertise Centre for Honour-Related Violence (LEC), actors within the emerging HRV field still suffered from an "our-institution" syndrome, which manifests itself when

> institutions no longer keep an eye on the working methods, opportunities, jurisdictions and objectives of their partner organizations, and moreover systematically believe that their own working style is preferable and only take action to enhance their own "honour and glory". (Janssen 2008: 135)

Jansen clearly felt that network collaboration was not yet institutionalized within the organizational practices of the partners concerned.

Others also seem to have been aware of this notion. One interviewee, for instance, indicated that the most difficult aspect of working in networks was implementing this method within his own organization. Even within municipal authorities that were responsible for the local administrative control, the network approach needed to be "sold" time and time again:

> The difficulty that you have within your own municipal organization in terms of clarifying the result you actually want to achieve, what everyone must contribute, you have to make a huge investment and that's where managers play an extremely important role. Coming together time after time for meetings, recounting the same story about what you want again and again, what you're working towards. This is difficult but you have to make time for it; you have to hold your people together. It doesn't happen of its own accord and it can't be enforced. Within the Board, you can decide how you're going to do it but you can't enforce it. You can only do that if people are interested and [they] realize that they're part of something bigger. And even then this only involves the municipal organization; you also have to externalize a great deal.

Partners in the networks evidently still struggled with their internal organizations. As a consequence, those internal organizations often lagged behind their external partnership arrangements, negatively affecting those external collaborative practices.

Thus, the findings indicate that new collaborative practices were evolving between actors who worked together to provide the protection of victims and prosecution of perpetrators of honour-related violence: the police, women's shelters, municipal authorities, the Youth Care Agencies, the Support Centres for Domestic Violence, the Public Prosecution Service, etc. These actors were asked to take part in this network collaboration on the basis of their specific regular-function roles.

The study also illustrates that while network collaboration was perceived as a very reliable way to tackle honour-related violence at the local level the complexity of its implementation – demanding both internal and external adjustments – meant that by 2007-2008 none of the existing networks was fully developed. Moreover, at that moment in time, the external collaborative practices were apparently more advanced than the internal adjustment to the method. This tension between *external and internal adjustment to network collaboration* perhaps contributed to the lack of trust that was at times apparent between separate network partners and between network partners and migrant organizations: with internal adjustment to network collaboration lagging behind, network partners were unable to properly fulfil the roles attributed to them by other network partners.

11.5 Network partners and migrant organizations: lack of trust

At the local level, the emergence of the issue of honour-related violence not only led to the development of network collaboration, it also gave rise to collaborative efforts between network organizations and migrant organizations. However, while both types of actors acknowledged that they needed each other to properly tackle honour-related violence, their collaborative efforts were characterized by a lack of trust. Various interviewees, representatives of both migrant organizations and government institutes, explicitly commented on this lack of trust. Strikingly, their comments focused primarily on the lack of trust that the other actors had in them. For instance, a representative of a women's shelter talked about the lack of trust that migrant organizations displayed with regard to the good intentions of government institutes:

> Interviewee: "The second step was to gather around the table with migrant organizations and with their national umbrellas, which represent the local umbrella organizations. We had about three or four of these meetings, which were difficult and devolved into a game of yes and no the first time. It basically came down to acknowledgment of positions. Migrant organizations don't feel recognized by the predominantly white government institutes and their partners, and say, 'Listen, we're part of this, we possess expertise in this area and you're ignoring us.' We didn't get together to discuss this, however, and you need to discuss this first before you can move forward."
>
> Interviewer: "So, acknowledging the problem within their communities was not a point of discussion?"
>
> Respondent: "No, they did in fact acknowledge that it was a problem, but at the same time they felt like, 'You can't tell us what to do!' Which we didn't want to anyway, (…) we wanted to see who had what kind of expertise and try to find a common ground. At the time we'd already realized that we couldn't simply walk into a community and tell them, 'This is the problem, this is what you need to do about it and this is what we're going to do.' It doesn't work that way, they have to do it themselves. They need us and we need them. If you want to tackle this problem at its roots, they need to communicate better with their grassroots and their committee members, talk to people in the districts and organize meetings."

In a similar vein, the following quote from a representative of an umbrella organization for migrant organizations illustrates the perceived lack of trust among network partners and their unwillingness to cooperate with migrant organizations:

> But you need to cooperate. It doesn't work if the police only see me as an informant; you need to trust each other. Also, if somebody becomes aware of his or her situation, I need to know from the police that they can provide shelter. I need to be sure of that, otherwise I can't refer someone to them. I need a guarantee of her safety, because I'm the one responsible.

Another representative of an umbrella organization added the following observation:

> Look, although migrants are the target group, they're not viewed as allies. These kinds of things occur especially within male professions like the police. Their definition of a

collaborative effort is completely different. Although we have regular meetings, what happens is that they say, "We'll report to you what we've done." That's their idea of working together.

Yet both groups of actors seemed to understand that they needed to trust each other in order to properly combat honour-related violence. The following quote also illustrates this:

> You can expect that in the future, once the contact and trust [have been established] between informal networks and the migrant organizations and the white assistance, shall we say, like the police, the judicial authorities and social workers, hopefully cases will be dealt with faster and more adequately, making sure that victims are brought into safety more quickly or preventing escalation. (Representative of a women's shelter)

The programme "On the right side of honour" also focused explicitly on tackling the perceived lack of trust:

> When local collaborative connections are being set up, creating a basis of trust between the parties involved is the priority. The professional authorities need to view Turkish organizations as serious and equal partners. Local organizations have to be willing to tackle the preconception (an oversimplified idea) that the police will only take action once someone has been murdered and that women's shelters are actually whorehouses. (IOT 2008: website)

Nonetheless, at the time of this study, the collaborative efforts between network organizations and migrant organizations did not go beyond explicitly demarcating each other's tasks and roles. For instance, when asked whether migrant organizations could and/or should play a part in the Dutch measures against honour-related violence, one interviewee stated,

> Definitely! They can definitely play a part in it; however, in my opinion that part should not be exaggerated. (…) [T]hey're obviously not replacing aid organizations. (…) [B]ut what they're especially good at are the informal networks. They have vast informal networks, they're very often, not always, but still very often informed at an early stage, often through their networks, that there's a problem, that there's a conflict or that something is about to happen. (Representative of a women's shelter)

This quote highlights a possible explanation for the identified lack of trust: a fear of role confusion. The interviewee appears to limit the role of migrant organizations in order to protect his own functional area.

The question is whether this concern is justified. In their explanation of the programme "On the right side of honour" the umbrella organizations explicitly note that they are not responsible for assisting victims of honour-related violence or and ensuring their safety. In their eyes, safety, the criminal-law measures and assistance are clearly the responsibility of network partners. At the same time, though, they were disappointed with the pace at which network collaboration was developing. Moreover, they perceived the slow pace as extremely problematic, given that in the meantime they were working to change migrants' attitude towards the service providers. They were worried that the network partners would not be ready for the people that they had convinced of the need to seek help.

At the same time, network partners felt that migrant organizations sometimes had unrealistic expectations. One interviewee expressed this as follows:

> Migrant organizations' expectations are sometimes not very realistic. For example, they look for a point of contact at the Dutch police, one person for the entire police force in the Netherlands. That doesn't work. (Police officer)

This example also illustrates another factor contributing to the lack of trust: poor understanding of each other's internal organizations. To an outsider, someone who is unaware of how the police are organized, the request makes sense, as this would facilitate the collaborative efforts with the police. However, to a police representative, someone who is aware of the autonomy of the twenty-five police forces, the request is unrealistic.

At the same time, this lack of trust and the subsequent demarcation processes also seem to be enhanced by the *othering discourses* that were part of the moral panic about honour killings. The question of whether migrant organizations could function as mediators in cases of honour-related violence exemplifies this proposition as this question is translated into questions about the loyalties of migrant organizations. The following quote from a network partner in Amsterdam illustrates this point:

> (…) [I]nvolvement of people from the target demographic in mediation so from the migrant communities, shall we say, is rejected. According to Rotterdam you just shouldn't do this. (…) Because these people are not isolated, and as soon as they do this, they're endangering not only themselves, but also other people. So it simply leads to potential danger for people in their own communities and in that case it's better to involve neutral, independent people in mediation attempts or, you know, see what still can be done.

This clearly illustrates the ambivalence that was felt about involving people from the communities concerned as informants or go-betweens.

On the one hand, a consensuses appears to have existed about the fact that people with a migrant background could be seen as "experts by experience", able to analyse and pinpoint how honour plays a role in a particular cases. On the other, some respondents also voiced their concerns about the ability of these migrant experts to remain "neutral", "independent", and "detached" from their cultural heritage. For example, I was regularly told stories about Turkish mediators and translators who, while working with the police, attempted to influence the individuals filing the reports to return to their families, or worse, who sought out the families and told them about the individual's whereabouts.

The ambivalence about involving "experts by experience" within the domains of prosecution and protection appears to be connected to a wider discussion within the integration discourse on migrants' loyalties. In this case, the loyalties of the migrant professionals and organizations were questioned: would they stand for the Dutch standards and values institutionalized in the Dutch law system, or would they act as representatives of "their" culture?

As a consequence, at the local level the cross-border collaborative practices were characterized by two paradoxical features. On the one hand, the parties lacked trust in one another, while on the other they had high hopes in terms of what the others could achieve in tackling honour-related violence. The explicit demarcation processes subsequently reveal the existence of two subfields within the emerging HRV field, one being formed by the government organizations responsible for protecting victims and prosecuting perpetrators of honour-related violence, and the second comprising primarily migrant organizations seeking to bring about a change in mentality within their grassroots.

This demarcation processes might have been amplified by two factors. Firstly, migrant organizations were new actors in the fight against violence. The police, the Public Prosecution Service and women's shelters were already working together to tackle other issues such as domestic violence, and as such had already developed a degree of partnership, whereas migrant organizations were taking on a new role within the HRV field. Secondly, the demarcation processes between the two subfields might also have ensued from the moral panic connected to this particular issue (see Chapter 7). An inevitable component of a moral panic is a demarcation between "us" and "them". This mentality might have contributed to the ambivalence among government organizations about working with migrant organizations, whose motives and loyalties were sometimes openly questioned.

11.6 Concluding remarks

According to Bourdieu, a field is not formed by a group of actors, but rather by the *relationship between the positions* that compose the field. Those positions in turn are defined by the type and amount of capital available to the actor occupying this position (Bourdieu & Wacquant 1992:107).

Chapter 9 describes which types of capital are of particular importance within the emerging HRV field and how these types of capital are distributed across the key actors within this field. In the present chapter I have focussed on how these actors are positioned within the emerging field. I have studied this by focussing on the type of interactions – i.e. collaboration practices – that could be witnessed within this particular field.

This analysis reveals four type of collaboration practices that dominated the emerging field. At a local level this concerns network collaboration (*ketensamenwerking*) between actors who are concerned with providing assistance to victims of honour-related violence and/or with coordinating criminal investigations into honour-related violence cases. These networks included actors such as women's shelters, the police, municipal authorities, Support Centres for Domestic Violence and Youth Care Agencies. These actors gained their central role within these local networks on the basis of their informational capital (e.g. their day-to-day knowledge about victims and perpetrators of honour-related violence).

A second collaboration practice that could be observed within the emerging field is the collaboration between the state and the umbrella organizations for migrant organizations. This collaboration preceded the emergence of the issue of honour-related violence and was officialized via the Minorities Policy (Consultation) Act. Still, the emergence of this particular issue meant that the value of the umbrellas' social capital increased as the state now needed these organizations to "implement" a change of mentality within their grassroots.

The state also depended on local network partners such as the police, municipalities and women's shelters to implement the next two pillars of the interministerial programme: prevention and prosecution. This dependence meant an increase in the value of the informational capital of the actors providing assistance to victims of honour-related violence and/or coordinating the criminal investigations. The state subsequently drew on its economic capital to push these actors to take action. In addition, the state worked on *theoretical unification* within the HRV field by funding conferences and developing course material, brochures and model agreements.

Finally, migrant organizations and their umbrella organizations wanted to collaborate with local network partners such as the police and women's shelters. Particularly this collaboration practice highlighted demarcation processes and struggles between field members. The comments made by representatives of network collaboration actors indicates a lack of trust in the migrant organizations' loyalties. The comments made by representatives of migrant organizations also show that they did not feel accepted as full and equal partners.

While the value of migrants' insider knowledge (i.e. informational capital) was acknowledged, this was apparently not perceived as sufficient incentive to fully accept each other as partners. In the following, I analyse the struggles that feature this collaboration practice in further detail by relating it to the *othering discourses* that are described in Chapters 6 and 7.

The above illustrates how the worth of the various types of capital depends on the field's logic and the issue at hand. For instance, in this case migrant organizations' social capital became particularly relevant, as one of the state's goals was to achieve a change of mentality within the policy target groups.

At the same time, general processes such as the Dutch decentralization trend and the rise of network collaboration as a way to organize local collaboration also influenced the HRV field's emerging configurations and struggles. This point is further addressed in the next section, where I discuss how the HRV field was nested within broader fields.

The HRV field as a nested field

This case study illustrates how a field's configurations are influenced by broader societal developments and thus the broader fields in which this particular subfield is nested (Emirbayer and Johnson 2008:22-32). The general *decentralization trend* meant that the state was not able to directly control organizations such as the police. In addition, the rise of network collaboration as a new organizing principle meant that actors within the HRV field needed to become acquainted not only with a new issue, but also with a new way of working together.

Finally, the HRV field's configuration indicates that both the othering discourses that accompanied the *moral panic* about honour killings and the Dutch approach towards integration (i.e. *categorical thinking*) strongly influenced the way in which the HRV field was structured.

According to Ghorashi (2006, 2010) categorical thinking combines an *essentialist perceptive* on culture in which migrants are not seen as individuals but as representatives of a different culture (thus being presented as cultural others), with a *deficit approach*, an approach in which migrants are seen as a policy target group that needs to be liberated from its disadvantaged position.

These processes can also be seen in the emerging HRV field. Migrants are positioned as cultural others with their own culturally embedded types of violence. Migrant organizations are subsequently asked to change this cultural "deficit" by seeking a change of mentality within their own rank and file. In line with what Ghorashi (2006, 2010) describes this creates a delineation between Dutch and non-Dutch violence. Moreover, this case study illustrates how this approach towards honour-related violence structured the emerging HRV field, eventually leading to the development of two subfields: one representing the established order and one representing migrant organizations and their umbrella organizations.

Conclusion and discussion

When I first began this research back in 2007, I was confronted with a myriad of actors and activities surrounding the issue of honour-related violence. These included actors as diverse as a theatre maker, migrant organizations, schools, scholars, politicians, women's shelters, police investigators and victims of honour-related violence. I was intrigued by this widespread attention for the issue and searched for a theoretical framework that would help me to make sense of this puzzle. I found that framework in the concepts of *organizational field emergence* and *issue-based organizational fields*, which had both been developed within institutional theory in organizational analysis. I combined this institutional framework with Bourdieu's *theory of practice*, as his work appeared to offer a solution to institutional theory's enduring quest for a balanced theory of action and power.

This research therefore served two purposes. On the one hand, I wished to empirically explore the actors and processes involved in the emergence of an issue-based organizational field, leading to the following research question:

> *What actors and processes contributed to the emergence of the issue-based organizational field on honour-related violence in the Netherlands?*

On the other hand, I wished to explore the potential of Bourdieu's work for institutional theory in organizational analysis, resulting in the following research question:

> *How does Bourdieu's theory of practice contribute to an understanding of the processes involved in organizational field emergence?*

In this final chapter I answer these questions and reflect on both the theoretical and practical implications of this study. I start by briefly recapitulating the results of the case study. I then describe the empirical contribution of this study, focusing primarily on the critical preconditions for organizational field emergence and on the processes that shape the emerging field configurations. I then turn to the second question and consider the added value of Bourdieu's framework. I end with a series of practical recommendations for actors working in the public domain.

The emergence of the Dutch honour-related violence field

This study reconstructed the emergence of the issue of honour-related violence by tracing the emergence of the labels of *eerwraak* (i.e. honour killing) and *eergerelateerd geweld* (honour-related violence) within the Dutch media field and political field. This reconstruction reveals that the issue of honour-related violence first emerged in the Dutch public discourse around the new millennium (Chapter 4).

The emergence of the issue was facilitated by *evolving macro-cultural discourses* on multiculturalism, gender equality, nationalism, citizenship and social cohesion (Chapter 6) and was driven by four *field-configuring events*, the shootings of Kezban, Hassan, Zarife and Gül (Chapter 5). This combination of macro-level and micro-level processes contributed to a *reconceptualization* of domestic violence against migrant women into honour-related violence. Moreover, the extensive media coverage of these incidents, the subsequent court cases and the warnings issued by various actors contributed to a *moral panic* about this issue: honour killings were perceived as a sign of the failing integration of migrants (Chapter 7). Together these three interrelated processes provide an explanation for the widespread public attention for the issue of honour-related violence at the beginning of the new millennium.

This case study shows that the attention for honour-related violence quickly spread to other fields, including the political field, where Gül's murder functioned as a catalyst for heated parliamentary debates between MPs and ministers about reliable solutions to the problem. These debates triggered a number of state actions, for example the development of a clear problem definition, the development of an interministerial programme to combat honour-related violence and the allocation of funding. In this manner the state *officialized* the problem of honour-related violence, a new stage in the development of an issue-based organizational field (Chapter 8).

The actors, actions and processes described above all contributed to the issue's emergence and the subsequent field emergence. Moreover, they influenced the *emerging field configurations*. However, these configurations (e.g. the emerging theoretical unification, the relevant types of capital and the positioning of the actors) were also food for debates between the actors entering this emerging field. It was through those debates and struggles that the HRV field's configurations eventually took shape.

Data from the field ethnography show that by 2007-2008 many actors had joined the honour-related violence field: the police, women's shelters, municipal authorities, support centres for domestic violence, schools, the Public Prosecution Service, the immigration service and migrant organizations Moreover, some of these actors could be labelled as *key actors*, having gained that position by combining multiple types of capital that were deemed important within this particular field – *economic capital, social capital* and various types of *informational capital*. Within the emerging field the struggle over the relevant types of capital particularly revolved around informational capital, with different actors having access to different forms of knowledge: expert knowledge (e.g. subject-matter experts), practical knowledge (e.g. police, women's shelters, schools) and insider knowledge (migrant organizations) (Chapter 9).

The ethnographic data also reveal that by 2007-2008 various actors were "*translating*" the official problem definition to their own working environments. These separate translations led to differences in interpretation between actors. For instance, some focused primarily on the escalated forms of violence (e.g. the police) while others focused on early signs of honour-related violence (e.g. schools). Although these translations are an essential part of field emergence (Grodal 2007), they also caused disputes between actors, who felt that not everyone had incorporated the definition in a suitable way (Chapter 10).

Yet the greatest struggle within this emerging field concerned the position of the migrant organizations. Migrant organizations were seen as bridge builders between state policy and the targeted migrant communities. Despite this key role, migrant organizations did not feel accepted as full and equal partners. For instance, they were not accepted as partners within the organizations involved in network collaboration. Based on this finding, it is my conclusion that the Dutch HRV field in fact comprised two distinct subfields: one consisting of the state and the various network partners and the other of the migrant organizations. Actors in the first field focused on protecting victims and prosecuting perpetrators. Actors in the second field worked on preventing of honour crimes by seeking to bring about a change in mentality within migrant communities.

Field emergence: a multi-layered process

This case study illustrates that the emergence of an issue-based organizational field is a multi-layered process in which various actors, actions and processes come together and influence each other. In the following I discuss the empirical contribution of this case study in greater detail, focusing on 1.) the phases in field emergence, 2.) the critical preconditions for field emergence, and 3.) the processes that shape the emerging field configurations. In doing so I present an answer to the question *What actors and processes contributed to the emergence of the issue-based organizational field on honour-related violence in the Netherlands?*

The three phases of issue-based field emergence

This case study illustrates that several phases can be distinguished in the process of field emergence: the emergence of the issue, the officialization of the issue as a social problem and the emergence of the related issue-based organizational field. These different phases flow into one another and influence one another, yet remain distinct. In the following I discuss these phases in the emergence of the Dutch HRV field in greater detail.

Phase 1: issue emergence

An issue-based field can only emerge once an issue has emerged in the public discourse. I therefore studied how the issue of honour-related violence emerged in the Dutch public discourse. The preceding analysis reveals that a set of interrelated processes, actors and actions contributed to the issue's emergence: a number of *unplanned field-configuring events* – honour killings – triggered the attention of a diverse group of actors. These actors were subsequently able to sound the alarm over these events within *the media field*, which was facilitated by both *changes within macro-cultural discourses* and the *development of a label* (i.e. eerwraak) that was compatible with the media field's logic. The media's representation of these events then led to the development of a *moral panic* about these honour killings, which were framed as non-Dutch types of violence (Part II).

Phase 2: officialization of the social problem

A next phase in the emergence of an issue-based field is the transformation of the issue into a discrete social problem. As Bourdieu et al. (1994) previously established, the findings of this case study illustrate how the *state* played a crucial role in *officializing the problem* of honour-related violence.

The *moral panic* that developed within the media field was seized and enhanced by several MPs (e.g. Hirsi Ali and Albayrak), who subsequently sounded the alarm about this type of violence within the political field. During the parliamentary debates that followed (*planned field-configuring events*) these MPs used a range of instruments (e.g. motions and priority project status) to push the Members of Cabinet to take action against this type of violence. This eventually resulted in the development of a clear-cut definition of the problem, the start of a pilot to establish the problem's extent, the allocation of funding to various projects and pilots and lastly the development of an interministerial programme to combat honour-related violence. Together these actions helped to 1.) legitimize honour-related violence as a discrete social problem and 2.) demark honour-related violence from domestic violence (Chapter 8).

Phase 3: field emergence

While described as distinct and separate, the foregoing phases overlap and influence each other. This also holds true for the phase of *field emergence*. This study illustrates that various actors were already working to combat honour-related violence before the state took any action. This particularly holds true for a number of migrant organizations. However, these bottom-up initiatives were not always connected. What the *involvement of the state* facilitated, particularly through the development of the interministerial programme, was that the organizations fighting honour-related violence now knew about each other and each other's activities. In the words of Hoffman (1999), they realized that they were partaking in a common debate.

As a consequence, the actors began to interact more and started to *struggle* with one another about the emerging field configurations. For example, once the migrant organizations became aware that other actors were working to fight honour-related violence through network collaboration, they started to demand a position within this network. Besides struggles for position, these conflicts with migrant organizations also included struggles about what type of knowledge had the greatest relevance (i.e. informational capital). Moreover, Zeynep Boral's murder in 2007 reignited the debate about the applicability of the "honour killing" label. While her family and various migrant organizations claimed that the incident was indeed an honour killing, the government initially followed the explanation of a scholarly expert and claimed that it was a case of domestic violence[122].

The above is summarized in the Figure 8. The subsequent section, in addition, describes the pivotal processes, actors and actions that contribute to the emergence of the Dutch HRV field greater detail.

---

122. According to the expert this murder was not an honour killing, as it did not correspond to the traditions connected to honour killings. For instance, by committing suicide Zeynep's husband broke with the tradition that the husband should turn himself in to himself to the police immediately after committing the honour killing.

Figure 8. Key events in the emergence of the Dutch HRV field

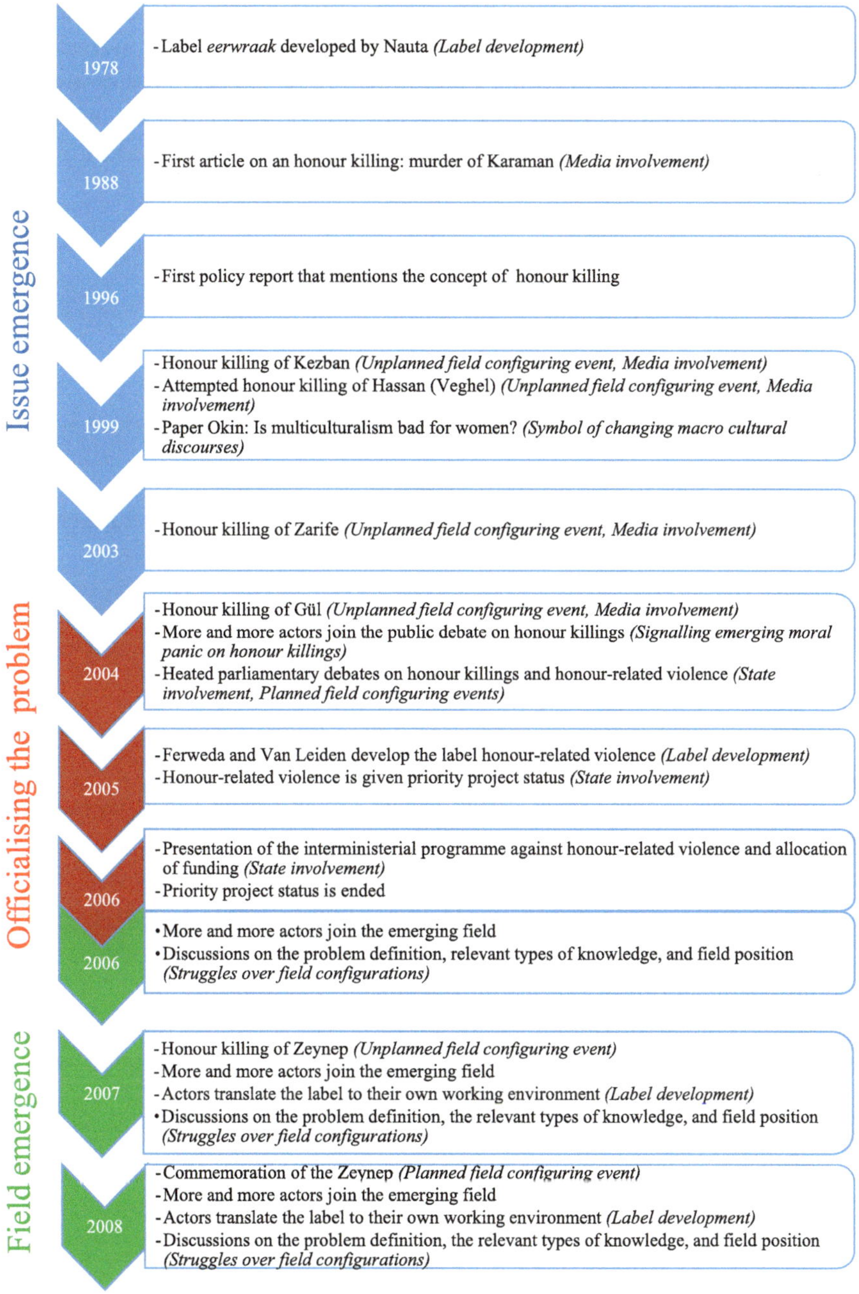

Issue emergence

1978
- Label *eerwraak* developed by Nauta *(Label development)*

1988
- First article on an honour killing: murder of Karaman *(Media involvement)*

1996
- First policy report that mentions the concept of honour killing

1999
- Honour killing of Kezban *(Unplanned field configuring event, Media involvement)*
- Attempted honour killing of Hassan (Veghel) *(Unplanned field configuring event, Media involvement)*
- Paper Okin: Is multiculturalism bad for women? *(Symbol of changing macro cultural discourses)*

2003
- Honour killing of Zarife *(Unplanned field configuring event, Media involvement)*

Officialising the problem

2004
- Honour killing of Gül *(Unplanned field configuring event, Media involvement)*
- More and more actors join the public debate on honour killings *(Signalling emerging moral panic on honour killings)*
- Heated parliamentary debates on honour killings and honour-related violence *(State involvement, Planned field configuring events)*

2005
- Ferweda and Van Leiden develop the label honour-related violence *(Label development)*
- Honour-related violence is given priority project status *(State involvement)*

2006
- Presentation of the interministerial programme against honour-related violence and allocation of funding *(State involvement)*
- Priority project status is ended

Field emergence

2006
- More and more actors join the emerging field
- Discussions on the problem definition, relevant types of knowledge, and field position *(Struggles over field configurations)*

2007
- Honour killing of Zeynep *(Unplanned field configuring event)*
- More and more actors join the emerging field
- Actors translate the label to their own working environment *(Label development)*
- Discussions on the problem definition, the relevant types of knowledge, and field position *(Struggles over field configurations)*

2008
- Commemoration of the Zeynep *(Planned field configuring event)*
- More and more actors join the emerging field
- Actors translate the label to their own working environment *(Label development)*
- Discussions on the problem definition, the relevant types of knowledge, and field position *(Struggles over field configurations)*

Critical preconditions for field emergence

According to Hoffman (1999:352) the emergence of an issue-based field is signalled by 1.) increased interaction between particular actors, 2.) an increase in the shared information load and 3.) the development of a mutual sense of awareness between actors that they are involved in a common debate. However, he does not examine in further detail how this increased interaction and shared information load comes about.

Based on my case study, it can be concluded that several distinct *processes*, *actors* and *actions* come together in the emergence of the Dutch HRV field, described here as *critical preconditions for field emergence*.

Table 6: Critical preconditions for the emergence of the Dutch HRV field

Process	Actor	Action
Field-configuring event	Media involvement	Label development
Changes in macro-cultural discourses	State involvement	Struggles over the emerging field configurations
Moral panic		

Process: field-configuring events

The emergence of a new issue is strongly facilitated by the occurrence of *critical events*: events that trigger the attention of the media and are used by actors (i.e. key instigators) to draw attention to a specific issue. According to Hoffman and Ocasio (2001:414) these types of events "focus sustained public attention and invite the collective definition or redefinition of social problems".

In this case the actual and attempted honour killings of Kezban, Hassan, Zarife and Gül functioned as critical events. Each generated a great deal of media attention and debate about the applicability of the "honour killing" label. Moreover, each successive incident caused the group of actors sounding the alarm on this particular issue to grow: first a friend, then an expert, a school director, women's shelters and finally politicians (Chapter 5).

Besides functioning as critical events, these murders therefore functioned as *field-configuring events*: they shaped the configurations of the emerging issue-based field by 1.) bringing together actors that would later become key actors within the Dutch HRV field and 2.) stimulating debates about the problem's definition. This perspective on field-configuring events matches the definition of Meyer et al. (2005:1026), who described field-configuring events as events that "encapsulate and shape" the development of a field.

Nonetheless, Meyer at al. (2005) attributed this function to temporary social organizations such as conferences and tradeshows, not to the types of *unplanned* field-configuring events described here. This can be explained by the fact that Meyer et al. (2005) did not study the development of issue-based fields, but focused on fields developing around particular products and technologies. As a consequence, they were not interested in events that triggered issue emergence.

Yet the type of events described by Mayer et al. (2005), denoted here as *planned* field-configuring events, were also present in the emerging HRV field. The debates between MPs and Members of Cabinet could, for instance, be described as classical field-configuring events, having strongly contributed to the emergence and shape of the HRV field (Chapter 8). The same applies to the various conferences and meetings that were organized by other actors such as the police, municipal authorities and women's shelters. These conferences and meetings contributed to field emergence by enabling the development of a shared information load and contributing to network building between the various actors.

Based on this case study I therefore posit that the occurrence of both unplanned and planned field-configuring events forms a critical precondition for field emergence. Unplanned events are necessary to stimulate issue emergence, while planned events are a condition for developing a network of actors with a shared understanding of the problem.

Process: evolving macro-cultural discourses

Following the work of Lawrence and Phillips (2004), this study also shows that the emergence of the issue of honour-related violence was facilitated by evolving macro-cultural discourses. Changes at the macro level create an opening to challenge issues at the micro level. In this case, the intertwinement of gender issues with multicultural discourses led to disenchantment with the multicultural ideal, which in turn made it possible to criticize culture-linked forms of violence. In addition, evolving discourses on nationalism, citizenship and social cohesion created a climate in which such criticism was welcomed as a means of enforcing moral boundaries between what is Dutch and what should not become Dutch (Chapter 6). Macro-cultural discourses therefore not only provide the discursive backdrop for an issue-based field, changes in these macro-cultural discourses form a critical precondition for issue and field emergence.

The inclusion of an analysis of these evolving discourses also makes it possible to explain why this particular issue emerged when it did. As explained in Part II, honour killings and honour-related violence were already happening in the Netherlands long before they were labelled as such. It was only after these changes in these macro-cultural discourses occurred that people started to separate these forms of violence from domestic violence.

Besides facilitating the emergence of a particular issue, macro-cultural discourses can also influence the actions taken to tackle the issue, actions that in turn reinforce those discourses. In this case, these discourses enabled actors within the political field to view honour-related violence as an integration issue, rather than seeing it as a specific type of domestic violence. As a consequence, a programme was developed to tackle this "new" type of violence. In this manner, the state not only officialized the problem as a distinct social problem, it also reinforced the boundary between what was Dutch (i.e. domestic violence) and what was not Dutch (i.e. honour-related violence) (Chapter 8).

Process: moral panic

The general argument behind the concept of a moral panic is that the attention given to a particular social problem does not correlate to the "objective" gravity of the problem. Instead, the moral panic that develops over a social problem indicates concerns about broader societal changes and challenges (Chapter 7).

In this thesis I argue that the attention given to honour-related violence in the Netherlands is a case in point. While honour killings are serious crimes, the number of honour killings does not correlate to the extensive attention that these murders received. Moreover, I follow the reasoning of scholars such as Pratt Ewing (2008:154) by arguing that the sudden attention given to honour killings should be considered against the backdrop of evolving macro-cultural discourses on multiculturalism, gender inequality, nationalism, citizenship and social cohesion. The anxiety about the lack of integration by migrants subsequently facilitated the emergence of the HRV field, as the moral panic about honour killings united actors within and outside the political field to take action against this type of violence (Chapters 7 and 8).

Interestingly, what the emerging field addressed was not these underlying anxieties, but rather the symbol representing these anxieties: the honour killings. Moreover, by reaffirming the boundaries between Dutch violence (e.g. domestic violence) and migrant violence (e.g. honour killings), the field's emergence paradoxically seems to have reaffirmed these anxieties rather than alleviating them.

The moral panic about honour killings not only facilitated the emergence of the Dutch HRV field but also structured the Dutch HRV field into two distinct sub-fields: one formed by network organizations that focused on protecting victims and prosecuting perpetrators, and a second formed by migrant organizations which focussed on achieving a change of mentality within their rank and file (Chapter 11, Figure 7). The othering discourses that accompanied the moral panic about honour killings and the underlying anxieties about migrants lacking integration contributed to a climate in which migrant organizations were not trusted as partners within the local collaboration networks.

Actor: the media as a gatekeeper

While issue-based organizational fields only emerge after multiple actors have committed to that particular issue, the involvement of two specific actors appears to be a critical precondition for any issue-based field emergence: the media and the state.

The involvement of the media is a precondition for field emergence given that the emergence of an issue depends strongly on the media's role. The media field acts as a gatekeeper by deciding what actors to quote and what stories to tell. For instance, the present study illustrates how the media selected specific types of "stories" that matched the *rules of the game* applied by the media field. Only those honour killings that fitted those rules received extensive coverage in the media, while others received barely any mention whatsoever. Moreover, each honour killing involved a specific actor whom the media would quote at length when describing the incident (Chapters 4 and 5).

Actor: the state as the constructor of social problems

Similar to the media's involvement, the state's involvement seems to be a critical precondition for field emergence. As already argued by scholars such as Clegg (2010) and Bourdieu et al. (1994) this case study also illustrates the state's extensive power to steer a field to a particular direction. The development of both the policy definition and the interministerial programme should be seen in this light. Together they contributed to the construction of honour-related violence as a distinct social problem.

Moreover, occurrences within the political field impacted the emerging configurations of the Dutch HRV field. For instance, this study reveals that one of the state's key values – developing a solid knowledge base – carried over from the political field to the HRV field. Not only did all the key actors have access to some type of informational capital, one of the key struggles within the emerging field also concerned the question of what type of informational capital was the most valuable.

Lastly, by commissioning the development of a clear-cut definition of the problem the state contributed to *theoretical unification* within the emerging field. The ethnographic field study shows that the interviewees had indeed developed a shared understanding of the issue of honour-related violence: although they were unable to quote the policy definition, their descriptions generally corresponded to its key elements.

Irrespective of the major role that the state plays, this study also illustrates that the state's power is limited by factors such as the general decentralization processes in the Netherlands. As a consequence, the state could not exert any direct control over other key actors such as the police, women's shelters and municipal authorities (Chapter 11).

Action: labels and translation

In her work on the emergence of the nanotechnology field, Grodal (2007:172-175) draws attention to the importance of a common label for field emergence. She argues that the adoption of a label by new actors (i.e. developing a shared information load) is a critical precondition for field emergence. However, she also finds that while it is important to have a common label it is similarly important to leave actors enough freedom to translate the label to their own working environments, arguing that this facilitates their commitment to the emerging field.

In this case, not one but two labels contributed to the emergence of the HRV field: *eerwraak* (i.e. honour killing) and *eergelateerd geweld* (honour-related violence) (Chapter 4). The label *eerwraak* facilitated the emergence of the issue in the public discourse. It made the issue relevant to the media field, which revels in reporting on these types of critical events, i.e. events that a.) occur at public locations, b.) carry sufficient dramatic features, c.) are illustrative of failing government agencies and d.) provoke the interest of various actors who are willing to voice their concerns about the issue (Chapter 5).

The policy definition of honour-related violence subsequently facilitated the emergence of the field by enabling other actors to join. This new label and definition encompassed a much wider range of types of violence, making it feasible for other actors to see roles for themselves in combatting and preventing honour-related violence. Moreover, the ambiguity of the definition made it possible for the separate actors to translate it to their own working environments (Chapter 10). This process of translation signals a next stage in the emergence of fields.

As such, this case study supports Grodal's proposition (2007) that the development of a common label and its subsequent translation to the respective working environments of the actors involved forms a critical precondition for field emergence.

Action: struggles over the emerging field configurations

Still, fields do not only come into being by exogenous forces (e.g. evolving discourses, critical events and state involvement). In fact, the actions of actors inside the field are what eventually facilitate field emergence and shape the emerging field configurations. Actors need to join the field first – in other words the issue needs to trigger their interest, their *illusio*. Next, they must acknowledge their participation in a common debate and develop a shared information load (Hoffman 1999). In other words, they need to interact with one another. Moreover, Bourdieu (1977:190) indicates that these interactions will often include struggles for power.

This case study into field emergence reveals that the issue of honour-related violence did indeed trigger the interest of a wide variety of actors. It also illustrates how those actors interacted and how they were positioned in respect of each other. Moreover the findings confirm Bourdieu's argument by illustrating how actors *struggled* with one another over the *relevant types of capital, the problem definition* and their *positions* within the field. These struggles chiefly concerned the relevant type of knowledge (i.e. informational capital) and the position of migrant organizations within the field. It is through these struggles that the field's eventual shape is determined (Chapters 9, 10 and 11). Still, those field configurations were also shaped by other interrelated processes. Those processes are addressed in the following section.

Processes shaping the emerging field configurations

Besides shedding light on the critical preconditions for field emergence, this case study also provides information about the processes that influence the emerging configurations of an issue-based field. In the foregoing, I have already highlighted the importance of struggles over definition and capital and for position in shaping of the emerging field configurations. In the following I examine three additional processes. First, I discuss the interrelatedness between how the issue emerged and the emerging field configurations. I then consider how an issue-based field is always nested in another, broader field. Lastly, I describe how the habitus of the various actors influences the emerging field configurations.

The interrelatedness of issue emergence and field emergence

Above I have argued that the *emergence of the issue* of honour-related violence was amplified by three interrelated processes: evolving macro-cultural discourses, unplanned field-configuring events and the moral panic about honour-related violence. However, these processes not only drove the emergence of the issue, they also *shaped the field's emerging configurations*. For instance, the macro-cultural discourses facilitated the framing of honour-related violence as an integration issue rather than as a typical form of domestic violence, which in turn strongly contributed to the development of a distinct issue-based organizational field.

This study also illustrates how the actors that functioned as key instigators of the media's attention for the issue of honour-related violence later all became key actors within the emerging HRV field (e.g. women's shelters and schools). The same holds true for actors who contributed to the "officialization" of the problem by developing a clear-cut definition (e.g. experts) and carrying out a pilot to determine the extent of the problem (e.g. the Multi-Ethnic Policing Unit). Evidently, being involved in the emergence of the issue helps actors to later become key actors within the emerging field.

One possible explanation for this mechanism lies in the field's focus on informational capital: actors with an early involvement in the issue possessed knowledge that other actors did not. Moreover, that knowledge gave them standing within the political field: all these actors were given regular mention within the political field as important actors in the battle against honour-related violence. Their positions as key actors were therefore confirmed by actors within the political field and became incorporated into the emerging HRV field's logic.

Nested fields

A second aspect that shaped the emerging HRV field's configurations is how the broader field within which it is nested is configured. New organizational fields do not emerge in a vacuum: they are nested in and influenced by other fields. The HRV field, for instance, is nested in and influenced by the broader societal discourses described in this study. In addition, it is nested within the larger governmental field, where decentralization is a key development. This general decentralization process also influenced the emerging configurations of the HRV field, as it affected the state's power (i.e. capital) to control actors such as municipal authorities, the police and women's shelters from the top down (Chapter 11).

At the same time, the emerging HRV field was made up of organizations that could be studied as fields in their own right. What happened within these *organizations-as-field* also impacted the larger HRV field. The present case study for instance illustrates that events within the political field affected the configurations of the HRV field. A case in point is the decision to set up an interministerial programme to fight honour-related violence: by highlighting the interconnectedness of the various actions against honour-related violence, this programme helped other actors to feel that they were partaking in a common debate.

Habitus and emerging field configurations

The emerging configurations of the HRV field were also informed, albeit less directly, by events in other fields: through the habitus of the actors. The habitus of the actors that joined the emerging HRV field was developed within other organizational fields. As a consequence, they imported knowledge and working methods developed in those fields into the HRV field.

In this case this meant, for instance, that the various actors interpreted the honour-related violence definition slightly differently in order to adapt it to their own particular working environments. Moreover, following Bourdieu (1977:79), who states that the habitus has a strong historical component, this case illustrates that previous experiences shape an actor's habitus. This is shown by the women's shelter organizations, which in the past had been confronted with the honour killings of women staying in their shelters (e.g. Kezban and Gül). As a consequence, they highlighted those elements of the definition that made it possible to assess the risks involved. This meant that they were particularly interested in learning whether people outside the family knew about a possible shameful event, which would push family members to take action against the individual who had supposedly shamed the family honour (Chapter 10).

Bringing Bourdieu back into institutional theory: an update

In the above, I have provided an answer to the empirical question driving this research. In the following I focus on the case study's theoretical contribution. In Part 1 I argued that to date institutional theory has been plagued by some persistent challenges, for example the development of a reliable *theory of action* that strikes the right balance between *structure and agency*, between *macro-level* developments and *micro-level* activities, and a clear conceptualization of processes of *power* and *domination* (Chapter 1). I subsequently argued that Bourdieu's *theory of practice* offers institutionalists the necessary framework, as long as they apply the entirety of his theoretical concepts (i.e. *habitus, field* and *capital*). Yet the proof of the pudding is in the eating (Chapter 2). In this section I therefore formulate an answer to the question *How does Bourdieu's theory of practice contribute to an understanding of the processes involved in organizational field emergence?*

Bourdieu and the structure-agency dilemma

Bourdieu's solution to the structure-agency dilemma lies in his conceptualization of action (i.e. practice). According to Bourdieu (1977) an actor's perception of a given situation and his subsequent action are informed by both his habitus and his position within the field, which in turn is determined by the amount and value of his capital within that particular field: *[(Habitus) (Capital)] + Field = Practice*. Bourdieu adds a historical component to his theory of practice, by arguing that each action feeds back into both the actor's habitus and the field's logic:

This means that each action, viewed here as an expression of *agency*, is informed by various components: the situation causing the action, the actor's habitus and his position within the field. Based on this combination of components, the actor calculates what action is feasible (i.e. *calculation of possibilities*). His actions are consequently "*structured*" by his past experience (i.e. his habitus) and by his position within the field (i.e. the amount and value of his capital within that field) (Chapter 2).

Figure 1: The interrelationship between habitus, field and capital

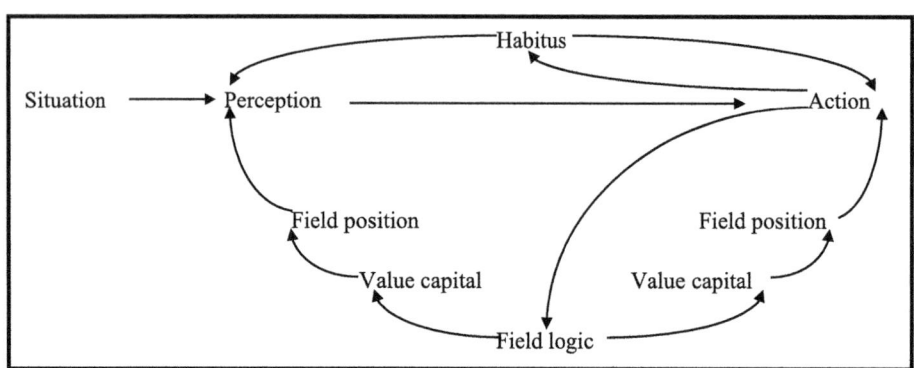

Field emergence and evolving field configurations can then be explained by the fact that the decision to act brings together these various components. For instance, actors may be confronted with a new and unexpected situation (i.e. a critical event), and therefore arrive at a new calculation of possibilities. Moreover, through the feedback loop into the habitus and the field's logic, Bourdieu ensures that each new action is informed by a slightly different habitus and field logic, as these have been informed by a previous action. Actors can therefore incrementally change their actions, even where the situation has not changed significantly.

The fact that an actor's calculation of possibilities takes both the field's logic (macro) and the actor's habitus (micro) into consideration also helps Bourdieu to surmount the micro-macro divide within a single act, as both components influence the eventual action. In addition, the concept of *nested fields* helps to interrelate various levels of analysis (micro, meso and macro), since the processes can inform the action taken by the individual, organization or field.

Lastly, Bourdieu's concept of capital and his conceptualization of fields as *fields of power* and *fields of struggle* make it possible to include a clear *power conceptualization* within his theory of practice. Bourdieu compares how a field functions to playing a game. The purpose of the game is to retrieve the trump card, i.e. the type of capital that is perceived as the most valuable type of capital within that specific field. At the same time, the actor's ability (i.e. his power) to play the game is determined by the amount and value of the capital already in his possession (Bourdieu and Wacquant 19992: 98-99). Bourdieu's concept of *symbolic violence* (1977:196-197) also directs attention to the more subtle *processes of domination*, which lie in the structuring function of both the field's logic and the actor's habitus, even though actors are mostly unaware of this (Chapter 2). Finally, Bourdieu explicitly directs attention to the power of states to determine a field's configuration (introduction to Part III).

This discussion of Bourdieu's theoretical concepts illustrates that the added value of his theory of practice lies in the combined use of his concepts. It is through the interrelationship between habitus, field, capital and action that Bourdieu strikes a balance between structure and agency, between micro-level and macro-level developments, while incorporating a multi-layered power conceptualization. By focusing solely on the concept of field, institutionalists have lost that balance and remain unable to restore it. Moreover, they have lost the ability to incorporate a balanced approach to processes of power and domination (Clegg 2010).

The added value of Bourdieu's theory in practice

By applying Bourdieu's framework to this case study I have illustrated that the entirety of his theory is indeed greater than the sum of its parts. Using Bourdieu's framework enables the study of the myriad processes, actors and actions involved in the emergence of an issue-based organizational field. Moreover, by applying his theory at multiple levels of analysis I was able to study the interrelatedness of the organizational field practices at the micro level, the meso level and the macro level.

For example, at the micro level Bourdieu's framework enabled me to understand the dynamics within the political field. Actors here were confronted with a "new" type of violence: honour killings. Within this highly structured and formalized field, both MPs and ministers subsequently acted according to the rules of that particular field (i.e. the field's logic). During parliamentary debates MPs would ask critical questions and use the instrument of motions to steer the government in a particular direction. In response the ministers would write letters to parliament explaining why they first sought to gain a better understanding of the extent and nature of the problem. Each successive debate then led to new actions and responses, ultimately combining to contribute to the officialization of honour-related violence as a distinct social problem.

At the meso level, Bourdieu's theory of practice enabled me to understand the dynamics within the emerging HRV field. In particular his conceptualization of fields as *fields of struggle* and *fields of power* helped me to make sense of the debates between the separate actors. The concept of capital, in addition, allowed me to understand why certain actors gained positions as key actors within the emerging HRV field. These key actors all combined various types of capital. They especially had access to various types of informational capital, which turned out to be the *trump card* within this particular field. Moreover, his concept of habitus helped to explain why the actors highlighted different aspects of the definition of honour-related violence.

At the same time, attention for macro-level developments enhanced my understanding of the processes at a meso and micro level. For instance, attention for the general decentralization processes made it possible to explain why the state was unable to direct the emerging HRV field from the top down. Instead, the state used a variety of instruments, for example commissioning studies, developing a problem definition and allocating funding to relevant actors, to enhance field development. Attention for changing macro-cultural discourses, in addition, helped to explain why honour-related violence was framed as an integration issue rather than as a distinct type of domestic violence.

Updating Bourdieu's framework with the addition of institutional concepts

At the same time, the present case study illustrates that some of the concepts from institutionalism can be useful additions to Bourdieu's work. As explained above, this holds true in particular for the concepts *of issue-based organizational fields, field-configuring events* and *label development*. The concept of *moral panic* is another useful addition for studying the emergence of issue-based fields, shedding light on why a particular issue suddenly appears in public discourses and subsequently generates large amounts of organizational activity. Moreover, the moral panic concept helps to explain the lack of trust between organizations making up local collaboration networks and migrant organizations, and thus the development of two distinct sub-fields within the emerging HRV field.

Future research

Although it is at times challenging, I feel that applying Bourdieu's framework (i.e. painting the bigger picture, focusing on micro-level, meso-level and macro-level developments, and on both structure and agency) has enhanced our understanding of the processes and actors involved in the emergence of issue-based fields. Bourdieu's theory of practice, his work on state power and social problems, makes it possible to study these processes in a balanced manner. I therefore wholeheartedly recommend that others follow this example and further explore Bourdieu's potential for institutional theory.

For instance, it would be interesting to apply Bourdieu's framework to another case of field emergence, to establish whether the same mix of processes, actors and actions is present. It would also be interesting to see whether the emergence of an issue-based field is always preceded by a moral panic about the issue at hand. Moral panic literature includes some mention of "institutional legacies" of moral panic (Goode and Ben-Yehuda 1994:158, Garland 2008:15-16), yet no mention is made of the emergence of an entirely new organizational field. In a similar vein, I have not encountered any studies of issue-based fields that mention the concept of moral panic. This implies that while a moral panic may enhance the emergence of an issue-based field it is not a critical precondition for field emergence. Further study of issue-based field emergence will be necessary to answer this question once and for all.

Lastly, it would be interesting to study the decline of issue-based fields. In his work on issue-based fields, Hoffman (1999:352) hints that issue-based fields might not always be in use. He states, "Field membership may also be for a finite time period, coinciding with an issue's emergence, growth, and decline." Together with Wooten he goes on to urge scholars to focus on the moment that "fields come alive" to study the processes involved in field emergence (Wooten and Hoffman 2008:139). In this thesis I took up this invitation and studied the emergence of the HRV field. I now encourage others to study the processes involved in field decline. Do issue-based fields indeed collapse once the issue has subsided from the public discourse? What processes, actors and actions contribute to a field's decline? And do fields, once degenerated, leave behind any institutional legacies?

Lessons for the public domain

The matter of honour-related violence described here is an interesting case for anyone working in the public domain, with the potential to be confronted with a new issue at any moment. Macro-cultural discourses change, critical events happen and actors such as the national government, municipal authorities and the police are subsequently confronted with a new issue that needs their attention. Recent examples include the financial crisis, the terrorist attacks in Paris and Brussels and the sudden influx of refugees into Europe.

The present case study teaches that actors within the public domain have a number of options for what action they can take when confronted with a new issue. These actions can have a major impact on how the issue is addressed. The development of a clear-cut label and definition, for instance, impacts what actors feel responsible for handling a particular problem. Moreover, by organizing field-configuring events such as conferences and other types of meetings, actors within the public domain can contribute to the development of a shared understanding of the problem and its solution.

At the same time, this case study brings into view that the emergence of a specific issue sometimes points towards other underlying anxieties. This is particularly the case when a moral panic drives the attention for an issue. In these situations, it is advisable not only to focus on the symbolic issue, but also to address the underlying anxieties. Focusing on the symbolic issue alone will potentially amplify the underlying anxieties rather than diminishing them.

Epilogue: Newsletter of the Platform for Honour and Freedom

The Dutch Platform for Honour and Freedom (*Platform Eer en Vrijheid*) had its first national conference of 2016 on 12 May. *Bar Beton Rijnsweerd* in Utrecht played host to 120 professionals and volunteers who encounter issues such as honour-related violence, forced marriage, abandonment and marital captivity on a daily basis. Among the attendees were lawyers and representatives of domestic violence organization *Veilig Thuis*, lawyers, women's centres, municipal authorities, the Central Agency for the Reception of Asylum Seekers (COA) and the police.
(7 June 2016)

The purpose of the conference was to bring together all the different professionals and volunteers who spend their days fighting various forms of honour-related violence. These organizations utilize very different methods, and the national conference offers them an opportunity to talk to each other and form new partnerships. Since the Platform for Honour and Freedom is all about meeting people, sharing knowledge and broadening perspectives, the route chosen was that of a networking conference. A number of organizations gave presentations about themselves, offering information about ongoing campaigns and about methods and processes and taking time to talk directly to the attendees. The attendees of the networking conference operate in different regions and combat honour-related violence in a variety of ways. *Kompaan en de Bocht*, *Fier Fryslan*, *Stichting Hindustani*, the Ministry of Social Affairs and Employment, *Landelijke Werkgroep Mudawwannah*, the International Women's Centre in Den Helder, the Dutch Centre for Forced Marriage and Abandonment and *Emancipatie Expertisecentrum Feniks* were at the conference.

The theme for the plenary session was sharing methods and instruments that are available to all attendees. The chair for the day, Ms Naima Azough, was pleased to find that the Platform for Honour and Freedom is continually increasing in depth, as evidenced by the diversity of the topics in the workshops. For example, besides its regular topics of discussion such as forced marriage and abandonment, the Platform now also addresses shelter for refugees experiencing situations of domestic violence, sexuality and resilience, and child abduction. The diversity of the attendees is also remarkable: not only professionals from widely-known organizations, but also experts from the field and migrant organizations. As a consequence, these conferences are not opportunities to talk about the target demographic, but with them. The network is growing organically all the time. Diversion's Norah van Leest, the project leader for the Platform for Honour and Freedom, announced that we are reaching more and more new members and that this is undoubtedly thanks to the fact that the Platform for Honour and Freedom is part of the debate at the national level.

Situations in which honour plays a major role often involve young people who want to make their own decisions. Making your own decisions and talking about those decisions are the central elements in the campaign presented by Daniëlle Kretz, programme coordinator for the Ministry of Social Affairs and Employment. The new campaign, "Talking about your choices", offers young people tools for talking to the people around them about making their own decisions. Examples include deciding whether or not to move away from home to study, whether or not to marry and whether to study for a degree. It also serves as a source of inspiration by telling the stories of young people who have already made these moves. Offering inspiration is also the purpose of Zina Platform's campaign entitled "Not without you anymore". Kim Zonneveld and Seval Okyay from Zina Platform gave a creative presentation explaining how difficult it still is to talk about self-determination in closed communities, and what resistance doing so can trigger.

The final contribution of the plenary opening session came from Federatie Opvang and Fischer Groep. Liesbeth van Bemmel and Else Weijsenfeld provided a brief outline of the framework of national and international laws for sheltering women without official status, and explained what changes are in the works. This is valuable knowledge with immediate relevance now, given the changes that professionals and volunteers are experiencing in their work as a result of the influx of refugees.

Visit our website to read the specifics of the plenary discussion, or to find out what the nine workshops were about. The presentations are also available there. The website also contains the photographs that David Hup took during the event.

On behalf of the Platform for Honour and Freedom, we would like to once more thank everyone who attended the event, as well as all our knowledge partners, for their time and effort. The next national conference is scheduled for Thursday, 8 December. If you have an idea for a workshop, a speaker or a theme that was not discussed at the last event, let us know using this form. Alternatively, you can contact us by telephone at +31 (0)20 3059283 or by e-mail at platform.eer.en.vrijheid@gmail.com.

Source: Ministry of Social Affairs and Employment 2016: website

References

Aa van der, A. & T. Konijn (2004). *Ketens, ketenregisseurs en ketenontwikkeling. Het ontwikkelen van transparante en flexibele samenwerkingsverbanden in netwerken.* Utrecht: Lemma.
Abu-Lughod, L. (2002). Do Muslim Women Really Need Saving? Anthropological Reflections on Cultural Relativism and Its Others. *American Anthropologist,* 104 (3), 783-790.
Akin, Y. (2008) *Black Pearls.* Alkmaar
Albrecht, M. (2006). *Uitvoeringsprogramma 2006-2010. Rotterdamse aanpak eergerelateerd geweld.* Rotterdam: GGD Rotterdam-Rijnmond.
ANP (1999). Herdenking moorden tevens protest tegen geweld. *Stichting Algemeen Nederlands Persbureau,* 1 July 1999.
ANP (2001). Vijf jaar cel voor 18-jarige schutter school Veghel. *Stichting Algemeen Nederlands Persbureau,* 13 February 2001.
ANP (2003a). Turkse vader doodt dochter uit eerwraak. *Stichting Algemeen Nederlands Persbureau,* 28 September 2003.
ANP (2003b). School wil openbaar debat na eerwraak op scholiere. *Stichting Algemeen Nederlands Persbureau,* 29 September 2003.
ANP (2004). "Turkse vrouw niet vermoord om eerwraak". *Stichting Algemeen Nederlands Persbureau,* 26 March 2004.
Arslan, Z. (2003). Uitbannen eerwraak vergt collectieve inzet. *Dagblad Tubantia/Twentsche Courant.* 4 October 2003.
Ayşe (2005). *Op de vlucht voor eerwraak.* Baarn: Uitgeverij De Kern, De Fontein bv
Bate, S.P. (1994). *Strategies for cultural change.* Eastbourne: Antony Rowe Ltd.
Battilana, J. (2006a). Agency and institutions: the Enabling role of Individuals' Social Position. *Organization,* 13 (5), 653-676.
Battilana, J. (2006b). *The Role of Individuals in Institutional Change: When Individuals act as Institutional Entrepreneurs.* Dissertation presented at INSEAD.
Beemer, F.A., M.A.R. van Roost, H. de Ruigh-Hortsmanshof, A.H.E. van der Aa. & T.P.J. Konijn (2003). *Ruimte voor regie. Handreiking voor ketenregie in het openbaar bestuur.* Den Haag: Ministerie van Binnenlandse Zaken en Koninkrijksrelaties.
Berendse, M. (2013). *Authoring Cultural Change. Discursive (de)Legitimation within Rijkswaterstaat.* Enschede: Ipskamp Drukkers BV.
Berger, P.L. & T. Luckmann (1967). *The Social Construction of Reality: A treatise in the sociology of knowledge.* Garden City: Doubleday/Anchor Books.
Bessems, K. (2003). Een tragische omstandigheid; Eewraak. *Trouw.* 1 October 2003.
Best, J. (1993). But seriously folks: The limitations of the strict constructionist interpretation of social problems. In: Holstein, J.A. & G. Miller (Eds.). *Reconsidering social constructionism* (337-354). New York: Aldine de Gruyter.
Best, J. (2002). Constructing the Sociology of Social Problems: Spector and Kitsuse Twenty-Five Years Later. *Sociological Forum,* 17 (4), 699-706.
Bloemraad, I., A. Korteweg, G. Yurdakul (2008). Citizenship and Immigration: Multiculturalism, Assimilation, and Challenges to the Nation-State. *Annual Review of Sociology,* 34, 153-179.

Blumer, H. (1971). Social problems as collective behaviour. *Social Problems,* 18 (winter), 298-306.

Boer, de M. (2008) *Samenwerken voor de veiligheid van (potentiële) slachtoffers van eergerelateerd geweld. Stappenplan om te komen tot lokale samenwerkingsafspraken en Voorbeeldconvenant.* Den Haag: Ministerie van Justitie / Ministerie van Binnenlandse Zaken en Koninkrijksrelaties.

Boogers, M., L. Schaap, E.D. van den Munckhof and N. Karsten (2008). *Decentralisatie als opgave. Een evaluatie van het decentralisatiebeleid van de Rijksoverheid, 1992-2008.* Tilburg: Tilburgse School voor Politiek en Bestuur.

Boonstra, J.J., K.M. Bennebroek Gravenhorst & R.A. Werkman (2003). Het veranderingsvermogen van organisaties. In: Y.D. Burger, R. in 't Veld en S.J.M. Cortlever-Keus (Eds.) *Facetten van Sioo.* Utrecht: LEMMA bv (32-50).

Bosman, F. (1999). Aldus. *Het Parool.* 17 December 1999.

Bourdieu, P. (1977). *Outline of a Theory of Practice.* Cambridge, UK: Cambridge University Press.

Bourdieu, P. (1996) *The State Nobility: Elite Schools in the Field of Power.* Stanford: Stanford University Press.

Bourdieu, P. & L. Wacquant (1992). *An invitation to reflexive sociology.* Chicago: University of Chicago Press.

Bourdieu, P. L.J.G. Wacquant and S. Farage (1994). Rethinking the State : Genesis and Structure of the Bureaucratic Field. *Sociological Theory,* 12 (1), 1-18.

Bovenkerk, F., Van San, M., Boone, M., Korf, D. & T. Boekhout van Solinge (2009 [2006]). *Loverboys of Modern Pooierschap.* Amsterdam: Pandora pockets.

Boxenbaum, E. & S. Jonsson (2008). Isomorphism, Diffusion and Decoupling. In Greenwoord, R., C. Oliver, K. Sahlin & R. Suddaby (Eds.). *The Sage Handbook of Organizational Institutionalism.* London, Thousand Oaks, New Dehli & Singapore: Sage Publications

Brenninkmeijer, N., M. Geerse, C. Roggeband, H. Ghorashi & M.Veenswijk (2009). *Eergerelateerd geweld in Nederland, Onderzoek naar de beleving en aanpak van eergerelateerd geweld.* Den Haag: Sdu Uitgevers.

Butler, J. (2008). Sexual politics, torture, and secular time. *The British Journal of Sociology,* 59 (1), 1-23.

Çalişkan, A. (2006). *De nootjes van het huwelijk. Het waargebeurde en hartverscheurende verhaal van een geëmancipeerde Turkse immigrante.* Amsterdam: Uitgeverij Thoeris b.v.

Child, J., Y. Lu & T. Tsai (2007). Institutional Entrepreneurship in building an Environmental Protection System for the People's Republic of China. *Organization Studies,* 28 (07), 1013-1034.

Christensen, S., P. Karnøe, J. Strangaard Pedersen & F. Dobbin (1997). Actors and Institutions, Editors' Introduction. *American Behavioral Scientist,* 40 (4), 392-396.

Clegg, S. (2010). The State, Power, and Agency: Missing in Action in Institutional Theory? *Journal of Management Inquiry,* 19 (1), 4-13.

Cohen, J., M. Howard & M.C. Nussbaum (Eds.) (1999). *Is Multiculturalism Bad for Women. Susan Moller Okin with respondents.* Princeton, New Jersey: Princeton University Press.

Cohen, S. (1972). *Folk devils and moral panics: the creation of the Mods and Rockers.* London: MacGibbon and Kee.

Cooper, J.D., M. Ezzamel & H. Willmott (2008). Examining Institutionalization: A Critical Theoretic Perspective. In Greenwoord, R., C. Oliver, K. Sahlin & R. Suddaby (Eds.). *The Sage Handbook of Organizational Institutionalism.* London, Thousand Oaks, New Delhi & Singapore: Sage Publications

Critcher, C. (2003). *Moral Panics and the Media*. Buckingham & Philadelphia: Open University Press.

Dacin, M.T., J. Goodstein & W.R. Scott (2002). Institutional Theory and Institutional Change: Introduction to the Special Issue Forum. *Academy of Management Journal*, 45 (1), 45-57.

De Dordtenaar (1999). Verschillende organisaties zijn tekort geschoten. *De Dordtenaar*. 25 June 1999.

Dekker, A. & F. Özgümüş (2008). *Vluchtelingen als Changemakers in de strijd tegen eergerelateerd geweld, Manifest*. Amsterdam: Vluchtelingen Organisaties Nederland.

De Stenor/Veluws Dagbald (2004). "Geen sprake van eerrwaak". *De Stenor/Veluws Dagbald*, 18 March 2004.

De Telegraaf (1999). Moord op Kezban Vural (29) en Naciye Kurt (30) boezemt Turkse vrouwen angst in. Tot de dood ons scheidt. *Telegraaf*, 29 September 1999.

De Volkskrant (1999). "Geschonden eer is verzachtende omstandigheid". *De Volkskrant*. 17 December 1999.

DiMaggio, P.J. (1988). Interest and agency in institutional theory. In: L.G. Zucker (Ed.) *Institutional patterns and organizations: Culture and environment*. Cambridge, MA: Ballinger.

DiMaggio, P.J. & W.W. Powell (1983). The iron cage revisited: Institutional isomorphism and collective rationality in organizational fields. *American Sociological Review*, 48 (2), 147-160.

DiMaggio, P.J. & W.W. Powell (1991). Introduction. In: DiMaggio, P.J. & W.W. Powell (Eds.). *The New Institutionalism in Organizational Analysis*. Chicago & London: The University of Chicago Press.

Djura (2005). *Een sluier van stilte. Op de vlucht voor eerwraak*. Amsterdam: Uitgeverij Maarten Muntinga.

Dobbernack, J. (2010). "Things fall apart": social imaginaries and the politics of cohesion. *Critical Policy Studies*, 4 (2), 146-163.

Dobbin, F. (2008). The poverty of organizational theory: comment on: "Bourdieu and organizational analysis". *Theory and Society*, 37 (1), 53-63.

Downs, A. (1972). Up and down with ecology – the "issue-attention cycle". *Public Interest* 28 (summer), 38-50.

Dubbelman, M. (1999). "Eerwraak is een reinigingsritueel". *Algemeen Dagblad*. 9 December 1999.

Dustin, M. (2006). *Gender Equality, Cultural Diversity: European Comparisons and Lessons*. London: Gender Institute, London School of Economics and Political Science.

Eck, C. Van (2001). *Door bloed gezuiverd, Eerwraak bij Turken in Nederland*. Amsterdam: Uitgeverij Bert Bakker.

Eijberts, M. & H. Ghorashi (2017). Biographies and the doubleness of inclusion and exclusion. *Social Identities, Journal for the Study of Race, Nation and Culture*, 23 (2), 163-178.

Ekis, F. (2003). Advocaat vader Zarife: "Eerwraak niet motief". *Rotterdams Dagblad*. 12 November 2003.

Emirbayer, M. & V. Johnson (2008). Bourdieu and organizational analysis. *Theory and Society* 37 (1), 1-44.

Ermers, R.J.H.M. (2007). *Eer en Eerwraak: Definitie en analyse*. Amsterdam:Bulaaq.

Fatusch Productions (2007). *Differences of Opinion are a Blessing. Contemporary Interpretations in Islam*.

Fauwe, L., de (2003). Twentse Turke noemen eerwraak een achterlijk gebruik. *Het Parool*. 30 September 2003.

Ferweda, H. & I. van Leiden (2005). *Eerwraak of eergerelateerd geweld? Naar een werkdefinitie*. Den Haag: WODC, Ministerie van Justitie.

Ferwerda, H. & M. Hardeman (2013). *Kijk...dan zie je het! Huiselijk geweld geteld en verdiept.* Arnhem: Beke groep.

Fijnaut, C. and F. Bovenkerk (1996),"Georganiseerde criminaliteit in Nederland: Een analyse van de situatie in Amsterdam", *Enquête Opsporingsmethoden,* Bijlagen XI, Deelonderzoek IV, Kamerstuk 24072 nr. 20, Tweede Kamer, vergaderjaar 1995–1996. The Hague: SDU.

Fijnaut, C. J. C. F., F. Bovenkerk, G. J. N. Bruinsma, & H. G. van de Bunt (1996). *Enquête Opsporingsmethoden, eindrapport Georganiseerde Criminaliteit in Nederland.* Bijlagen VII, Kamerstuk 24072 nr. 16, Tweede Kamer, vergaderjaar 1995–1996. The Hague: SDU.

Fligstein, N. (1997). Social Skill and Institutional Theory. *The American Behavioural Scientist,* 40 (4), 297-405.

Fligstein, N. (2001). Social Skill and the Theory of Fields. *Sociological Theory,* 19 (2), 105-125.

Fligstein, N. & D. McAdam (2011). Towards a General Theory of Strategic Action Fields. *Sociological Theory,* 29 (1), 1-26.

Fox, J.E. & C. Miller-Idriss (2008). Everyday nationhood. *Ethnicities,* 8 (4), 536-576.

Fritz, N.J. & D. L. Altheide (1987). The Mass Media and the Social Construction of the Missing Children Problem. *The Sociological Quarterly,* 28 (4), 473-492.

Garland, D. (2008). On the concept of moral panic. *Crime Media Culture,* 4 (1), 9-30.

Garud, R., C. Hardy & S. Maguire (2007). Institutional Entrepreneurship as Embedded Agency: an Introduction to the Special Issue. *Organizational Studies,* 28 (7), 957-969.

Gashi, H. (2006). *Mijn leed draagt jouw naam.* Amsterdam: Muntinga Pockets & Uitgeverij Sirene bv.

Ghorashi, H. (2003). Ayaan Hirsi Ali: daring or dogmatic? Debates on multiculturalism and emancipation in the Netherlands. *FOCAAL-UTRECHT* , 163-172.

Ghorashi, H. (2006). *Paradoxen van culturele erkenning. Management van Diversiteit in Nieuw Nederland.* Amsterdam: Vrije Universiteit.

Ghorashi, H. (2010). From absolute invisibility to extreme visibility: emancipation trajectory of migrant women in the Netherlands. *Feminist Review,* 94 (1), 78-86.

Gietman, C. (2010). *Republiek van adel: eer in de Oost-Nederlandse adelscultuur (1555-1702).* Arnhem: Uitgeverij Van Gruting.

Gilman, S. (1999). Barbaric rituals? In: J. Cohen, M. Howard & M. Nussbaum (Eds.) *Is multiculturalism bad for women?* (53-58). Princeton: Princeton University Press.

Glaser, B.G. & A.L. Strauss (1967). *The discovery of grounded theory, strategies for qualitative research.* New Brunswick and London: Aldine Transaction.

Goedee, J. & A. Entken (2006). *(Ont)Keten, implementeren van werken in ketens.* Den Haag: Lemma.

Golsorkhi, D., B. Leca, M. Lounsbury & C. Ramirez (2009). Analysing, Accounting for and Unmasking Domination: On Our Role as Scholars of Practice, Practitioners of Social Science and Public Intellectuals. *Organization,* 16 (6), 779-797.

Goode, E. & N. Ben-Yehuda (1994). Moral Panics: Culture, Politics, and Social Construction. *Annual Review of Sociology,* 20 (1), 149-171.

Greenwoord, R., C. Oliver, K. Sahlin & R. Suddaby (Eds.) (2008). *The Sage Handbook of Organizational Institutionalism.* London, Thousand Oaks, New Dehli & Singapore: Sage Publications.

Grodal, S. (2007). *The emergence of a new organizational field – labels, meaning and emotions in nanotechnology.* Dissertation at Stanford University.

Grodal, S. & N. Granqvist (2014). Great Expectations: Discourse and Affect During Field Emergence. In: Ashkanasy, N.M., W.J. Zerbe, C.E.J. Härtel (Eds.) *Emotions and the Organi-*

zational Fabric (Research on Emotion in Organizations, Volume 10). Emerald Group Publishing Limited, (139 – 166).

Gustafsson, R. (2010). *Awareness, Institutional Entrepreneurship, and Contradictions in Emerging Technological Fields*. Helsinki: Helsinki University of Technology.

Haagsche Courant (2004). OMOM – Eer. *Haagsche Courant*, 17 March 2004.

Haar, M. van der, K. Völke & D. Yanow (2010). *Naar Nederland*, the movie: Doing Dutchness for immigrants. Paper presented at the Migration and Diversity Centre, VU University, Amsterdam, 28 June 2010.

Hall, S., C. Critcher, T. Jefferson, J.Clarke & B. Roberts (1978). *Policing the crisis: mugging, the state and law and order*. London: MacMillan.

Haverland, M. & D. Yanow (2012). A Hitchhiker's Guide to the Public Administration Research Universe: Surviving Conversations on Methodologies and Methods. *Public Administration Review*, 72 (3), 401-408.

Heijmans, T. (2001a). "Ali wilde echt niemand doodschieten"; Moeder Fatma en zus Yeliz:'Op tv zeiden ze dat het om eerwraak ging. Onzin!' *De Volkskrant*. 22 January 2001.

Heijmans, T. (2001b). "Ik was best wel boos," antwoordt Ali. *De Volkskrant*. 31 January 2001.

Heijmans T. (2004). Politie onderzoekt omvang eerwraak. *De Volkskrant*. 5 April 2004.

Hellgren, Z. & B. Hobson (2008). Cultural dialogues in the good society. The case of honor killings in Sweden. *Ethnicities*, 8 (3), 385-404.

Het Parool (2004). Vreeman: beter beveiliging bedreigde vrouwen. *Het Parool*. 16 March 2004.

Hilgartner, S. & C.L. Bosk (1988). The Rise and Fall of Social Problems: A Public Arenas Model. *American Journal of Sociology*, 94 (1), 53-78.

Hirsch, P.M. & M. Lounsbury (1997). Ending the Family Quarrel. Toward a Reconciliation of "Old" and "New" Institutionalism. *The American Behavioral Scientist*, 40 (4), 406-418.

Hirsch, P. & M. Lounsbury (2014). Toward a More Critical and "Powerful" Institutionalism. *Journal of Management Inquiry*, 24 (1), 96-99.

Hirsi Ali, A. (2003). Pak huiselijk geweld effectiever aan. *NRC Handelsblad*. 3 October 2003.

Hirsi Ali, A. (2004). Ik bevraag de islam, een religie zonder zelfreflectie; De kritiek op de islam moet van binnenuit komen, van mensen die zijn opgevoed met de islam, die de moedervlekken zien. *De Volkskrant*. 30 October 2004.

Hoesseini, S. & R. Masto (2004). *Ik, Safiya. Het autobiografische verhaal van een Nigeriaanse vrouw die gered werd van de dood door steniging*. Amsterdam: Uitgeverij Mouria.

Hoffman, A.J. (1999). Institutional Evolution and Change: Environmentalism and the U.S. Chemical Industry. *Academy of Management Journal*, 42 (4), 351-371.

Hoffman, A.J. & W. Ocasio (2001). Not All Events Are Attended Equally: Toward a Middle-Range Theory of Industry Attention to External Events. *Organization Science*, 12 (4), 414-434.

IOT (2008). *Deelplan eergerelateerd geweld 2007-2010. Naar een gezamenlijke aanpak*. On: http://www.iot.nl/artikel_lees.php?lang=nl&artikelID=1307 (visited on 20 November 2008).

IOT (2016). *Doelstelling*. On: http://www.iot.nl/?page=sayfa&sayfa_id=33 (visited on 11 December 2016).

Janssen, J. (2006). *Eindrapportage. Pilot Eergerelateerd geweld in Haaglanden en Zuid-Holland-Zuid*. Den Haag: Politie Haaglanden.

Janssen, J. (2008). Organisaties, cultuur en eergevoel. Over complexe institutionele samenwerking bij de aanpak van eergerelateerd geweld. *Proces*, 2008/4.

Jansen, J. & R. Sanberg (2010). *Inzicht in cijfers, Mogelijke eerzaken in 2007, 2008 en 2009*. Den Haag: Ministerie van Binnenlandse Zaken en Koninkrijksrelaties, Ministerie van Justitie,

Programmabureau Eergerelateerd Geweld en Landelijke Expertises Centrum Eer Gerelateerd Geweld.

Janssen, J. & R. Sanbergen (2013). *Univormiteit in cijfers. Mogelijke eerzaken in 2010, 2011, 2012.* Den Haag: Landelijke Expertise Centrum Eer Gerelateerd Geweld.

Jongerius, S. (2000). In het theehuis wordt gezwegen over eerwraak. *Brabants Dagblad.* 18 March 2000.

Kiewiet, J. (2008). *De aanpak van eergerelateerd geweld binnen een Amsterdams ROC-ASA* Master thesis. Amsterdam: Vrije Universiteit

Klutzz, D.N. & N. Fligstein (2016). Varieties of Sociological Field Theory. In: Abrutyn, S. (Ed.). *Handbook of Contempory Sociological Theory.* Switzerland: Springer International Publishing.

Knegt, de, M. (2002). Turken hangen vuile was buiten. *Leeuwarder Courant.* June 08, 2002.

Koot, W.C.J. & E. Dobbinga (2004). Vertraagd vernieuwen. De weerbarstigheid van departementale culturen. *Bestuurskunde,* 13 (3), 110-18.

Korteweg, A. & G. Yurdakul (2009). Islam, gender, and immigrant integration: boundary drawing discourses on honor killing in the Netherlands and Germany. *Ethnic and Racial Studies,* 32 (2), 218-238.

Korteweg, A. & G. Yurdakul (2010). *Religion, Culture and the Politicization of Honor-Related Violence. A Critical Analysis of Media and Policy Debates in Western Europe and North America.* Geneva: United Nations.

Kruijff, de A. (2010). *Student counsellors 'using' diversity discourses. A case study on honor related violence and diversity discourses in the work of student counsellors at the Vrije Universiteit Amsterdam.* Master thesis. Amsterdam: Vrije Universiteit

Kurunmäki, L. (1999). Professional vs financial capital in the field of health care-struggles for the redistribution of power and controle. *Accounting, Organizations and Society,* 24 (2), 95-124.

Kvinnoforum (2003). *A Resource Book for Working Against Honor Related Violence.* Stockholm: Kvinnoforum.

Kvinnoforum (2005). *Honor Related Violence, European Resource Book and Good Practices.* Stockholm: Kvinnoforum.

Laan, E. van der (2008). *Handelingsprotocol tegen eergerelateerd geweld.* On: http://www.min-vrom.nl/ pagina.html?id=38044 (visited on 27 November 2008).

Lammers, C.J., A.A. Mijs & W.J. van Noort (2000). *Organisaties vergelijkenderwijs: ontwikkeling en relevantie van het sociologisch denken over organisaties.* Utrecht: Spectum

Lampel, J. & A.D. Meyer (2008). Guest Editor's Introduction, Field-Configuring Events as Structuring Mechanisms: How Conferences, Ceremonies, and Trade Shows Constitute New Technologies, Industries, and Markets. *Journal of Management Studies,* 45 (6), 1025-1035.

Lange, H. De (1999). Nieuwe wet komt te laat voor Kezban Vural; Stalking. *Trouw.* 2 July 1999.

Lange, Y. (1999). Turken bezinnen zich op plegen van eerwraak. *NRC Handelsblad.* 15 December 1999.

Langvasbråten, T. (2008). A Scandinavian Model? Gender Equality discourse on Multiculturalism. Sweden. *Social Politics,* 15 (1), 32-52.

Lawrence, T.B. & N. Phillips (2004). From Moby Dick to Free Willy: Macro-Cultural Discourse and Institutional Entrepreneurship in Emerging Institutional Fields. *Organization.* 11 (5), 689-711.

Lawrence, T., R. Suddaby & B. Leca (2011). Institutional Work: Refocusing Institutional Studies of Organization. *Journal of Management Inquiry,* 20 (1), 52-58.

Leeuwarder Courant (2004). Vermoorde Gül wist dat haar man zou komen. *Leeuwarder Courant.* 16 March 2004.

Lettinga, D.N. (2011). *Framing the hijab. The governance of intersecting religious, ethnic and gender differences in France, the Netherlands and Germany.* Ridderkerk: Ridderprint Offsetdrukkerij BV.

Levy, D. & M. Scully (2007). The Institutional Entrepreneur as Modern Prince: The Strategic Face of Power in Contested Fields. *Organization Studies,* 28 (7), 971-991.

Lewis, G. (2006). Imaginaries of Europe: Technologies of Gender, Economies and Power. *European Journal of Women's Studies,* 13 (2), 87-102.

LOM Samenwerkingsverband (2008). *Wet overleg minderhedenbeleid.* On: http://www.minderheden.org/ lom.html (visited on 22 November 2008).

Loseke, D.R. (1999). *Thinking about Social Problems. An Introduction to Constructionist Perspectives.* New York: Walter de Gruyter Inc.

Lutz, H. (2002). Zonder blikken of blozen. Het standpunt van de (nieuwe) realisten. *Tijdschrift voor Genderstudies,* 5 (3), 7-17.

Maguire, S., C. Hardy & T.B. Lawrence (2004). Institutional Entrepreneurship in Emerging Fields: HIV/AIDS Treatment Advocacy in Canada. *Academy of Management Journal,* 47 (5), 657-679.

Mantel, A. (2003). Vuist tegen eerwraak. *De Telegraaf.* 30 September 2003.

Marrewijk, van A., M. Veenswijk & S. Clegg (2010). Organizing reflexivity in designed change: the ethnoventionist approach. *Journal of Organizational Change Management,* 23 (3), 212-229.

Martin, J. (1992). *Cultures in organizations. Three perspectives.* New York, Oxford: Oxford University Press.

Mayer, A.D., V. Gaba & K.A. Colwell (2005).Organizing Far from Equilibrium: Nonlinear Change in Organizational Fields. *Organization Science,* 16 (5), 456-473.

Meetoo, V. & H. Safia Mirza (2007). "There is nothing 'honorable' about honor killings": Gender, Violence and the limits of multiculturalism. *Women's Studies International Forum,* 30 (3) 187-200.

Mepschen, P., J.W. Duyvendak, & E.H. Tonkens (2010). Sexual politics, Orientalism and Multicultural Citizenship. *Sociology,* 44 (5), 962-979.

Meyer, J.W. & B. Rowan (1977). Institutionalized Organizations: Formal Structure as Myth and Ceremony. *The American Journal of Sociology,* 83 (2), 340-363.

Ministry of Justice (2010). *Eergerelateerd geweld.* On: http://www.justitie.nl/onderwerpen/criminaliteit/eergelateerd_geweld/ (visited on 16 February 2010).

Ministry of Social Affaires and Employment (2016). *Nieuwsbrief Platform Eer en Vrijheid* On: https://abonneren.rijksoverheid.nl/nieuwsbrieven/archief/nieuwsbrief-platform-eer-en-vrijheid/690/editie/24669cae-da36-4e54-88e8-14cba5d9ec87 (visited on 7 December 2016).

Munir, K.A. (2014). A Loss of Power in Institutional Theory. *Journal of Management Inquiry,* 24 (1), 90-92.

Mutch, A. (2007). Reflexivity and the Institutional Entrepreneur: A Historical Exploration. *Organizational Studies,* 28 (07), 1123-1140.

Narayan, U. (2000). Undoing the "Package Picture" of Cultures. *Signs,* 25 (4), 1083-1086.

Nauta, A. & T. Nauta (2011). *Nauta & Nauta, Experts in eergerelateerd geweld vraagstukken, Profiel.* On: http://www.eerwraak.be/index.php?option=com_content&task=view&id=27&Itemid=37&PHPSESSID=f7v7fehpsgnvf74p15gj6evqg4 (visited on 18 March 2011).

Nieuwenhuis, A. & H. Ferwerda (2010). *Tot de dood ons scheidt. Een onderzoek naar de omvang en kenmerken van moord en doodslag in huiselijke kring.* Arnhem: Beke groep.

Nijdam, H. (2008). *Lichaam, eer en recht in middeleeuws Friesland. Een studie naar de Oudfriese boeteregisters*. Hilversum: Uitgeverij Verloren in cooperation with the Fryske Akademy.

NOVA (7-6-2008). *Moeder over de moord op haar dochter Zeynep Boral*.

NRC Handelsblad (1999). Turken bezinnen zich op plegen van eerwraak. *NRC Handelsblad*. 15 December 1999.

NRC Handelsblad (2003). Man doodt dochter (18) in Turkije om eerwraak. *NRC Handelsblad*. 29 September 2003.

Oakes, L.S., B. Townley & D.K. Cooper (1998). Business Planning as Pedagogy: Language and Control in a Changing Institutional Field. *Administration Science Quarterly*, 43 (2), 257-292.

Okin, S.M. (1999). Is Multiculturalism Bad for Women? In: Cohen, J., M. Howard & M.C. Nussbaum (Eds.) *Is Multiculturalism Bad for Women. Susan Moller Okin with respondents*. Princeton, New Jersey: Princeton University Press.

Pascall, G. & J. Lewis (2004). Emerging Gender Regimes and Policies for Gender Equality in a Wider Europe. *Journal of Social Policy*, 33 (3), 373–394.

Perkmann, M. & A. Spicer (2007). "Healing the Scars of History": Projects, Skills and Field Strategies in Institutional Entrepreneurship. *Organizational Studies*, 28 (07), 1101-1122.

Philips, G.J. (2008). *Scholenproject: Eergerelateerd geweld in en om de school*. PowerPoint presentatie G4 overleg Den Haag.

Phillips, A. & S. Saharso (2008). Guest editorial: The rights of women and the crisis of multiculturalism. *Ethnicities*, 8(3), 291-301.

Port, M. Van der (2001). *Geliquideerd, Criminele afrekeningen in Nederland*. Amsterdam: J.M. Meulenhoff bv.

Pratt Ewing, K. (2008). *Honor in Berlin: Stigmatizing Muslim Men in Berlin*. Stanford University Press.

Prins, B. (2002). The Nerve to Break Taboos: New Realism in the Dutch Discourse on Multiculturalism. *Journal of International Migration and Integration*, 3 (3-4), 363-379.

Prins, B. & S. Saharso (2010). From toleration to repression. The Dutch backlash against multiculturalism. In: Vertovec, S. & S. Wessendorf (Eds.) (2010). *The Multicultural Backlash. European discourses, policies and practices*. London & New York: Routledge

Raad, van der S. (2015). *Othering and Inclusion of Ethnic Minority Professionals, A Study on Ethnic Diversity Discourses, Practices and Narratives in the Dutch Legal Workplace*. Amsterdam: VU University Press.

Reimers, E. (2007). Representations of an Honor Killing. Intersections of discourses on culture, gender, equality, social class, and nationality. *Feminist Media Studies*, 7 (3), 239-255.

Reysoo, F. & K. Ouchan (1999). *Nooit geschreven brief aan mijn vader*. Amsterdam: Uitgeverij Bulaaq.

Rodríguez-García (2010). Beyond Assimilation and Multiculturalism: A Critical Review of the Debate on Managing Diversity. *Journal of International Migration & Integration*, 11 (3), 251-271.

Roggeband, C. & Verloo, M. (2007). Dutch Women are Liberated, Migrant women are a Problem: the Evolution of Policy Frames on Gender and Migration in the Netherlands, 1995 – 2005. *Social Policy & Administration*, 41 (3), 271- 288.

Roggeband, C. & D. Lettinga (2016). In Defence of Gender Equality? Comparing the Political Debates about Headscarves and Honor-Related Crimes in France and the Netherlands. *Social Politics*, 23 (3), 239-262.

Rotterdams Dagblad (1999). "Onze vriendin Kezban moet het laatste slachtoffer zijn". *Rotterdams Dagblad*. 25 June 1999.

Saharso, S. (2002). Een vrouw met twee missies. Reactie op Helma Lutz. *Tijdschrift voor Genderstudies,* 5 (3), 18-23.

Said, E. (1978). *Orientalism.* London: Penguin Group.

Santing, F. (2004). "Moord Gül geen eerwraak, wel om de eer"; Turkolge van Eck over effect gekrenkte trots. *NRC Handelsblad,* 21 December 2004.

Schinkel, W. (2008). Contexts of Anxiety: the Moral Panic over "Senseless Violence" in the Netherlands. *Current Sociology,* 56 (5), 735-756.

Schinkel, W. (2010). The Virtualization of Citizenship. *Critical Sociology,* 36 (2), 265-283.

Schneider, J.W. (1985). Social Problems Theory: The Constructionist View. *Annual Review of Sociology,* 11 (1), 209-229.

Schwartz-Shea, P. & D. Yanow (2012). *Interpretive Research Design, Concepts and Processes.* New York: Routledge.

Scott, W.R. (1987). The Adolescence of Institutional Theory. *Administrative Science Quarterly,* 32 (4), 493-511.

Scott, W. R. (2008a). Approaching adulthood: the maturing of institutional theory. *Theory and Society,* 37 (5), 427-442.

Scott, W.R. (2008b) (third edition). *Institutions and Organizations. Ideas and Interests.* Thousand Oaks, New Delhi, London, Singapore: Sage Publications.

Scuzzarello, S. (2008) National Security versus Moral Responsibility: An Analysis of Integration Programs in Malmö, Sweden. *Social Politics,* 15 (1), 5-31.

Siim, B. & H. Skejei (2008). Tracks, intersections and dead ends, Multicultural challenges to state feminism in Denmark and Norway. *Ethnicities,* 8 (3), 322-344.

Smits, K. (2013). *Cross Cultural Work. Practices of collaboration in the Panama Canal Expansion Program.* Delft: Next Generation Infrastructures Foundation.

SMN (2008). *Van taboe naar aanpak: Notitie over de Marokkaanse gemeenschap en eergerelateerd geweld.* Utrecht: SMN.

SMN (2008). *Wie zijn wij?* On: http://www.smnnet.nl/organisatie.php?id=1&PHPSESSID=c43eb7c36067a3ceb92beaccd33ab077 (visited on 20 November 2008).

Soeteman, F. (2004). Jaloerse Turk (37) schoot gevluchte ex aan flarden. *De Telegraaf.* 7 December 2004.

Souad (2004). *Geschonden, Ik overleefde de aanslag op mijn leven.* Amsterdam: Arena.

Spector, M. & J.I. Kitsuse (1973). Social Problems: A Re-Formulation. *Social Problems,* 21 (2), 145-159.

Spector, M. & J.I. Kitsuse (1977). *Constructing Social Problems.* Menlo Park: Cummings Publishing Company, Inc.

Steinmetz, B. (2004). Traditionele Turkse erecode is nog steeds springlevend. *Het Parool.* 16 January 2004.

Stichting Kezban (2008). *Wat doet stichting Kezban.* On: http://www.st-kezban.nl/pages/doel.htm (visited on October 20, 2008).

Suddaby. R. (2010). Challenges for Institutional Theory. *Journal of Management Inquiry,* 19 (1), 14-20.

Swartz, D.L. (1997). *Culture and Power: the sociology of Pierre Bourdieu.* Chicago: The University of Chicago Press.

Swartz, D.L. (2008). Bringing Bourdieu's master concepts into organizational analysis. *Theory and Society,* 37 (1), 45-52.

Tennekes, J. (1995). *Organisatiecultuur: Een antropologische visie.* Leuven/Apeldoorn: Garant Uitgevers n.v.

Thiel, S. van (2003). Sturen op afstand. Over de aansturing van verzelfstandigde organisaties door kerndepartementen. *Management in overheidsorganisaties*, 93, A5215.

Thompson, J.B. (1991). "Editor's Introduction" In: Bourdieu, P (1991). *Language and Symbolic Power*. Cambridge, MA: Harvard University Press.

Thornton, P. W. Ocasio & M. Lounsbury (2012). *The Institutional Logics Perspective: a New Approach to Culture, Structure and Processes*. New York, NY: Oxford University Press.

Tolbert, P.S. & L.G. Zucker (1983). Institutional Sources of Change in the Formal Structure of Organizations: The Diffusion of Civil Service Reform, 1880-1935. *Administrative Science Quarterley*, 28 (1), 22-39.

Torre, E.J. van der en L. Schaap (2005). *Ernstig eer gerelateerd geweld: een casus onderzoek*. Den Haag: COT Instituut voor Veiligheids- en Crisismanagement.

Tweede Kamer (2015a), *The debate*. On: https://www.houseofrepresentatives.nl/debate (visited on 10 October 2015).

Tweede Kamer (2015b). *Over het Presidium*. On: http://www.tweedekamer.nl/kamerleden/presidium (visited on 10 October 2015).

Tweede Kamer (2015c). *Commissie voor de Rijksuitgaven* On: http://www.tweedekamer.nl/kamerleden/commissies/ru (visited on 11 October 2015).

Tweede Kamer (2016). Grote Projecten. On: http://www.tweedekamer.nl/kamerleden/commissies/ru/grote_projecten (visited on 18 February 2016).

Utrechts Nieuwsblad (2003). Het motief was waarschijnlijk eerwraak. *Utrechts Nieuwsblad*

Vaughen, D. (2008). Bourdieu and organizations: the empirical challenge. *Theory and Society*, 37 (1), 65-81.

Veenswijk, M. (1995). *Departementale cultuur: IJzeren kooi, bron van versplintering of politiek werktuig?* Delft: Eburon.

Verdwaalde Gezichten (2008). On: http://www.verdwaaldegezichten.nl/index.php?option=com_content&task=section&id=9&Itemid=59 (visited on 20 October 2010).

Verloo, M. (Ed.) (2007). *Multiple Meanings of Gender Equality: A Critical frame Analysis of Gender Policies in Europe*. Budapest: Central European University Press.

Vermeulen, D. (2000). Strijd tegen vrouwengeweld op de agenda. *De Dordtenaar*. 23 June 2000.

Vermeulen, F. (1990). "Eerwraak in onze samenleving niet te tolereren". *NRC Handelsblad*, 9 August 1990, p. 2

Vertovec, S. & S. Wessendorf (2010). Introduction: assessing the backlash against multiculturalism in Europe. In: Vertovec, S. & S. Wessendorf (Eds.) (2010). *The Multicultural Backlash. European discourses, policies and practices*. London & New York: Routledge

Vieten, U.M. (2007) *Situated Cosmopolitanisms: the notion of the Other in contemporary discourses on cosmopolitanism in Britain and Germany*, Ph. D. Thesis, University of East London.

Visser, E. de (1999). Turkse na scheiding vaak bedreigt. *De Volkskrant*. 2 July 1999.

Voorde, J. ten (2007). *Cultuur als verweer. Een grondslagentheoretische studie naar de ruimte en grenzen van culturele diversiteit in enige leerstukken van materieel strafrecht*. Nijmegen: Legal Publishers.

Vries, G. de (2000). Eis 12 jaar voor schietpartij Veghel. *NRC Handelsblad*. 19 May 2000.

Waquante, L. (2004). Following Bourdieu into the field. *Ethnography*, 5 (4), 387-414.

Westenholz, A., J. Strandgaard Pedersen & F. Dobbin (2006). Introduction, Institutions in the Making: Identity, Power, and the Emergence of New Organizational Forms. *American Behavioral Scientist*, 49 (7), 889-896.

Wikan, U. (2008). *In honor of Fadime, Murder and Shame.* Chicago/ London: University of Chicago Press.
Willmott, H. (2015). Why Institutional Theory Cannot Be Critical. *Journal of Management Inquiry,* 24 (1), 105-111.
Wit, H. de (2000). Geweld in huis geen zeldzaamheid. *Het Parool.* 5 June 2000.
Witschge, T. (2007). *(In)difference online. The openness of public discussion on immigration.* Amsterdam: Universiteit van Amsterdam.
Wooten, M. & A.J. Hoffman (2008). Organizational Fields: Past, Present and Future. In: Greenwood, R., C. Oliver, K. Sahlin & R. Suddaby (Eds.). *The Sage Handbook of Organizational Institutionalism.* London, Thousand Oaks, New Dehli & Singapore: Sage Publications.
Wright, A.L. (2009). Domination in Organizational Fields: It's Just Not Cricket. *Organization,* 16 (6): 855-885.
Ybema, S., D. Yanow, H. Wels & F. Kamsteeg (2009). *Organizational Ethnography. Studying the complexities of Everyday Life.* London: SAGE Publications Ltd.
Young, J. (2005). Book review: Moral panics, Margate and Mary Poppins: Mysterious happenings in south coast seaside towns. *Crime, Media, Culture,* 1 (1), 100-105.
Young, Y. (2009). Moral Panic, Its Origins in Resistance, Ressentiment and the Translation of Fantasy into Reality. *British Journal of Criminology,* 49 (1), 4-16.
Zee, R. van der (2007). Hij wilde haar niet doden, maar kon de druk niet aan. Zelfdoding eermoordenaar is atypisch; eerwraak. *NRC Handelsblad.* 4 July 2007.
Zijlstra, A. (1999). Familie van vermoorde Kezban vangt zwaar getraumatiseerde kinderen op, "Ik mis Mama, Ik haat mijn vader!", *De Telegraaf.* 13 November 1999.
Zucker, L.G. (1977). The Role of Institutionalization in Cultural Persistence. *American Sociological Review,* 42 (5), 726-743.

Appendixes

Appendix 1: Occurrences of the "honour killing" and "honour-related violence" labels in the media and in politics

All numbers presented below are based on either an analysis of Dutch national and regional newspapers using the search engine LexisNexis on 24 March 2011 and/or on an analysis of "official announcements" by the Dutch national government using the search engine Overheid.nl on 30 March 2011.

Table showing occurrences of the "honour-killing" (eerwraak) label in Dutch newspapers 1990-2010

Years 1990-2000	Occurrences	Years 2000-2011	Occurrences
1990	1	2001	140
1991	0	2002	91
1992	0	2003	595
1993	3	2004	1341
1994	1	2005	1213
1995	3	2006	876
1996	2	2007	1182
1997	1	2008	753
1998	3	2009	580
1999	53	2010	683
2000	79		

Table showing occurrences of the "honour killing" (eerwraak) label in Dutch parliament 1996-2010

Years 1996-2003	Occurrences	Years 2004-2011	Occurrences
1996	3	2004	73
1997	0	2005	99
1998	1	2006	41
1999	1	2007	69
2000	6	2008	54
2001	6	2009	47
2002	2	2010	64
2003	40		

Table showing occurrences of the "honour-related violence" or HRV (eergelateerd geweld) and "honour killing" (eerwraak) labels in Dutch parliament and in the media 2004-2010

Year	HRV in newspapers	Honour killing in newspapers	HRV in Parliament	Honour killing in parliament
2004	0	1341	8	73
2005	70	1213	48	99
2006	114	876	56	41
2007	242	1182	103	69
2008	234	753	109	54
2009	153	580	105	47
2010	160	683	135	64

Appendix 2: Example from the matrix on Gül's murder

Date	Actor	Claims
16 March 2004	Cocky Roel, director of the Alkmaar women's shelter	– We need to take honour killings more seriously in the Netherlands.
	FO, umbrella organization for women's shelter organizations	– We call on the Dutch government to take action with regard to the safety of women's shelters.
	Neighbours of Gül in Apeldoorn	– We are in shock, Gül was highly educated, though we knew that her freedom was restricted.
	Ruud Vreeman, Mayor of Zaanstad	– If need be these women need to be given new identities. – We need safe women's shelters. – The Turkish community needs to take action, they need to take responsibility.
	Johan Gortworst, director of FO	– We need money for the women's shelter organizations. – The police need to investigate how a secret address became public. – This is the third victim in ten months.
	A Turkish women staying in a women's shelter	– Turkish men want revenge if their wives walk away. A divorce shames the husband's honour. – This was done by a traditional Turkish man.
	Sadet Metin, on behalf of the Kezban Foundation	– We call on the Turkish community to go to the police if they suspect an attempted honour killing. – The Turkish community needs to stop educating their children with these kinds of antisocial standards and values, and learn to respect women. – This murder shows similarities with Kezban's murder. – We have been working on this topic in a variety of ways, for example a film about honour killings. – Subsidies take long to be granted, which makes our work difficult. – We need to take action, talk alone is not enough.

Appendix 3: Observations

1. Conference on Honour-Related Violence: June 2007, WTC Rotterdam.
2. Rob Ermers's book presentation: 21 September 2007, WTC Rotterdam.
3. Kezban conference: 4 March 2008, Forum Utrecht.
4. Network consultation in Amsterdam: 11 March 2008.
5. Network consultation in Amsterdam: 1 April 2008.
6. Movisie conference: 6 April 2008, Podium Mozaïek Amsterdam.
7. Sounding board group for the project for schools in Rotterdam and Twente: 20 May 2008.
8. Presentation of police film *Uw eer, onze zaak* ("your honour, our business") in Amsterdam: 29 May 2008, Amsterdam City Hall.
9. Care coordinators' conference of the ASA regional training centre: 4 June 2008, Amsterdam.
10. G4 conference (of the four largest Dutch municipalities): 4 June 2008, The Hague City Hall.
11. Women's shelters conference: 5 June 2008: "Het Vechthuis" Utrecht.
12. Memorial service for Zeynep Boral: 11 June 2008, De Hertenkamp, Alkmaar.
13. National conference for points of contact for honour-related violence at police forces: 24 June 2008, Badhotel Scheveningen.
14. G4 conference (of the four largest Dutch municipalities): 4 September 2008, The Hague City Hall.

Appendix 4: Information on the respondents and their backgrounds

Number	Respondent's name	Organization	Title	Location
1.	Anonymous	Stichting Vangnet	Staff member	Amsterdam
2.	Akın, Yeter	Stichting Verdwaalde Gezichten	Project leader	Haarlem
3.	Albrecht, Marcia	Municipal Health Service, Municipality of Rotterdam	Network manager, honour-related violence	Rotterdam
4.	Altuntas, Celal	Stichting Zebra	Social worker	The Hague
5.	Ayrancı, Mustafa	HTIB	Chair	Amsterdam
6.	Azdural, Ahmet	Inspraak Orgaan Turken (IOT)	Director	Utrecht
7.	Bakker, Hilde	Movisie	Adviser, domestic and sexual violence	Utrecht
8.	Bartels, Edien	VU Univeristy Amsterdam	Academic staff member	Amsterdam
9.	Batem, Serpil	Stichting Yasmin	Social and cultural worker	The Hague
10.	Bergen, Diana van	VU Univeristy Amsterdam	Academic staff member	Amsterdam
11.	Kışın, Sidar	Multicultureel Instituut (MCI)	Social worker	The Hague
12.	Boer, Marjolijne van den	Advies- en Meldpunt Kindermishandeling	Service team member	Amsterdam
13..	Brouwer, Lenie	VU Univeristy Amsterdam	Academic staff member	Amsterdam
14.	Bourri, Fatima	Sja-Meidenplaza	Senior girls' worker	Amsterdam
15.	Bouman, Annemarie	Police force, Amsterdam Amstelland	Academic staff member	Amsterdam
16.	Cornelissen, Agnes	Advies- en onderzoeksbureau Beke	Researcher	Arnhem
17.	Dalkıran, Seren	Stichting Verdwaalde Gezichten	Project leader	Haarlem
18.	Dekker, Anne-Floor	Vluchtelingen Organisaties Nederland	Project coordinator	Amsterdam

Number	Respondent's name	Organization	Title	Location
19.	Doğan, Carola	Inspraak Orgaan Turken (IOT)	Project coordinator	Utrecht
20.	Driessen, Daan	National Expertise Centre for Honour-Related Violence (LEC)	Police Chief Superintendent	The Hague
21.	El Houari, Lahbib	Stichting Meander	Adviser	Haaglanden region
22.	Ermers, Rob	Midden Oosten Perspectief	Specialist in Arabic and Turkish studies	Den Bosch
23.	Gerrits, Patricia	Dutch Ministry of Housing, Communities and Integration	Project leader, social prevention	The Hague
24.	Gortworst, Johan	Federatie Opvang (FO)	Director	Utrecht
25.	Heerschap, Hans	Police force, Rotterdam Rijnmond	Policy officer	Rotterdam
26.	Heide, Maimunah van der	Stichting Vangnet	Founder	Amsterdam
27.	Horst, Ingrid	Dutch Ministry of Justice	Project leader, domestic violence	The Hague
28.	Imbens, Annie		Researcher	Utrecht
29.	Janssen, Janine	National Expertise Centre for Honour-Related Violence (LEC)	Academic staff member	The Hague
30.	Jasai, Bea	Stichting Arosa, women's shelter Rotterdam	Manager	Rotterdam
31.	Kamp, Trix van der	Stichting Meander	Support staff member	Haaglanden region
32.	Karadeniz, Arzu	Stichting IDEA/ Turkse Vrouwen Komitee	Project leader	Utrecht
33.	Keuzenkamp, Saskia	VU Univeristy Amsterdam/SCP	Academic staff member	Amsterdam
34.	Kiewiet, Hillegonde	NVA Centrum voor duurzame inburgering	Director	Amersfoort
35.	Kışın, Sidar	Multicultureel Instituut (MCI)	Social worker	The Hague

Number	Respondent's name	Organization	Title	Location
36.	Kok, Riekje	Stichting Toevlucht, advice and support centre for domestic violence in Groningen	Director	Groningen
37.	Koning, Martijn de	International Institute for the Study of Islam in the Modern World (ISIM)	Academic staff member	Amsterdam
38.	Kop, Joke	Vrouw & Vaart	Coordinator	Amsterdam
39.	Korkmaz, Şahin	Koerdische Arbeiders Unie – Komkar	Volunteer	The Hague
40.	Kriens, Jantien	Municipality of Rotterdam	Alderman	Rotterdam
41.	Kuppens, Jos	Advies- en onderzoeksbureau Beke	Researcher	Arnhem
42.	Linden, Peter van der	Dutch Ministry of Housing, Communities and Integration	Policy officer	The Hague
43.	Marcouch, Ahmed	Slotervaart urban district council	Urban district council chair	Amsterdam
44.	Meihuizen Hassoun, Tomador	Arabisch-Nederlandse vrouwenliga	Chair	The Hague
45.	Molenaar, Mariet	Police force Amsterdam - Amstelland	Project leader, domestic and honour-related violence / police inspector	Amsterdam
46.	Mouaddab, Nadia	Samenwerkingsverband Marokkanen in Nederland (SMN)	Policy officer	Utrecht
47.	Müjde, Melda		Former police employee / mediator	Amersfoort
48.	Navruzoğlu, Mürüvet	Stichting Yasmin	Social and cultural worker	The Hague
49.	ocal, Neriman	Hayrun Nisa	Chair	Amsterdam
50.	Okumuş, Rahime	NVA centrum voor duurzame inburgering	Project supervisor	Amersfoort
51.	Ouchan, Karima	Regional training centre (ROC) Twente	Project leader	Almelo

Number	Respondent's name	Organization	Title	Location
52.	Oudheusen, Vera	Dutch Ministry of Health, Welfare and Sport	Project team member, protection	The Hague
53.	ozcan, Garip	Multicultureel Instituut (MCI)	Social and cultural worker	The Hague
54.	ozgümüş, Fatma	Vluchtelingen Organisaties Nederland	Director	Amsterdam
55.	Pattiselanno, Margie	Municipality of Amsterdam	Project leader, honour-related violence	Amsterdam
56.	Paulissen, Riesje	Municipality of Eindhoven	Network manager, honour-related violence	Eindhoven
57.	Pepe, Francisco	"Love and Hate" academic network	Researcher	Amsterdam
58.	Péres Yánes, Cecilia	advice and support centre for domestic violence/honour-related violence report line	Subject matter coordinator	Amsterdam
59.	Phagoe,	Stichting Vikaash	Chair	Amsterdam
60.	Philips, Goverdien	Albeda College Rotterdam	Project leader	Rotterdam
61.	Roosen, Adelheid	Stichting Female Economy	Director, Is.man	Amsterdam
62.	Saharto, Sawitri	VU Univeristy Amsterdam	Academic staff member	Amsterdam
63.	Schaik, Ineke van	Hippe Heks	Volunteer	Amsterdam
64.	Teerds, Bram	Dutch Ministry of Justice	Project leader, criminal law measures	The Hague
65.	Uppelschoten, Marc	Municipality of Amsterdam	Project leader, honour-related violence	Amsterdam
66.	Uyar, Canan	Milli Görüş Northern Netherlands	Chair of the women's federation	Amsterdam
67.	Velde, Jan Willem van der	Blijfgroep, a women shelter	Project leader	Amsterdam
68.	Vlaanderen, Rijk van	ASA regional training centre	Coordinator, combatting honour-related violence	Amsterdam

Number	Respondent's name	Organization	Title	Location
69.	Vogelsanger, Andrea	Schorer Stichting	Senior project team member	Amsterdam
70.	Voorthoren, Marianne	Platform for Islamic Organizations in Rijnmond (SPIOR)	Policy officer	Rotterdam
71.	Wassie, Najla	Pharos (Dutch Centre of Expertise on Health Disparities)	Senior adviser / trainer	Utrecht
72.	Weert, Paul van	Municipality of Amsterdam, Municipal Health Service	Team leader	Amsterdam
73.	Wielkens, Marjorie	VU University Amsterdam	Student counsellor	Amsterdam
74.	Yalım, Özden	Fatusch Productions	Freelancer	Rotterdam
75.	Zee, Renate van der		Reporter	Utrecht
76.	Zuthem, Harm van	Inspraak Orgaan Turken (IOT)	Policy officer	Utrecht

Appendix 5: Interview schedule

Introduction
We are researching two topics: 1. how organizations combat honour-related violence (policies, detection, prevention, shelter for victims, measures against offenders etc.); and 2. how immigrants view honour-related violence, for example what it is for women to live with the pressure resulting from prevailing views of honour.

The purpose of this interview is to find out about various matters including:
X's organizational structure
How X handles honour-related violence (HRV)/what measures X takes against HRV
X's position in the spectrum of organizations that are concerned with honour-related violence

Recording the interviews offers us practical benefits. These recordings are purely for our own purposes and we will treat them confidentially. Do you have any objection to being recorded?

We intend to list the individuals and/or organizations that we interviewed in our report. Is that alright with you, or would rather that we did not? We can also render the responses anonymous.

We understand that because of your position you are not permitted or are unwilling to share certain information. We would appreciate it if you could tell us when this occurs.

(It is important for our purposes to keep asking open questions throughout the interview, rather than giving you options such as "does this happen, or that, or that?")

The actual interview starts

To establish for ourselves how the work relating to HRV is embedded in X, the first few questions are about the organization. Before we begin, though, we should ask how much time you have for this interview. Alright.

Organization X:
What are the **principal responsibilities** of X?
What are the **principal objectives** of those responsibilities?
What organization levels, departments, services, teams, projects etc. does X include?
Does the organization have core activities and separate projects or ….
How does the work relating to HRV **fit in**?
Do the women/migrants/members of the "targeted demographic" **find their way to** X?
How do they find their way to you?
How do you think that the migrants/targeted demographic **view** X?
What can you do to improve the organization's visibility/accessibility/image?

Role of the respondent at X:
What is currently **your role/job** at X/on the team/in the work/on the project?
Since when have you been doing this job?
Were you already working for X before that? What was **your responsibility/job before**?
How did you **first encounter** HRV?
How did you decide to become **actively** involved in policy/efforts to combat HRV etc.?
How did you acquire your **expertise** relating to HRV (experience, in the field, individuals, training, formal education, learned from other initiatives)?

This work/project:
How did X **decide** to develop a dedicated policy/team/project for combatting honour-related violence?
How did the work/project **come about**?
At what level was the **initiative** taken for this work/project?
What is the **purpose/mission** of the work/project?
What is the **substance** of the work/project (in what phases)?
Which individuals/departments/units of the organization are involved in this work/project?
How are **collaborative efforts** between them given shape (how often do they communicate, about what issues)?
To what extent does **support** exist for this work/project within X?
How are important **decisions** made about work relating to HRV?
How is the work/project **financed**?
Is the work/project part of the **Honour-Related Violence Programme**?

If so, how did X/this project become part of that programme? If not, would it offer any benefits to become part of that programme?
What are your views on how the work/project **is proceeding**?
Assuming that such work/projects inevitably encounter difficulties, what have been the most important **obstacles** in this work/project?
What could other organizations **learn** from the experiences gained in this work/project?
What practices could they adopt? What should be done differently?

You have now explained how X is set up, what the work/project involves and what your own role is. We would also like to find out whether you have partnerships with other organizations, and if so how they work.

Partner organizations/individuals of X:
With **what organizations** have you formed partnerships in connection with HRV?
How did that partnership **come about**?
Whose initiative was it?
How is this partnership **organized** (how often, on what subjects, which individuals at that organization)?
What are the separate organizations' **responsibilities** in this partnership?
Is this an informal partnership, or has it been **formally established**?
How is the partnership **proceeding**?
What could be done to **improve** the partnership?
What is your view on the **role that X** plays in this network of partner organizations? Is it clear/feasible?
What role do you yourself believe that X should fulfil?
Are there any organizations with which you would like to form partnerships?
How could those partnerships be given shape/why have these partnerships not been formed?
Do you have any partnerships with organizations in countries of origin?

Now we would like to take a more specific look at the HRV with which you are concerned/as X encounters it.

Honour-related violence (extent, definition, etc.)
What groups are involved in honour-related violence?
What **types of violence** do you consider to be HRV?
What is the **extent** of the **problem** in this region/town/city, how many victims?
What **types of victims** (male, female, age, etc.) do you encounter (numbers)?
What **types of offenders** do you encounter/know?

What is the **essence of the problem** of HRV? Where does this violence originate? (Role of religion? Gossip?)
How does HRV relate to "standard" domestic violence?
What should **NL/the government/the organizations/society/migrants** do to eliminate HRV?

The government believes that a wide range of different institutions and organizations should be concerned with HRV: the courts and the Public Prosecution Service, the police, social workers, educators, self-help organizations, women's shelters.

What organizations you do personally believe play the most important roles? What areas require the most focus/work at present?
Regarding your own project/work: what do you need in terms of resources/financing etc. to **maintain the results** that have been achieved? To continue the work in the way you want to?

Media
HRV is being given more and more attention in the media.
What is your opinion of how the media **report** on HRV/how it is **discussed** (e.g. following the murder in Alkmaar)?
How **do you yourself deal with the media** in matters concerning HRV?
What **impact** do you think the media have on existing and potential victims and offenders?
Does the media attention **impact how X handles** HRV? In what way?

We have taken up quite a bit of your time, and it might be a good idea to bring this interview to a conclusion. We have just a few more questions.
Is there anything that you would like to **add**? Is there anything important that we have missed?
What do you personally believe is **the most important issue to research** in connection with HRV?
Whom else do you think we **should interview,** to obtain a clear understanding of how people at Y deal with HRV?
Can you recommend any interesting **local initiatives** concerning measures, prevention, etc.?

If the respondent mentions anything that would be interesting for us to attend, inquire about the possibilities.

Summary

When I first started on this research back in 2007, I was confronted with a myriad of actors and activities surrounding the issue of honour-related violence. These included actors as diverse as a theatre maker, migrant organizations, schools, scholars, politicians, women's shelters, police investigators and victims of honour-related violence. I was intrigued by this widespread attention for the issue and went in search of a theoretical framework that would help me to make sense of this puzzle. I found the framework that I needed in the concepts of *organizational field emergence* and *issue-based organizational fields*, which had both been developed within institutional theory in organizational analysis. I combined this institutional framework with Bourdieu's *theory of practice*, as his work appeared to offer a solution to institutional theory's enduring quest for a balanced theory of action and power.

This research therefore served two purposes. On the one hand, I wished to empirically explore the actors and processes involved in the emergence of an issue-based organizational field, leading to the following research question:

What actors and processes contributed to the emergence of the issue-based organizational field on honour-related violence in the Netherlands?

On the other hand, I wished to explore the potential of Bourdieu's work for institutional theory in organizational analysis, resulting in the following research question:

How does Bourdieu's theory of practice contribute to an understanding of the processes involved in organizational field emergence?

I therefore conducted a case study of firstly the emergence of the issue and secondly the emergence of the honour-related violence field. This case study encompassed three components: 1.) a media analysis of Dutch national newspapers between 1990 and 2010, 2.) an analysis of the parliamentary debates on honour-related violence between 1990 and 2010 and 3.) an ethnographic field study that took place in 2007-2008.

I start this summary by briefly recapitulating the results of the case study. I then describe the empirical contribution of this study, focusing primarily on the critical preconditions for organizational field emergence and on the processes that shape the emerging field configurations. I then turn to the second question and consider the added value of Bourdieu's framework.

The emergence of the Dutch honour-related violence field

This study reconstructed the emergence of the issue of honour-related violence by tracing the emergence of the labels of *eerwraak* (i.e. honour killing) and *eergerelateerd geweld* (honour-related violence, 'HRV') within the Dutch media field and political field. This reconstruction reveals that the issue of honour-related violence first emerged in the Dutch public discourse around the turn of the millennium (Chapter 4).

The emergence of the issue was facilitated by *evolving macro-cultural discourses* on multiculturalism, gender equality, nationalism, citizenship and social cohesion (Chapter 6) and was driven by four *field-configuring events*: the shootings of Kezban, Hassan, Zarife and Gül (Chapter 5). This combination of macro-level and micro-level processes contributed to a *reconceptualization* of domestic violence against migrant women as honour-related violence. Moreover, the extensive media coverage of these incidents, the subsequent court cases and the warnings issued by various actors contributed to a *moral panic* about this issue: honour killings were perceived as a sign of migrants' failure to integrate (Chapter 7). Together these three interrelated processes provide an explanation for the widespread public attention for the issue of honour-related violence at the beginning of the new millennium.

This case study shows that the attention for honour-related violence quickly spread to other fields, including the political field, where Gül's murder functioned as a catalyst for heated parliamentary debates between MPs and ministers about reliable solutions to the problem. These debates triggered a number of state actions, for example the development of a clear problem definition, the development of an interministerial programme to combat honour-related violence and the allocation of funding. In this manner the state *officialized* the problem of honour-related violence, and heralded a new stage in the development of an issue-based organizational field (Chapter 8).

The actors, actions and processes described above all contributed to the issue's emergence and the subsequent field emergence. Moreover, they influenced the *emerging field configurations*. However, these configurations (e.g. the emerging theoretical unification, the relevant types of capital and the positioning of the actors) were also food for debates between the actors entering this emerging field. It was through those debates and struggles that the HRV field's configurations eventually took shape.

Data from the field ethnography show that by 2007-2008 the honour-related violence field had acquired a large number of actors: the police, women's shelters, municipal authorities, support centres for domestic violence, schools, the Public Prosecution Service, the immigration service and migrant organizations. Moreover, some of these actors could be labelled as *key actors*, having gained that position by combining multiple types of capital that were deemed important within this particular field – *economic capital, social capital* and various types of *informational capital*. Within the emerging field the struggle for the relevant types of capital particularly revolved around informational capital, with different actors having access to different forms of knowledge: expert knowledge (e.g. subject-matter experts), practical knowledge (e.g. the police, women's shelters, schools) and insider knowledge (migrant organizations) (Chapter 9).

The ethnographic data also reveal that by 2007-2008 various actors were "translating" the official problem definition to their own working environments. These separate translations led to differences in interpretation between actors. For instance, some focused primarily on the escalated forms of violence (e.g. the police) while others focused on early signs of honour-related violence (e.g. schools). Although these translations are an essential part of field emergence (Grodal 2007), they also caused disputes between actors, some of whom felt that not everyone had incorporated the definition in a suitable way (Chapter 10).

Yet the greatest struggle within this emerging field concerned the position of the migrant organizations. Migrant organizations were seen as bridge builders between state policy and the targeted migrant communities. Despite this key role, migrant organizations did not feel accepted as full and equal partners. For instance, they were not accepted as partners within the organizations involved in network collaboration. Based on this finding, it is my conclusion that the Dutch HRV field in fact comprised two distinct subfields: one consisting of the state and the various network partners and the other of the migrant organizations. Actors in the first field focused on protecting victims and prosecuting perpetrators. Actors in the second field worked on preventing of honour crimes by seeking to bring about a change in mentality within migrant communities.

Field emergence: a multi-layered process

This case study illustrates that the emergence of an issue-based organizational field is a multi-layered process in which various actors, actions and processes come together and influence each other. In the following I discuss the empirical contribution of this case study in greater detail, focusing on 1.) the phases in field emergence, 2.) the critical preconditions for field emergence, and 3.) the processes that shape the emerging field configurations. In doing so I present an answer to the question *What actors and processes contributed to the emergence of the issue-based organizational field on honour-related violence in the Netherlands?*

The three phases of issue-based field emergence

This case study illustrates that several phases can be distinguished in the process of field emergence: the emergence of the issue, the officialization of the issue as a social problem and the emergence of the related issue-based organizational field.

These different phases flow into one another and influence one another, yet remain distinct. In the following I discuss these phases in the emergence of the Dutch HRV field in greater detail.

Phase 1: issue emergence

An issue-based field can only emerge once an issue has emerged in the public discourse. I therefore studied how the issue of honour-related violence emerged in the Dutch public discourse. The preceding analysis reveals that a set of interrelated processes, actors and actions contributed to the issue's emergence: a number of *unplanned field-configuring events* – honour killings – triggered the attention of a diverse group of actors. These actors were subsequently able to sound the alarm over these events within *the media field*, which was facilitated by both *changes within macro-cultural discourses* and the *development of a label* (i.e. eerwraak) that was compatible with the media field's logic. The media's representation of these events then led to the development of a *moral panic* about these honour killings, which were framed as non-Dutch types of violence (Part II).

Phase 2: officialization of the social problem

A next phase in the emergence of an issue-based field is the transformation of the issue into a discrete social problem. As Bourdieu et al. (1994) previously established, the findings of this case study illustrate how the *state* played a crucial role in *officializing the problem* of honour-related violence.

The *moral panic* that developed within the media field was seized and amplified by several MPs (e.g. Hirsi Ali and Albayrak), who subsequently sounded the alarm about this type of violence within the political field. During the parliamentary debates that followed (*planned field-configuring events*) these MPs used a range of instruments (e.g. motions and priority project status) to push the Members of Cabinet to take action against this type of violence. This eventually resulted in the development of a clear-cut definition of the problem, the start of a pilot to establish the problem's extent, the allocation of funding to various projects and pilots and lastly the development of an interministerial programme to combat honour-related violence. Together these actions helped to 1.) legitimize honour-related violence as a discrete social problem and 2.) demark honour-related violence from domestic violence (Chapter 8).

Phase 3: field emergence

While described as distinct and separate, the foregoing phases overlap and influence each other. This also holds true for the phase of *field emergence*. This study illustrates that various actors were already working to combat honour-related violence before the state took any action. This was the case in particular with a number of migrant organizations. However, these bottom-up initiatives were not always connected. What the *involvement of the state* facilitated, particularly through the development of the interministerial programme, was that the organizations fighting honour-related violence now knew about each other and each other's activities. In the words of Hoffman (1999), they realized that they were partaking in a common debate.

As a consequence, the actors began to interact more and started to *struggle* with one another about the emerging field configurations. For example, once the migrant organizations became aware that other actors were working to fight honour-related violence through network collaboration, they also demanded a position within this network. Besides struggles for position, these conflicts with migrant organizations also included struggles about what type of knowledge had the greatest relevance (i.e. informational capital).

Critical preconditions for field emergence

According to Hoffman (1999:352) the emergence of an issue-based field is signalled by 1.) increased interaction between particular actors, 2.) an increase in the shared information load and 3.) the development of a mutual sense of awareness between actors that they are involved in a common debate. However, Hoffman does not examine in further detail how this increased interaction and shared information load comes about.

Based on my case study, it can be concluded that several distinct processes, actors and actions came together in the emergence of the Dutch HRV field, described here as critical preconditions for field emergence.

Table 6: Critical preconditions for the emergence of the Dutch HRV field

Process	Actor	Action
Field-configuring event	Media involvement	Label development
Changes in macro-cultural discourses	State involvement	Struggles over the emerging field configurations
Moral panic		

Process: field-configuring events

The emergence of a new issue is strongly facilitated by the occurrence of critical events: events that trigger the attention of the media and are used by actors (i.e. key instigators) to draw attention to a specific issue. According to Hoffman and Ocasio (2001:414) these types of events "focus sustained public attention and invite the collective definition or redefinition of social problems".

In this case the actual and attempted honour killings of Kezban, Hassan, Zarife and Gül functioned as critical events. Each generated a great deal of media attention and debate about the applicability of the "honour killing" label. Moreover, each successive incident caused the group of actors sounding the alarm on this particular issue to grow: first a friend, then an expert, a school director, women's shelters and finally politicians (Chapter 5).

Besides functioning as critical events, these murders therefore became field-configuring events: they shaped the configurations of the emerging issue-based field by 1.) bringing together actors that would later become key actors within the Dutch HRV field and 2.) stimulating debates about the problem's definition. This perspective on field-configuring events matches the definition of Meyer et al. (2005:1026), who describes field-configuring events as events that "encapsulate and shape" the development of a field.

Nonetheless, Meyer at al. (2005) attributes this function to temporary social organizations such as conferences and tradeshows, not to the types of unplanned field-configuring events described here. This can be explained by the fact that Meyer et al. (2005) did not study the development of issue-based fields, but focused on fields developing around particular products and technologies. As a consequence, they were not interested in events that triggered issue emergence.

Yet the type of events described by Mayer et al. (2005), denoted here as planned field-configuring events, were also present in the emerging HRV field. The debates between MPs and Members of Cabinet could, for instance, be described as classical field-configuring events, having strongly contributed to the emergence and shape of the HRV field (Chapter 8). The same applies to the various conferences and meetings that were organized by other actors such as the police, municipal authorities and women's shelters. These conferences and meetings contributed to field emergence by enabling the development of a shared information load and contributing to network building between the various actors.

Based on this case study I therefore posit that the occurrence of both unplanned and planned field-configuring events forms a critical precondition for field emergence. Unplanned events are necessary to stimulate issue emergence, while planned events are a condition for developing a network of actors with a shared understanding of the problem.

Process: evolving macro-cultural discourses

Following the work of Lawrence and Phillips (2004), this study also shows that the emergence of the issue of honour-related violence was facilitated by evolving macro-cultural discourses. Changes at the macro level create an opening to challenge issues at the micro level. In this case, the intertwinement of gender issues with multicultural discourses led to disenchantment with the multicultural ideal, which in turn made it possible to criticize culture-linked forms of violence. In addition, evolving discourses on nationalism, citizenship and social cohesion created a climate in which such criticism was welcomed as a means of enforcing moral boundaries between "what is Dutch" and "what should not become Dutch" (Chapter 6). Macro-cultural discourses therefore not only provide the discursive backdrop for an issue-based field, changes in these macro-cultural discourses also form a critical precondition for issue and field emergence.

The inclusion of an analysis of these evolving discourses also makes it possible to explain why this particular issue emerged when it did. As explained in Part II, honour killings and honour-related violence were already happening in the Netherlands long before they were labelled as such. It was only after the changes in these macro-cultural discourses occurred that people started to separate these forms of violence from domestic violence.

Besides facilitating the emergence of a particular issue, macro-cultural discourses can also influence the actions taken to tackle the issue, actions that in turn reinforce those discourses. In this case, these discourses enabled actors within the political field to view honour-related violence as an integration issue, rather than seeing it as a specific type of domestic violence. As a consequence, a programme was developed to tackle this "new" type of violence. In this manner, the state not only officialized the problem as a distinct social problem, it also reinforced the boundary between what was Dutch (i.e. domestic violence) and what was not Dutch (i.e. honour-related violence) (Chapter 8).

Process: moral panic

The general argument behind the concept of a moral panic is that the attention given to a particular social problem does not correlate to the "objective" gravity of the problem. Instead, the moral panic that develops over a social problem indicates concerns about broader societal changes and challenges (Chapter 7).

In this thesis I argue that the attention given to honour-related violence in the Netherlands is a case in point. While honour killings are serious crimes, the number of honour killings does not correlate to the extensive attention that these murders received. Moreover, I follow the reasoning of scholars such as Pratt Ewing (2008:154) by arguing that the sudden attention given to honour killings should be considered against the backdrop of evolving macro-cultural discourses on multiculturalism, gender inequality, nationalism, citizenship and social cohesion. The anxiety about the lack of integration by migrants subsequently facilitated the emergence of the HRV field, as the moral panic about honour killings united actors within and outside the political field to take action against this type of violence (Chapters 7 and 8).

Interestingly, what the emerging field addressed was not these underlying anxieties, but rather the symbol representing these anxieties: the honour killings. Moreover, by reaffirming the boundaries between Dutch violence (e.g. domestic violence) and migrant violence (e.g. honour killings), the field's emergence paradoxically seems to have reaffirmed these anxieties rather than alleviating them.

The moral panic about honour killings not only facilitated the emergence of the Dutch HRV field but also structured the Dutch HRV field into two distinct sub-fields: one formed by network organizations that focused on protecting victims and prosecuting perpetrators, and a second formed by migrant organizations which focussed on achieving a change of mentality within their rank and file (Chapter 11, Figure 7). The othering discourses that accompanied the moral panic about honour killings and the underlying anxieties about migrants lacking integration contributed to a climate in which migrant organizations were not trusted as partners within the local collaboration networks.

Actor: the media as a gatekeeper

While issue-based organizational fields only emerge after multiple actors have committed to that particular issue, the involvement of two specific actors appears to be a critical precondition for any issue-based field emergence: the media and the state.

The involvement of the media is a precondition for field emergence given that the emergence of an issue depends strongly on the media's role. The media field acts as a gatekeeper by deciding what actors to quote and what stories to tell. For instance, the present study illustrates how the media selected specific types of "stories" that matched the rules of the game applied by the media field. Only those honour killings that fitted those rules received extensive coverage in the media, while others received barely any mention whatsoever. Moreover, each honour killing involved a specific actor whom the media would quote at length when describing the incident (Chapters 4 and 5).

Actor: the state as the constructor of social problems

Similar to the media's involvement, the state's involvement seems to be a critical precondition for field emergence. As already argued by scholars such as Clegg (2010) and Bourdieu et al. (1994) this case study also illustrates the state's extensive power to steer a field in a particular direction. Both the development of the policy definition and the interministerial programme should be seen in this light. Together they contributed to the construction of honour-related violence as a distinct social problem.

Moreover, occurrences within the political field impacted the emerging configurations of the Dutch HRV field. For instance, this study reveals that one of the state's key values – developing a solid knowledge base – carried over from the political field to the HRV field. Not only did all the key actors have access to some type of informational capital, one of the key struggles within the emerging field also concerned the question of what type of informational capital was the most valuable.

Lastly, by commissioning the development of a clear-cut definition of the problem the state contributed to theoretical unification within the emerging field. The ethnographic field study shows that the interviewees had developed a shared understanding of the issue of honour-related violence: although they were unable to quote the policy definition, their descriptions generally corresponded to its key elements.

Irrespective of the major role that the state plays, this study also illustrates that the state's power is limited by factors such as the general decentralization processes in the Netherlands. As a consequence, the state could not exert any direct control over other key actors such as the police, women's shelters and municipal authorities (Chapter 11).

Action: labels and translation

In her work on the emergence of the nanotechnology field, Grodal (2007:172-175) draws attention to the importance of a common label for field emergence. She argues that the adoption of a label by new actors (i.e. developing a shared information load) is a critical precondition for field emergence. However, she also finds that while it is important to have a common label it is similarly important to leave actors sufficient freedom to translate the label to their own working environments, arguing that this facilitates their commitment to the emerging field.

In this case, not one but two labels contributed to the emergence of the HRV field: *eerwraak* (i.e. honour killing) and *eergerelateerd geweld* (honour-related violence) (Chapter 4). The label *eerwraak* facilitated the emergence of the issue in the public discourse. It made the issue relevant to the media field, which revels in reporting on these types of critical events, i.e. events that a.) occur at public locations, b.) carry sufficient dramatic features, c.) are illustrative of failing government agencies and d.) provoke the interest of various actors who are willing to voice their concerns about the issue (Chapter 5).

The policy definition of honour-related violence subsequently facilitated the emergence of the field by enabling other actors to join. This new label and definition encompassed a much wider range of types of violence, making it feasible for other actors to see roles for themselves in combatting and preventing honour-related violence. Moreover, the ambiguity of the definition made it possible for the separate actors to translate it to their own working environments (Chapter 10). This process of translation signals a next stage in the emergence of fields.

As such, this case study supports Grodal's proposition (2007) that the development of a common label and its subsequent translation to the respective working environments of the actors involved forms a critical precondition for field emergence.

Summary

Action: struggles over the emerging field configurations

Still, fields do not only come into being by exogenous forces (e.g. evolving discourses, critical events and state involvement). In fact, the actions of actors inside the field are what eventually facilitate field emergence and shape the emerging field configurations. Actors need to join the field first – in other words the issue needs to trigger their interest, their illusio. Next, they must acknowledge their participation in a common debate and develop a shared information load (Hoffman 1999). In other words, they need to interact with one another. Moreover, Bourdieu (1977:190) indicates that these interactions will often include struggles for power.

This case study into field emergence reveals that the issue of honour-related violence did indeed trigger the interest of a wide variety of actors. It also illustrates how those actors interacted and how they were positioned in respect of each other. Moreover, the findings confirm Bourdieu's argument by illustrating how actors struggled with one another over the relevant types of capital, the problem definition and their positions within the field. These struggles chiefly concerned the relevant type of knowledge (i.e. informational capital) and the position of migrant organizations within the field. It is through these struggles that the field's eventual shape is determined (Chapters 9, 10 and 11).

In the above, I have provided an answer to the empirical question driving this research. In the following I focus on the case study's theoretical contribution. In Part 1 I argued that to date institutional theory has been plagued by some persistent challenges, for example the development of a reliable theory of action that strikes the right balance between structure and agency, between macro-level developments and micro-level activities, and a clear conceptualization of processes of power and domination (Chapter 1). I subsequently argued that Bourdieu's theory of practice offers institutionalists the necessary framework, as long as they apply the entirety of his theoretical concepts (i.e. habitus, field and capital). Yet the proof of the pudding is in the eating (Chapter 2). In this section I therefore formulate an answer to the question, *How does Bourdieu's theory of practice contribute to an understanding of the processes involved in organizational field emergence?*

Bourdieu and the structure-agency dilemma

Bourdieu's solution to the structure-agency dilemma lies in his conceptualization of action (i.e. practice). According to Bourdieu (1977) an actor's perception of a given situation and his subsequent action are informed by both his habitus and his position within the field, which in turn is determined by the amount and value of his capital within that particular field: [(Habitus) (Capital)] + Field = Practice.

Summary

Bourdieu adds a historical component to his theory of practice, by arguing that each action feeds back into both the actor's habitus and the field's logic.

This means that each action, viewed here as an expression of agency, is informed by various components: the situation causing the action, the actor's habitus and his position within the field. Based on this combination of components, the actor calculates what action is feasible (i.e. calculation of possibilities). His actions are consequently "structured" by his past experience (i.e. his habitus) and by his position within the field (i.e. the amount and value of his capital within that field) (Chapter 2).

Field emergence and evolving field configurations can then be explained by the fact that the decision to act brings together these various components. For instance, actors may be confronted with a new and unexpected situation (i.e. a critical event), and therefore arrive at a new calculation of possibilities. Moreover, through the feedback loop into the habitus and the field's logic, Bourdieu ensures that each new action is informed by a slightly different habitus and field logic, as these have been informed by a previous action. Actors can therefore incrementally change their actions, even where the situation has not changed significantly.

The fact that an actor's calculation of possibilities takes both the field's logic (macro) and the actor's habitus (micro) into consideration also helps Bourdieu to surmount the micro-macro divide within a single act, as both components influence the eventual action. In addition, the concept of nested fields helps to interrelate various levels of analysis (micro, meso and macro), since the processes can inform the action taken by the individual, organization or field.

Lastly, Bourdieu's concept of capital and his conceptualization of fields as fields of power and fields of struggle make it possible to include a clear power conceptualization within his theory of practice. Bourdieu compares how a field functions to playing a game. The purpose of the game is to retrieve the trump card, i.e. the type of capital that is perceived as the most valuable type of capital within that specific field. At the same time, the actor's ability (i.e. his power) to play the game is determined by the amount and value of the capital already in his possession (Bourdieu and Wacquant 19992: 98-99). Bourdieu's concept of symbolic violence (1977:196-197) also directs attention to the more subtle processes of domination, which lie in the structuring function of both the field's logic and the actor's habitus, even though actors are mostly unaware of this (Chapter 2). Lastly, Bourdieu explicitly directs attention to the power that states have to determine a field's configuration (introduction to Part III).

This discussion of Bourdieu's theoretical concepts illustrates that the added value of his theory of practice lies in the combined use of his concepts. It is through the interrelationship between habitus, field, capital and action that Bourdieu strikes a balance between structure and agency, between micro-level and macro-level developments, while incorporating a multi-layered power conceptualization. By focusing solely on the concept of field, institutionalists have lost that balance and remain unable to restore it. Moreover, they have lost the ability to incorporate a balanced approach to processes of power and domination (Clegg 2010).

The added value of Bourdieu's theory in practice

By applying Bourdieu's framework to this case study I have illustrated that the entirety of his theory is indeed greater than the sum of its parts. Using Bourdieu's framework enables the study of the myriad processes, actors and actions involved in the emergence of an issue-based organizational field. Moreover, by applying his theory at multiple levels of analysis I was able to study the interrelatedness of the organizational field practices at the micro level, the meso level and the macro level.

For example, at the micro level Bourdieu's framework enabled me to understand the dynamics within the political field. Actors here were confronted with a "new" type of violence: honour killings. Within this highly structured and formalized field, both MPs and ministers subsequently acted according to the rules of that particular field (i.e. the field's logic). During parliamentary debates MPs would ask critical questions and use the instrument of motions to steer the government in a particular direction. In response the ministers would write letters to parliament explaining why they first sought to gain a better understanding of the extent and nature of the problem. Each successive debate then led to new actions and responses, ultimately combining to contribute to the officialization of honour-related violence as a distinct social problem.

At the meso level, Bourdieu's theory of practice enabled me to understand the dynamics within the emerging HRV field. In particular his conceptualization of fields as fields of struggle and fields of power helped me to make sense of the debates between the separate actors. The concept of capital, in addition, allowed me to understand why certain actors gained positions as key actors within the emerging HRV field. These key actors all combined various types of capital. They especially had access to various types of informational capital, which turned out to be the trump card within this particular field. Moreover, his concept of habitus helped to explain why the actors highlighted different aspects of the definition of honour-related violence.

At the same time, attention for macro-level developments enhanced my understanding of the processes at a meso and micro level. For instance, attention for the general decentralization processes made it possible to explain why the state was unable to direct the emerging HRV field from the top down. Instead, the state used a variety of instruments, for example commissioning studies, developing a problem definition and allocating funding to relevant actors, to enhance field development. Attention for changing macro-cultural discourses, in addition, helped to explain why honour-related violence was framed as an integration issue rather than as a distinct type of domestic violence.

Updating Bourdieu's framework with the addition of institutional concepts

At the same time, the present case study illustrates that some of the concepts from institutionalism can be useful additions to Bourdieu's work. As explained above, this holds true in particular for the concepts of issue-based organizational fields, field-configuring events and label development. The concept of moral panic is another useful addition for studying the emergence of issue-based fields, shedding light on why a particular issue should suddenly appear in public discourses and subsequently generate large amounts of organizational activity. Moreover, the moral panic concept helps to explain the lack of trust between organizations making up local collaboration networks and migrant organizations, and thus the development of two distinct sub-fields within the emerging HRV field.

Although it is at times challenging, I feel that applying Bourdieu's framework (i.e. painting the bigger picture, focusing on micro-level, meso-level and macro-level developments, and on both structure and agency) has enhanced our understanding of the processes and actors involved in the emergence of issue-based fields. Bourdieu's theory of practice, his work on state power and social problems, makes it possible to study these processes in a balanced manner. I therefore wholeheartedly recommend that others follow this example and further explore Bourdieu's potential for institutional theory.

Acknowledgments

Not wholly unlike the emergence of an issue-based organizational field, the emergence of a Ph.D. thesis is a multi-layered process. It has its ups and downs, its challenges and victories, its evolving perspectives and meanings. Now that the book is finally finished, my overriding feeling is one of gratitude: gratitude for the opportunity to study at length and in great detail an issue that has fascinated and puzzled me; gratitude for the opportunity to meet interesting and inspiring people during my Ph.D. journey; but above all gratitude for the support that I received from so many colleagues, friends and family along the way.

First and foremost I must express my appreciation for my supervisors. Prof. Dr Halleh Ghorashi, Prof. Dr Marcel Veenswijk and Dr Conny Roggeband: thank you for staying with me during this long and winding road. I could not have finished this book without your support, your guidance and your comments – even the challenging ones. Halleh, I specifically want to thank you for nudging me into finishing this Ph.D. Your invitation to visit a writing retreat in Greece was a turning point in this process.

My thanks and appreciation also go out to the members of the reading committee, who gave their time and energy to review this manuscript: Prof. Dr Katherine Pratt Ewing, Prof. Dr Gily Coene, Prof. Dr Sawitri Saharso, Prof. Dr Willem Trommel and Prof. Dr Mirko Noordegraaf.

I also wish to express my particular gratitude to the colleagues with whom I conducted the initial research in 2007 and 2008: Dr Miriam Geerse, Najat Bay and Ouafila Bejja Essayah. I treasure the time that I spent working with you! Similarly, I wish to thank the students who contributed to this research: Jacquelien Kiewiet, Sanne van Strien and Anika de Kruijff. My thanks also go out to the respondents, who found time in their busy schedules to talk to me and who invited me to their meetings.

While many people believe that writing a Ph.D. thesis is a lonely process I never felt alone. During the first part of this Ph.D. journey I was surrounded by an amazing group of fellow Ph.D. candidates and colleagues at the Culture, Organization, and Management Department (which later merged into the Department of Organization Sciences of VU Amsterdam). Thank you all for making my time at the VU so enjoyable and so much fun! Hanneke and Myrte, I particularly want to thank you for helping me find my way around the academic world. Dear Sylvia, I am so happy that we were able to travel the greater part of this Ph.D. road together. Thank you for your support and your friendship. Marleen, Hyunghae, Floor, Petra and Maya, thank you for being such wonderful roommates. Finally,

Acknowledgments

dear members of the Ph.D. club: Karen, Melanie, Gea, Sander, Dhoya, Michiel, Femke and Caronlin, thank you for the enjoyable and enlightening discussions on our works in progress.

During the second part of my Ph.D. journey I took a job as a policy advisor for the Ministry of Justice and Security. My colleagues at the Migration Policy Department were just as supportive and as much fun to be around as my former colleagues at the VU: thank you for always showing an interest in my other "project". I particularly wish to thank Harke and Liesbeth for their efforts in helping me to arrange a study leave, which enabled me to finally finish this 10-year journey. I also wish to thank Michel and Peter[123] for their support and their friendship.

Finally, this Ph.D. journey took me to Greece, and specifically to ARTISA, an academic writing retreat in Epidaurus. My time at ARTISA was one of the most enjoyable and inspiring parts of my journey. Celeste, thank you for creating such a magical place! Frank, thank you so much for your valuable feedback; it lifted this thesis to another level.

I am quite sure some of my non-academic friends will have wondered whether finishing a Ph.D. was worth it all. Yet you always stuck by me and supported me despite everything. Dear Esther, Marianne, Stella, Jacobien, Peggy, Cecile, Ingrid, Amal and Linda, thank you for being my friends!

No words can describe how important it was to have the love and support from both sides of my family during this journey. I am blessed to be part of two wonderful families for whom having fun and helping and supporting each other are key values. Spending time with you and seeing our kids play together is all that really matters to me. I look forward to many more amazing times!

Dearest Gijs and Annika, you truly are the sunshine in my life! I love you and I cannot think of a better reason for being a little late in finalizing this book. Lastly, Rik, my rock, I could never have undertaken this journey without you. Thank you for always being there for me. I promise that our next journey will involve nothing but beaches, palm trees and lots of sunshine!

This book is the product of a long and winding Ph.D. road, to which many people contributed. Still, the responsibility for the foregoing, and for any errors that it contains, is mine and mine alone.

Nicole Brenninkmeijer

---

123. Dear Peter, when we first met you told me I should finish my Ph.D. quickly by simply putting all the "important stuff" in footnotes. This last one is for you. I am truly sorry that you are not here to see that I finally made it.

Rasmussen, O. Elstrup
(1994) The discontinuity of human existence. Part I. The fundamental concepts of human experience and the relation between the singular and the super singular. *Cognitive Science Research* 50, 34 p.

Rasmussen, O. Elstrup
(1994) The discontinuity of human existence. Part II. The general and the specific theories of discontinuity. *Cognitive Science Research* 51, p. 1-45.

Rasmussen, O. Elstrup
(1994) The discontinuity of human existence. Part III. Perspective text analysis. A methodological approach to the study of competence. *Cognitive Science Research* 52, p. 1-28.

Ravn, I., Emmeche, C., Køppe, S., Stjernfelt, F., Teuber, J.
(1995) *Chaos, Quark und schwarze Löcher*. München, Verlag Antje Kunstmann.

Schultz, E.
(1994) The hermeneutical aspects of activity theory. *Activity Theory* 15, p.13-16.

Shum, S., Hammond, N., Jørgensen, A.H., Aboulafia, A., Darzendas, J., Spyrou, T. & Benaki, E.
(1995) Modelling Encapsulations, Ideational Transfer and Designers Studies. In: *ESPRIT Basic Research Action 7040: AMODEUS, D12*.

Teasdale, T.W. & Owen, D.R.
(1994) Thirty-year secular trends in the cognitive abilities of Danish male school-leavers at a high educational level. *Scandinavian Journal of Psychology* 35, p. 328-335.

Willanger, R.
(1994) Neuropsychological syndroms and awareness. In: P. Cotterill et al. (eds.) *Brain & Mind*. København, Videnskabernes Selskab, p. 191-204.

Willanger, R.
(1994) Visuel Neglect. *Oftalmolog / nordiske øjenlæger*, p. 3-7.